Fostering Attachments
Long-term outcomes
in family group care

Fostering Attachments
Long-term outcomes
in family group care

Brian Cairns

Supported by

British Association for Adoption & Fostering
(BAAF)
Skyline House
200 Union Street
London SE1 0LX
www.baaf.org.uk

Charity registration 275689

British Library Cataloguing in Publication Data
A catalogue record for this book is available
from the British Library

ISBN 1 903699 54 1

Cover photographs of many members of the
Cairns family, Christmas 2003,
by Chris Stanway
Designed by Andrew Haig & Associates
Typeset by Avon DataSet, Bidford on Avon
Printed by Creative Print and Design Group

BAAF Adoption & Fostering is the leading
UK-wide membership organisation for all those
concerned with adoption, fostering and child
care issues.

Contents

*For all the family, and for everyone
who has helped us to grow.*

The author

Brian Cairns has worked as a schoolteacher in comprehensive and special education and as a social worker with many different service user groups. He currently works in a local authority emergency duty team, and additionally manages and presents training courses, acts as a social work practice teacher, and is a member of a fostering panel and a lay member of the Care Standards Tribunal. With his wife, Kate, he has brought up fifteen children, twelve of them placed by local authorities as long-term placements, whose development is the subject of this book.

Acknowledgements

Without my wife Kate, the course of my adult life would have been very different, and the events and experiences which have contributed to this book would never have happened. I am indebted to her for her vision, her commitment, her wisdom, her skill, her humour and her love, not only for me but for all our children.

To our children, both those born to us and those who arrived later in their lives, I am indebted for the joy and learning they have afforded me, for their love and companionship which I value more and more as life goes on, and for their continuing care and concern for one another.

To our parents, who not only concealed their understandable misgivings about what we were taking on, but also threw themselves into supporting us in every way they could and giving our children accessible and supportive grandparents, I owe my thanks.

To the many friends and professional colleagues, too numerous to name, who have listened to us, advised us, counselled us, shared their knowledge and experience with us, helped us to understand ourselves and our children, and encouraged us to write about our life together, I owe much of our strength as a family group.

Brian Cairns
January 2004

BAAF would like to thank Foster Care Associates for their kind support of this book.

Introduction

In the 1970s Professor Roy Parker began to use the term "separated children" to denote children who, whether through misfortune, design, or state intervention, do not live with a birth parent. This book looks at a group of twelve people who fell into this category in the 1970s and 1980s and who are now adults in their twenties and thirties. It also looks at the people who shared much of their childhood with them: my wife, Kate, and myself, and the three children born to us, Sal, Tom and Rich, now also in their twenties. It looks at what has become of us all, and tries to tease out those aspects of our shared life which may have helped us to become more coping and fulfilled people than we might otherwise have done.

As the adults in the house, Kate and I tried to take the long-term view, set the priorities, establish an ethos, and certainly accept a great deal of the responsibility when things went wrong. We also came to recognise that much valuable learning comes from reflection on apparent mistakes, and that few mistakes can not be corrected. But each of the other fifteen members of the family group which we became made a huge and invaluable and individual contribution, as did numerous other people who became part of our wider system over the years.

Most of what made a difference may have passed me by. This subjective, retrospective and eclectic look at how we lived and continue to relate may nevertheless yield some clues about how the experience of other "separated children", most of them in the care system, might be improved.

1   Groups and groupings

Models of care

There are so many models for the care of children who by misfortune or design do not live with a birth parent. Some are brought up by other kin, in an environment which may or may not have a good deal of overlap or similarity with what their parent(s) might have provided. Some are sent to boarding schools, where the environment will be very different from anyone's family home. Israel has pioneered kibbutzim, where children often live together in groups with professional carers, but spend short periods of "quality time" with their parents.

The children growing up within these arrangements are not generally stigmatised in the societies in which they live. Whilst some may feel in later life that their childhood experience was damaging, there is no general agreement that children who grow up in these settings must be disadvantaged by comparison with the majority of the population who grow up with birth parents in nuclear families.

However, for children who are cared for by the state, the debate continues to rage about the merits and demerits of various ways of organising their care. There is a general assumption that state care can be provided in "children's homes" – places where several, even many, children live together and are cared for by staff provided by the agency which runs the institution – or in foster homes – places where children share the homes of "ordinary" households and are cared for by foster carers, the adults who live there. Kinship care has traditionally been regarded as an alternative to state care: it is only recently that supported kinship care has increasingly found favour as an alternative way for the state to arrange care for children. Boarding-school education is rarely state-provided and is usually alternated at regular intervals with periods of parental care.

It is generally assumed – at least in the UK at the beginning of the 21st century – that a larger number of children will live together in a children's home than in a foster home. It is also assumed that children's home staff will work in the home on a rota basis, returning to their own separate living accommodation elsewhere at the end of each work shift.

In the UK currently, children's homes are generally believed to be a "bad" experience for children, and fostering a "better" one. Neither, however, is currently seen as the best long-term solution for children whose birth parents or kin are unable to resume caring for them after a relatively short time. These children are generally believed to need adoption, where children become "full life members" of families with whom they are placed. Government and media portray these children, whose new families still often receive little financial or professional support from the agencies responsible for the placement, as "secure" by comparison with children in residential (children's homes) or foster care.

Various assumptions flourish in this simplistic world with its confusing vocabulary. Why are children's homes described as "residential" care? Surely children "reside" wherever they live, whether in their Dad's flat, their foster carers' bungalow or their Gran's palace? Or has the term crept across from the world of residential care for adults, where the adjective indicates that care and housing are provided as part of the same package for the minority of adults in need of personal care who are also unable to provide and maintain housing for themselves? But all children are by definition dependent and unable to provide and maintain their own housing, and therefore receive residential care. Nevertheless, much of the stigma which lingers around residential care for adults, with its folk memories of the workhouse, attaches itself to the concept of "residential care" for children.

Foster carers are still portrayed at times as "in it for the money" – baby-farmers who live off the immoral earnings gained from bringing up children in exchange for money. The contrast, of course, in the current climate, is made with adopters, who "do it for love" and are therefore assumed to give more, emotionally and materially, to their children than do the mercenary foster carers with an eye on the bottom line. The increasing prevalence of the payment of adoption allowances may gradually change this popular prejudice, but for the moment the sense that it is somehow inappropriate to pay people "just" to bring up chidlren not born to them remains common, particularly, perhaps, among people who would never consider doing it. Yet would we have more trust in our teachers, our doctors, our postmen if they were volunteers rather than paid professionals with training and systems of accountability?

These and many more assumptions about the three commonest ways of organising and defining state-facilitated care of separated children –

	Assumptions about residential care	Assumptions about fostering	Assumptions about adoption
Placement duration	Temporary or short term	Temporary short-term/ medium-term	Permanent
Placement stability	Carers and children "move on" frequently	Children move frequently between placements	Children become part of a new family for life
No. of children placed together	Several children of similar age placed together	Usually <3 children of various ages at any one time	Usually just one or two children
Carers' living arrangements	Adults (staff) live off-site and work set hours	Adults (carers) share living accommodation with children	Adults (parents) share living accommodation with children
Intensity of "professional" involvement	Constant therapeutic professional input	Regular social work input	Less professional input after placement made
Level of public accountability	Open to inspection by statutory bodies	Open to inspection by social workers	Open to statutory inspection pre-placement only
Long-term support post-placement	Ongoing contact between staff and adult ex-residents rare	Ongoing contact between carers and adult ex-residents sometimes	Ongoing family relationship between adopters and adult adoptees expected
Perceived outcomes	Prognosis for children very poor	Prognosis for children rather poor	Prognosis for children good

residential care, fostering and adoption – lead us to believe that the three are easily distinguishable, each with its own distinct ethos and practices. Certainly each is governed by a different legal panoply of legislation and regulation. But how many of the general assumptions on the previous page HAVE to be true? I could extend this table almost indefinitely. But it is my contention that, simply because we assume that the prognosis for adopted children is better than for children who grow up within the other two systems, we may also falsely assume that all the features in the right-hand column of the table are universally positive, and, conversely, that all those differing features associated with residential care or foster care always have a negative effect. Should we be asking whether the assumption of poor outcomes for children who grow up in residential care is a consequence of the living arrangements of the staff, or the number of children thrown together under one roof? Or should we be looking at more subtle factors? And might there be a case for suggesting that, for some children, a living arrangement which combined elements of all three models might provide a setting where positive outcomes could be achieved?

In the late 1980s, I wrote – with Kate – a short article called 'The family as a living group', which was published as a chapter in a book called *Groups and Groupings* (Cairns and Cairns, 1989). In this article I outlined some of our approaches to living with our three "home-grown" children and our growing number of others who had been permanently placed with us by local authorities. In the intervening years I have been pleased to discover a steady stream of people with experience of living or working with separated children who found the chapter interesting or helpful or challenging, and who wanted to know more, and particularly, "did it work?"

Since the 1970s there has been a succession of studies looking at the comparative "success rates" of various models of meeting the basic needs of children who cannot live with their parents or other relatives. I don't intend this to be an "academic" book, so I shall not plunge into a lengthy review of all the literature, but for any reader who wishes to trace this history, the following short selection will provide some landmarks (George, 1970; Napier, 1972; Parker, 1980; Rowe *et al*, 1984; Stein and Carey, 1986; DoH, 1991; Fratter *et al*, 1991; Parker *et al*, 1991; Broad, 1998; Schofield *et al*, 2000). Many of the earlier studies defined "success" as "permanence" i.e. did the children remain in the new place for a certain number of years or until reaching a certain age? More recent studies have broadened the picture to give more consideration to the quality of the children's and young people's experience. Frequently the concern has been about structures – do separated children develop "better" in foster families, adoptive families, or residential care?

Our "mix-and-match" model

The environment in which we have lived and worked since 1975 is both all and none of these. The house in which we lived until 1994 was registered as a voluntary children's home for up to ten children. It was – officially – a children's home. It belonged to a voluntary organisation, which employed us to live in it and care for children. In it we were subject to the regulations of the time governing residential homes for children. It was subject to regular inspection by government bodies with whose representatives we had lengthy – and almost always amicable – debates about our differing interpretation of those regulations and their applicability to the real needs of children and young people.

But that house, like the one owned by ourselves to which we moved in 1994 with the last five children to "leave home", was also our family home. We had no separate accommodation, no designated "off-duty" time, no staff rota. The "imported" children knew that the plan on placing them with us – at ages varying between 4 and 14 – was that they would stay with us until they were ready to move on as independent adults at whatever age that might be. They knew that, for whatever reason, their families of origin were unable to bring them up and that we were going to be their effective parents – until death intervenes – if that long-term relationship is what they wanted. We would encourage them to relate to each other as brothers and sisters, and to our extended families as aunts, grandparents, etc. We would allow them to use our surname informally if that was their wish, and to call us Mum and Dad. In such ways we offered the experience of security ideally found in adoptive families.

And yet, they had a safety net. We know, in research terms, very little about the outcomes of adoption, other than anecdotally. Statistics of family breakdown, of children coming into care, of children on Child Protection

Registers, of teenage pregnancies, of youth offending, of educational achievement, do not record separately children and young people who have been adopted. Our children remained subject to Care Orders, the responsibility of the local authority which had taken their case to court in the first place to protect them from the risks posed by absent, abusive, or incapable parents. Throughout their childhood they each had a social worker to check on their progress, to be a listening ear and an observing eye, to help us identify and meet their changing needs and to maintain channels of communication with their families of origin. Every six months the local authority had to conduct a review of the arrangements for their care – which some of our children hated some of the time – and discuss ways in which they could be geared more closely to their needs. In these important respects, those of our children who were placed with us rather than born to us had the same service and protection as foster children. Indeed, this is the term that they generally used to describe themselves when some sort of explanation for their particular presence in the family seemed to be required.

For some of our children, trust that we would keep our side of the bargain took a very long time to build up. After all, why should they trust us? We had to look for and grasp every opportunity to demonstrate our own commitment to them. And we had to remember during difficult times that this commitment was just as binding as our commitment to our marriage. Children, vulnerable through immaturity, dependence and previous loss, have more potential to be harmed, I believe, by rejection from a placement than do spouses by rejection from a marriage.

In this book, then, I shall attempt to show how we tried to make this unusual – but, I would contend, very appropriate – model of state care for children "work". It is not a model of universal application. A minority of children who come into care are deemed to need a permanent placement. I don't believe that our model in its totality could be applied to a home, of whatever sort, from which children are *expecting* sooner or later to return to the care of a birth parent or other close relative. Of those children who do need "permanence", many have needs which may be well met by adoption, particularly if post-adoption support becomes more widely available. More traditional residential homes may be right for older children whose experience of family life has been too damaging for them to accept willingly any living arrangement that seems to replicate it.

In 1989 I wrote that 'we believed that we could establish a base for our children which would include three important elements: a carefully planned environment, the constant, consistent presence of caring adults, and a group of sufficient size to develop a potentially therapeutic network of relationships and interactions' (Cairns and Cairns, 1989, p. 169). I would reword and reorder those a little now. I would also note how little we understood then about how children's brains develop and how they are damaged and distorted by the effects of early attachment deficit and/or early, unresolved and/or repeated trauma. Moreover, we were less aware of some of the damaging experiences that our children had actually had, because of the even greater prevalence of taboo, secrecy, disbelief and inadequate investigation. Somehow we muddled through on a combination of instinct, untested hypothesis, and trial and error. But now I would have to say that an awareness of these issues on the part of the adults, which they can share with the young people as they grow, is vital enough for special mention as a fourth essential element. We were constantly looking out for models, theories and insights that would guide us to a better understanding of the puzzles and messages inherent in the feelings, statements and behaviour of our children. We also needed to understand our own emotional reactions.

Reviewing outcomes

Reviews of arrangements for looked after children are now more focussed on identifiable outcomes than they were previously. When I studied social policy and social work in Bristol in the 1980s, I was privileged to be taught by both Roy Parker and Sonia Jackson, who shared my conviction that "outcomes" in substitute care were about more than simply maintaining a placement until a child reached the age of 16, or even 18 years. They were looking for ways of assessing the *quality* of the child's experience in care. They wanted to explore how the state, as corporate parent, had ensured that children in its care benefited from the experience and developed their potential to become healthy, educated, capable, convivial, confident human beings with a sense of their own worth. Out of this conviction grew the Looked After Children (LAC) recording system now in general use in England and Wales, and in particular the

Assessment and Action Record, newly completed for every statutory review of every child in state care, whether the subject of a Care Order (Children Act 1989, Section 31) or "accommodated" by a local authority (Children Act 1989, Section 20).

This ongoing record, which accompanies the child throughout his or her time in care, traces the child's progress within seven "dimensions" of growth and development. These dimensions are: Health; Education; Identity; Family and Social Relationships; Social Presentation; Emotional and Behavioural Development; and Self-Care Skills. Although there is plenty of scope for debate about the boundaries and scope of these seven dimensions, a complete record over several years should provide a clear and dynamic picture of a developing and growing person.

If such records were maintained in relation to all children, and not just those in care, we would have a precious assessment and research tool which would make life so much easier for care professionals and biographers alike. Unfortunately for us, they were only introduced at the very end of our twenty-plus years of directly caring for our children. Had they been around twenty years earlier, our work both in helping our children then and in writing this book now would have been aided greatly. As it is, they form a convenient way of structuring this attempt to examine "how it was" for our children to grow up in our unusual (at least in contemporary Britain) setting, and "how it is" for them living now as independent adults, citizens, partners, parents and workers.

There are various reasons for having waited until now to write this book. One is what a good friend calls my "rare talent for indolence". I am not particularly "driven" or ambitious, having gradually eased out of the competitive approach to life for which my early formal education prepared me, and noted that looking after children became easier as a result. But the demand has become too pressing. I am indebted to many colleagues, particularly those who have been assiduous for many years in research and thinking "outside the box" about what actually works for looked after children, for encouraging me to share our family experience eventually with a wider audience.

Another reason is my awareness that we all go on growing and developing throughout our lives, and that to look at "outcomes" for individuals who are still probably less than halfway through their lives seems a nonsense. I think of an old local character on his usual stool by the bar who was asked by a tourist passing through, 'Have you lived in this village all your life?' The considered answer was 'Not yet'. However, in this age of performance management we seem to be programmed to look at outcomes before we have even completed implementation, and it is possible that our experience may be able to contribute in some way to continuing practice in this country and developing child care policy elsewhere.

The final reason has been a concern for our children's privacy and the constraints of confidentiality. I have been anxious to avoid causing them embarrassment or distress. But most of them have now given me their support for the writing of this book – the two who have not are in less regular contact with us now, and I do not have current addresses – and I am sure that they are now all mature and capable enough to take pride in themselves and hold their heads high if they are recognised. Several have been immensely helpful in reading my draft chapters and contributing their own reflections and insights, many of which I have been able to incorporate. I hope that their families of origin and others who appear in these pages will find adequate the cloak of anonymity that I have been able to offer.

Structure of the book

The second chapter of this book offers as much "historical" detail as should be necessary to provide a context for the remaining chapters: some biographical information about us all, a brief chronology of our life together, and enough information about the circumstances in which we have lived (a kind of verbal ecomap) to make us seem real to you. It also draws on a recent article by Kate (Cairns, 2002b) which brings together some of the key words or theoretical concepts which struck us like thunderbolts over the years and helped us to inform or improve our understanding of what we were (or might have been) trying to do. If I had been aware of all these things at the outset, I might have given up there and then, since I at least embarked on this lifestyle with the breezy, confident naiveté of youth.

The following seven chapters (3–9) deal in turn with each of the seven dimensions of child development considered by the LAC Assessment and Action Record. I assess in broad terms how the children placed with us have developed, and attempt to identify contributory factors to positive outcomes. There are occasional references to negative outcomes, too. But since, in general, we appear to have been more "successful" than other studies of outcomes for Looked After Children might have led us to expect – and it would be hard to have been appreciably less successful, so dire have outcomes generally been – I have allowed myself to see most outcomes as positive. Each chapter ends with an attempt to identify key factors which seem to me to have fairly universal applicability for separated children.

There were five other people in the household who were growing and changing – Kate and I, and our three "home-grown" children. Unusually among foster carers, Kate and I were only in our mid-twenties when we embarked on our "project". In the years since 1975 we have learned and grown and changed ourselves. Our children, and the experience of sharing their lives, have taught us a great deal. Chapter 10 looks at some of these personal developments. Unusually for "children who foster", our birth children had no previous experience of life as a cosy nuclear family before the influx – some might say invasion – of the other children. I believe that this was very positive. There was never a huge change to which they had to adapt. Sal was five months old when our first children were placed with us. Ten months later, after the addition of a further four children, Tom was born. Rich followed after a further 18 months. Nevertheless, their experience of family life as they grew up was very different in many respects to that of their friends. They reflect on that experience in Chapter 11 and suggest how it has contributed to making them the people they are today.

The final chapter asks in general terms, "What's Transferable?". Are the outcomes for us entirely a product of the individual, peculiar people that we are? Were the children who came to us untypical of "separated children" generally? Did fortune smile on us with more than usual favour? Or have we identified in our own experience anything which might usefully influence the work and lives of others involved with separated children, such as social workers and their managers and policymakers, parents, relatives and carers in families, foster homes or other group care settings, teachers, doctors, therapists, family court judges, neighbours, friends, and of course the children themselves? I believe that we have.

There is an afterword. The first nine chapters of this book were shared in draft form with most of the family, and I have woven many of their subsequent reactions, comments and recollections from letters, emails and recorded conversations into the text. But there were some comments that it seemed better to allow to stand alone, and with the permission of those who made them I have reproduced them at the end.

2 Who are we?

Starting points

One of the greatest difficulties for new foster carers or adopters must be the change from being a close nuclear family or household, in which all the relationships are known and intimate, to being a larger group trying to incorporate unpredictable strangers. It must feel sometimes like the sparrows trying to come to terms with the cuckoo. The transition is difficult for everybody, and everybody has to change, not just the newcomers.

We did it differently. We were living in Sheffield in the 1970s, I a recently qualified teacher working in a new comprehensive school, and Kate an unqualified social worker in a big city hospital. We had met in our first year at university, so we had already been together for several years, and since moving to Sheffield we had shared our house for periods of time with others – a 19-year-old Asian refugee from Uganda for several months, and a teenager whose family circumstances had broken down who came to us during several holidays from his residential school. As we began to talk about a family of our own, we realised that neither of us particularly wanted to live in the conventional unit of Mummy, Daddy and the 2.4 children. For us it would either be a much larger group, or a decision to have no children, but to throw ourselves into working together in a residential school or care setting.

Our reasons for this were different. Kate had grown up in residential schools, for her parents had worked together in an approved school and then in a local authority residential special school, always living on site, and Kate had enjoyed that particular kind of community living where the boundaries between work and home become blurred. I had been the child of quiet, cautious, home-loving parents in Belfast, almost an only child since my only sister was nearly seven years younger than me, and had come to find the closeness almost oppressive, particularly in what I had come to perceive as a disturbed and dysfunctional society. Both of us were discovering enjoyment in working directly with people, tempered by frustration with the strictures of the organisational settings in which we worked. The idea of being able to combine the adventure of helping children to recover from earlier damaging experience with the warmth and spontaneity of family life appealed to us both.

Having agreed broadly the sort of family group we wanted to live in, we had to find a way to do it. We felt that a large group would have many advantages. After all, groupwork theory suggests that viable groups are no smaller than six in number, and that around ten is good. And from the outset we saw our family as a group, with ourselves as facilitators. In this plan we would be able to incorporate "home-grown" children as well as incomers, but in order for the incomers not to feel marginalised, there would need to be at least as many of them in number as there were of the "core" family. People living in groups – especially, perhaps, recovering children (and certainly myself!) – need space to escape from one another as well as to share, so we would need a large house, preferably with a large garden as well. We could also see many advantages in living in a semi-rural setting. The atmosphere of relative calm would assist stabilisation and recovery; the fresh air and the richness of natural sounds and smells would be healthy and stimulate awareness of the natural world; we hoped that the local community would be less fragmented than in the ever-changing city; and we felt that the environment would be safer and more child-friendly, with fewer temptations and malign influences.

We approached numerous organisations setting out what we wanted to do – and what we didn't. We didn't want to adopt, because we felt certain that older children with "histories" would need an ongoing regular input, as of right, from skilled, known social workers outside the family – and so would we. We wanted our children to know that there were concerned adults and an escape route at hand for them if they came to find living with us intolerable. We knew that we could not be dependent totally, or even largely, on our own financial resources if we were to do the job properly and meet the needs of the children. We didn't want a succession of short-term placements – in the numbers we were envisaging that would be too disruptive for the permanent members of the family group. And we certainly didn't want to go away and have our "own" two or three children and come back five years later if we still felt the same way. We were dubious, too, about taking on large sibling groups of six or seven children, for we felt that the intense loyalties often found within such groups could well jeopardise the degree of assimilation we hoped for, and lead to bullying and marginalisation of our home-grown children, or at least an unhealthy split into fixed, mutually hostile or suspicious groups. And we were certain that we would need to be able to offer children a lifetime commitment, and that would mean not throwing them out into lodgings or "independence" the moment they reached the age of 16, ready (unlikely) or not.

Most agencies politely showed us the door. One national voluntary organisation was interested but wanted to establish us in a city and to combine short-term and respite care with long-term care, with no opportunity to enable children to stay with us once they left school.

A local authority offered us more or less what we wanted – except that the house was the former surgery in a colliery village, opposite the Miners' Welfare. It was the only house in the village not in a Coal Board terrace. Kate and I, with our middle-class backgrounds and our educated accents, would have been fish totally out of water, and the children would have been an oddity within the close community from day one. We felt that our children needed to become part of a more socially diverse community. We were not prepared to accept terms which we felt could compromise successful outcomes in what we wanted to do, either for the children we hoped would join us or for ourselves. The stakes were too high.

Eventually we linked up with a voluntary organisation which could accommodate us, provide us with a suitable house, and introduce us to local authorities who would want to place with us children who were deemed to need permanent family care, but who were for a variety of reasons not "available" for adoption, nor ideally suited to foster place-ments in small families. The reasons included sibling pairings, histories of placement breakdown, behavioural difficulties, and "delicate" relation-ships with birth families. Planning for these children might be very different now, but their need for permanence and stability would not have changed.

There was still some negotiation to be done about where our new home might be. Our new employers (for we had an employment contract as "wardens" of a registered children's home, albeit with encouragement to live as a family, and for me, at least, to continue with some other suitable subsidiary employment outside home) were keen to move us into a former vicarage in an isolated Midland hamlet, which we rejected as too rural. We agreed after further discussion to move into another property they owned on the edge of a Gloucestershire country town. It was a beautiful 17th-century wool-merchant's house, mentioned in Pevsner's guide to the historic buildings of England, but it and its six acres had been abandoned and neglected for over a year, and its interior arrangements were not ideally designed for ease of management, warmth or child-friendliness. It had the great advantage of being only ten miles from Kate's parents, with their wealth of experience. We moved in with our daughter Sarah (Sal), then three months old (for after finding our new employers we had felt able to think about starting our family in the conventional way, and results were immediate) on the basis that we would try to breathe new life into the old house and begin to build up our family group while we looked for a house nearby that might suit us better in the long term.

A year later, in the summer of 1976, we moved on to Plainlands, a few hundred yards from the school where Kate's parents lived and worked, and just outside a smaller country town which provided an excellent community for our children as they grew. The house dated from the 1920s and sat in an acre and a half with wide-ranging views. It was spacious, but with a compact design, and not dissimilar from other houses around, most of which were lived in by families with school-age children (in one case, a family with seven children). The couple who were selling it had brought up their own five children there. Across a country lane and a field was a vast area of common land with a conical hill (for winter sledging), riddled with rabbit warrens and badger setts, a long windy ridge with wooded slopes, a disused quarry, reasonably safe but affording adventure. It was ideal, and remained our family home for 18 years.

Building the family group

The family group had grown in the intervening year. We had been joined by three sibling pairs, each consisting of an elder sister and slightly younger brother, and our second "home-grown" child, Tom, arrived a week after we moved in. Four of the children had to endure the disruption of a change of school when we moved, which we regretted, but the new school was so superior to the old one that we didn't find it a difficult decision, and we transported the children, and the pair who joined us at half-term, to the new school for the term before we moved.

I had continued to work as a teacher, and in fact had joined the staff of Kate's parents' school, for boys with emotional and behavioural difficulties, where I taught, mainly part-time, until 1982. Kate also began to do some work there in a voluntary capacity as social worker/counsellor. Some of the boys from the school were fairly regular visitors to our house, and our children often spent time on the school site. We were conscious of drawing a clear distinction between our relationships with "our" children and those we had with pupils at the school. But it was valuable for our children to be able to think of us as having "jobs" which were not simply looking after them, and for us to have horizons beyond home and family. This normalised them, and normalised us. An LS Lowry painting has always hung in our hallway – 'Father returning from work', a cheerful stick-man with jaunty rolled umbrella and briefcase – which was a family favourite. Symbols are important. In a way, too, our acceptance of and by the boys at the school, their expressed appreciation sometimes of help we and my parents-in-law were able to give them, helped our children to develop trust in us and an understanding of their own difficulties. Our involvement with the school provided objective evidence that our home might be a good place to belong to. It is easy to forget the huge leap of faith that we expect children to make when they are placed with a new family, and to take for granted the courage that they need to make that leap.

Our link with the school also gave rise to one of our biggest mistakes. One boy, slightly older than our oldest child, Sharon, became a regular visitor. An ebullient, bright, lively and sometimes belligerent lad, his relationship with his mother and stepfather became too difficult for him to live at home, even in school holidays. We were asked if he could live with us and become a day pupil at the school, and we agreed. This was taking the intertwining of the two parts of our life a step too far. He was unable to shift between relationships, and so, we acknowledged, were we. He could not commit to the family nor we, as it turned out, to him. He dominated the younger children and found it impossible to share time or space, in a way which we could have managed more easily with a younger child, using group pressure from older children. He left us by mutual agreement after ten months, which was an unsettling experience for everybody, and left the school too. He did well in a more structured environment, found himself a very different family from us at 16, and has built successful careers, first of all in catering and later as a pathology assistant. But we may have done him a disservice along the way. The experience helped us to develop very carefully our thinking about family boundaries and identity, to which I return in Chapter 5.

Throughout this book, I have referred to all the members of the family group by their real first names, where they have given me their permission. Where they have not, or where I have been unable to contact them since planning the book, I have used a pseudonym. This is an appropriate point to introduce each of them as individuals, with their own stories. They appear in the order in which they joined the family, so that I can indicate the processes we went through in deciding to increase the group size at each point.

Sarah (known in the family as Sal) was born in May 1975, shortly before we left Sheffield. Although younger than most of our foster children, she came to assume something of a leadership role in the family, and is a conscientious aunt to the next generation. She has, as it were, entered the family business, having taken a degree in social policy and become a probation officer. She lives with her partner since schooldays in Sussex, and is an important part of the cement that continues to hold the group together despite being geographically remote. It is Sal who is organising the next family shared holiday trip envisaged for 2004.

Lynn was born in a south coast port in August 1968. She and her brother **Mark** (born July 1969) were the first children to join us, in October 1975, after our move to Gloucestershire.

They were born to young parents who separated when Mum developed a paralysing and incurable neurological condition. The children were placed in a large convent nursery when Mark was six weeks old, and had become the oldest children there when placed with us after several attempts to find them a permanent family had failed. Mark was developmentally delayed, an anxious child with poor speech. Lynn was outgoing, but we soon realised that she had considerable hearing loss, never subsequently successfully restored despite many attempts at surgery. Lynn has worked in many settings – offices, factories, hotel reception desks, warehouses – but keeps returning to working as a waitress, which she loves. Having lived and worked in other parts of Gloucestershire and Warwickshire, she now lives a couple of miles from Plainlands with her electrician husband, also local, and their infant son, and is a central figure in the shared life of the family.

Mark worked for many years in farming, on which he thrived, for the most part remaining close to where he grew up. As the industry contracted, he moved on to be a hard-working delivery driver, living in a nearby town with his partner. Mark "came out" as gay some years ago, which was greeted by the family with equanimity and warm acceptance. Mark needed quite a long time to establish himself as an independent adult, moving out from home frequently in his early twenties and returning when things didn't quite work out, finally moving out to a bedsit a few doors from us at almost 26.

Josie and **Dan** came to us in December 1975, a few days before Christmas. Josie was born in June 1969, Dan in April 1971. They had also lived in a nursery in London for much of their young lives. They had been placed in a pre-adoptive placement, but the prospective adopters split up just before the adoption was finalised, and the placement consequently was ended. There appeared to have been other irregularities within the placement, which may have contributed to Josie's considerable social and behavioural difficulties when she came to us. Josie and Dan are of mixed heritage; their mother is the daughter of Polish/Russian Jewish refugees who had settled in Scotland, and their father, of whom very little is known, was believed to be Guyanese.

Issues for us to consider were whether Lynn and Mark, and indeed we ourselves, could cope with other newcomers so soon, whether it was right for us to accept a request to take children of mixed heritage in rural Middle England, whether Josie and Mark, who were in the same school year, could tolerate any perceived competition. I return to these issues elsewhere.

Josie became a chef, leaving college with a City and Guilds qualification at 18, and choosing to work in residential schools and works canteens, mainly in the Home Counties, where she now lives in a comfortable flat conscientiously bringing up her son, now at junior school. They visit other family members frequently, and regularly come to us for several days at Christmas, as well as "house-sitting" when we go on holiday. Kate and I are named as testamentary guardians for Josie's son.

Dan took a degree in media studies and continued to a Master's course before taking up employment with an airline. He lives with his present partner in a cottage in a picturesque Midlands village. His previous partner, a talented artist whom he married in 1997, died of brain cancer in 1999, and Dan nursed her devotedly and sensitively through the three years of her terminal illness, returning to his previous employer after her death. His gentle, self-deprecating humour and quiet common sense won him respect as a child within the family and beyond, and continues to do so.

Sharon and her brother **John** joined us from South Wales in May 1976. Sharon was born in July 1965 and John in August 1966. They had grown up on a rough, notorious estate in an atmosphere of neglect, alcohol-fuelled domestic violence and petty crime, and had been 19 times in care. They had been victims of physical and sexual abuse, the extent of which was not immediately fully known. After a further serious incident of domestic violence in the presence of the children, they had been made wards of court with a view to securing their situation elsewhere.

We had not been planning to extend the group further until we had moved to Plainlands and welcomed our new baby into the world, but had said that, once we were ready to expand, another sibling pair a little older than Lynn would be good. We didn't think we could manage another pre-school child at this point (besides, they were rarely offered), we wanted to avoid further bunching in the age group of our existing children, and we felt that the group of children could accommodate two strong personalities at the top of the age range. And the day after we made that statement, there was an urgent request from Sharon and John's local authority – how could we refuse?

Sharon now lives with her second husband and her teenage daughter from her first marriage, for whom we are also testamentary guardians, in a village about 30 miles from us. Her teenage stepson is also a frequent member of the household. We see them frequently. She has continued a determined battle with the emotional legacy of her early childhood, which has had implications for her health, and was a contributory factor in the breakdown of her first marriage. She has built a reputation as a conscientious worker in hotel, factory and retail settings, and has for several years been the supervisor of cleaning staff in her local leisure centre. She retains a loving concern for all the family, although her relationship with her natural brother John has not survived.

John was the joker of the family, a defence which he erected against the pain of his early years. He had artistic talent, and trained in picture framing and restoration, but as a young man he drifted, and had a restless few years, a variety of jobs and relationships in England and abroad, and spells of unemployment, before serving a prison sentence. He was out of contact with us for several years, but has more recently been back in touch. He is now a family man with a partner, two stepchildren and a baby girl, and has settled in North Wales having given up a job as a maintenance engineer working mostly abroad in order to be with his new family.

Tom arrived in July 1976, barely a week after we had moved into Plainlands. Kate was in labour while organising party games for Sharon's eleventh birthday party on Plainlands' parched lawns. He had some early hearing problems, and was very slow to talk, confirming the prejudices of health visitors about the development of children born into large (so obviously, in their view, noisy and chaotic) households. But when he did start to talk, it was in complete sentences, and was followed by reading very shortly afterwards. Small and bespectacled throughout his childhood, and usually lost in a book, Tom was at times a victim of bullying, but his genial nature and keen sense of humour combined with the growing family's solidarity and protectiveness to shield him, whilst having to hold his own in a large and varied group was valuable experiential learning for him. He developed into a sociable, outgoing teenager, a keen actor and occasional poet, studied and adventured in Mexico, lived at home again for a couple of years after graduation, and is now working as a publisher and designer in a Midland city where he lives in a busy household with his wife, lodgers and cats.

Rich is our third "home-grown" child, born in February 1978. More practical and physical than Tom as a child, he organised his dreamy older brother, and they were often taken for twins. Outwardly more rebellious and independent than Tom, he was more challenging of our decisions in raising the family, but has perhaps remained closer to the Quaker influences of his childhood than any of the others. He found adolescence challenging, coinciding as it did with our downsizing to our own house alongside the rapid diminution in the number of people living at home, and this was particularly so when he became the only birth child left at home. A combination of protracted ME-type illness, two uncompleted degree courses and a serious car accident forcing a total career change complicated his transition to adulthood, but he has found satisfaction and a genuine maturity in working as an accountant in London where he lives with his partner. He has built a good social network, and is becoming something of a financial adviser to other members of the family.

Expanding the initial group

Fred was born in London in December 1966 to an established actress who had developed mental health problems. Little is known about his father, who may have been Scandinavian. He lived in a residential nursery in West London from a few weeks old, and although there were many changes of staff he received good care. He remained in a children's home until he was eleven, when he was fostered by a middle-class Bristol couple with two younger boys and high aspirations. Fred became very attached to the foster father, but the relationship with the foster mother was difficult. The placement broke down shortly before the foster carers' marriage, and Fred came to us in August 1981. There were doubts about whether this "city boy" would adapt to our country living; in fact he took to it very quickly, immersing himself in farming and ferreting and discovering in himself the legacy of his mother's roots in rural Oxfordshire. (He now sees one of the highlights of his day as his morning run on country tracks and lanes.) After leaving school he took agricultural qualifications and worked briefly on farms before progressing into sales, marketing and business consultancy, fields in which he has become extremely successful. Always active, the sort of person who fits in five-a-side football after a fifteen-hour day and doesn't have enough ears for his mobile phones, Fred married a local woman (a close schoolfriend of Lynn, in fact), has two much-loved children, and continues to live a mile or two from us despite having spent a few years away in the North in his early twenties.

Kwesi was born in London in August 1979 of a Ugandan mother who had grown up in care in England, and a Ghanaian father whom he has never known. Unprepared for parenthood, his mother left him with many carers during his first year, but recognised his need for stability and took him to stay with her aunt and cousins in Uganda when he was a year old, leaving him there when she returned to London. As the short-lived period of relative post-Amin stability in Uganda crumbled, the Baganda people to which Kwesi's family belonged were ruthlessly attacked, and his mother fetched him back, perhaps at considerable risk to herself. His relatives appear not to have survived. Still unwilling to take on parental responsibilities, his mother placed him in the care of a London borough, and after a temporary placement, he came to us in November 1983. We were uncertain about the wisdom of placing this linguistically confused African child, traumatised and without secure attachments, in our large family in rural England. The local authority was clear that we represented the best available option, and Kwesi's mother was adamant that she wanted her child brought up in a preponderantly white family rather than in a black family which did not match his cultural background (as few would).

Throughout his schooldays, Kwesi lived for sport, particularly football. He was signed as a schoolboy by a Premier League club at the age of ten, and had no other career thoughts. Rejected by this club at 16, he joined a Midland club in a lower division, and stayed there for two years, winning a professional contract, but not, in the end, making the grade at this level. Returning to Gloucester he shared a flat (where he still lives) with Mark (see above), working in a leisure centre, a petrol station, and as a delivery driver whilst playing semi-professional football part time. A moderately serious injury prompted him to reassess his future and seek a career path, and he joined a major building society as a mortgage adviser, at the same time building up a local reputation as a club disc-jockey. He visits and phones us often, and for years has been particularly close to Fred (see above), who acted as unofficial coach and mentor during his footballing years, travelling thousands of miles to get him to matches. Indeed, without the help of Fred and other older members of the family, the demands of

Kwesi's football at this level would have been hard for Kate and me to sustain, although we would have found a way because it was so important to him.

By the end of 1984, our older children had begun to leave home. Sharon had been gone for over a year, working as a waitress in a hotel about twenty miles away and living in the staff hostel. John had decided to abandon the world of art and had gone to London to work as a helper in a hostel for homeless men, and Fred, having completed his basic agricultural qualification, was working on a farm thirty miles north of us and living in lodgings nearby. It was time for us to consider filling up the space they had left behind them, even though they knew that their place as members of the family was inviolate.

Martin came to us early in 1985, having been born in London in April 1971 (just a few days before Dan) and having lived since infancy with foster carers who had settled in Gloucestershire. The foster placement had broken down in consequence of an "assault" by Martin on his foster mother, felt to be out of character, but prompted, we felt increasingly sure, by Martin never having been treated as one of the family, expected to do a great deal of work on the family smallholding, and apparently discriminated against in a variety of little ways in favour of the foster carers' slightly older only son. Martin seemed to integrate well into our family group. After a social care course at our local FE college, he left home to work with adults with learning disabilities and challenging behaviour in a residential home in the Home Counties, and kept in touch much as young adults do. However, after his marriage to a somewhat older colleague, they moved back to our part of Gloucestershire and had a child. There were differences of assumption around the extent of our role as grandparents, and Martin appeared to become increasingly resentful about perceived historical inequalities within our family group. They distanced themselves from the family network, eventually moving away, and we no longer have contact. The door will remain open if Martin's wishes should change in the future.

Karen was born in Dublin in July 1974. Her family moved to the Birmingham area within a year or two, although Karen is convinced that the woman who moved with them is not her mother, and that there was a baby brother who died in mysterious circumstances. This has been a family of secrets and abusive behaviour. A bright child whose parents and four younger siblings were perhaps much less able, Karen rebelled against her abusive upbringing whilst remaining loyal to her family and very susceptible to their emotional pull. She was taken into care at the age of seven after persistent running away from home, and lived in a children's home, rarely attending school and putting herself at serious risk, until she joined us in April 1985. Her siblings remained at home, to our consternation, although her eldest sister was eventually removed in her mid-teens.

Karen was an emotionally volatile child, living on a wildly swinging emotional pendulum. She left us at her own wish at fourteen, and after two other unsatisfactory placements returned to us with relief several months later. But on leaving school she was off again, and her local authority placed her in the children's home she had lived in as a young child, close to her parents' home. Finding Social Services' controls intolerable, she eloped to Scotland as soon as she turned sixteen and married her boyfriend from school. They returned to Gloucestershire, had a baby and set up home in a council flat in a neighbouring town to ours. It was a couple of years before Karen initiated contact with us again. Her marriage ended after the birth of the second child (the husband, however, has become a social worker); Karen has remarried, had three more children, and lives with her husband and four of her children not far from us. We see the family frequently and the children see us as grandparents. In recent years Karen has returned to college and successfully completed an Access course to Higher Education, which she may take further when her child care responsibilities are less onerous. A vivacious woman despite persistent health problems, Karen seems more settled and grounded now than at any previous point in her life.

Four years later we had to consider again whether we would fill empty places around the table. We could have decided to stay as we were, but we had recognised the strength of living in a larger group. Lynn had long since embarked on her career in catering and was working and living in a luxury hotel in the Midlands; Mark was still living at home and working on a farm a few miles away, but planning to take the plunge soon into living more independently (he subsequently left and returned several times); Josie had finished at college, deciding that she wanted to cook in a non-commercial environment, had joined the staff of a residential school in the South-East, where she was living in during term, and was developing her liking for spending vacations travelling in the more exotic parts of the world. Dan was planning to go off to university, and Martin preparing to look for an interesting post caring for vulnerable adults wherever in the country he could find one. We decided that we would think of adding two more children to the group, but that Kwesi would remain our youngest, so that we could prepare for a big change in lifestyle when we reached fifty around the end of the century. I was working full-time in a social work team, and Kate was studying two days a week in London while continuing to experience considerable pain from injuries sustained in a road accident in 1988, circumstances which combined to convince us that we would take no more younger children, even if they had been available.

Pete was born in November 1974 in an eastern shire county. After his mother left home, he and his three older brothers went into care, and lived together for several years in a voluntary children's home. In the summer of 1989, as the third brother was preparing to move on to independent living, the home was closed down quite suddenly, and an alternative permanent home was sought for Pete. We seemed an odd choice, being a long way from the rest of his family, since he had close links with his brothers, and to a lesser extent with his father and grandfather, all of whom remained in his home area. Nevertheless we accepted him willingly since he was keen to come to us, and he joined us after the briefest of introductions. In the subsequent months we found reason to believe that the children's home may have had a culture of sexual abuse, which may have informed the decision to place Pete in a different part of the country. Attempts to investigate and find out more seemed to dribble away into sand.

Pete overcame some of his educational difficulties, and gained an agricultural qualification at college. He lived with us briefly after completing his college course, then moved to lodgings before returning to his home area, less dependent on his brothers than he might otherwise have been. He phones us occasionally, and tells us that he is settled in a flat with his girlfriend and in steady employment.

Liam came to live with us in April 1990, the final child to join our family group. He was born in London in May 1977. His mother had drug addiction problems and a violent partner. He suffered physical abuse, often witnessed his mother's drug use and violence meted out to her by her partner and was accommodated several times. He has a very high IQ, but not surprisingly exhibited disturbed behaviour at school, and was placed in a residential special school at the age of six. Here (as we later discovered) he was treated abusively, and was subject to physical abuse in school holiday foster placements. At nine he was told perfunctorily at school that his mother had died of a heroin overdose. He eventually left the special school to live in a London children's home where he experienced further sexual abuse, and having been excluded from school, received occasional "home tuition". Despite all this, he craved "normal" family life and schooling, and a new social worker gained his trust and sought a placement with us. We could see that Liam had many, many difficulties to work through, but also recognised his resilience and potential. Once we had established that our local comprehensive school was prepared to enrol him and give him a chance, we offered him a home and family.

Liam has survived. At times it was a close thing, as he struggled with little support from his local authority against deep-seated problems of post-traumatic stress which have led him through all sorts of self-harming behaviour until well into his twenties. We were not always able, for reasons of safety, to have Liam live with us when at his most troubled. But remarkably, the funeral of my father, to whom Liam felt especially close, in October 1996, marked a turning point, and although it took several years thereafter for him to reach his present level of stability, he has felt since then able to look to us (by which I mean all of us, not just Kate and myself) for the support he has often needed. He is now for the first time in his life established in safe independent accommodation (on the south coast), working regularly in a responsible job which he enjoys and where he is appreciated, and building social relationships which are neither dependent nor exploitative.

Transition

By 1994, most of the children had grown up and moved away from home, most at around seventeen or eighteen, but because of the demands of work or study, and not because of any pressure placed on them to move to "independent living". We had decided when Liam joined us that our family should expand no further. Partly this was due to our wish to move on to a different stage of life ourselves while we remained fit enough to enjoy it; partly it was our sense that the family feeling which had developed among the fifteen "brothers and sisters" could not survive infinite growth (a consideration currently for the European Community, perhaps!). After the summer only Liam, Rich and Kwesi would still be at school; Sal and Tom would only be at home outside university terms, and of the older children, only Mark was living with us, having moved back in when a lodging arrangement had broken down.

It was time to move, into a somewhat smaller house of our own.

This time of transition coincided with the most difficult period in our time as foster carers. There had been hard times before. Caring for distressed children often feels impossible at the time, and the more one appreciates the depths of the distress of many looked after children and lives with the disturbing, confusing, frustrating, sometimes frightening and traumatising messages in their behaviour telling us, if we can only hear it, what their experience has been and continues to be, the more impossible it can seem. The children's unhappiness could seem infectious, the strain of resisting it in oneself whilst trying, gradually, to dilute it, at times almost intolerable. Our brains would hurt from the effort of trying to puzzle out what prompted their behaviour and how we could encourage change. But the mid-1990s were the hardest, bleakest time. Liam's overwhelming experiences of loss and abuse in his earlier childhood almost destroyed him in adolescence. He became a grave risk to himself and to other members of the family, notably to Kate and Rich who understood him and felt his pain possibly more accurately than the rest of us. In his blind rage, over which he could then exercise little control when traumatic memories overtook him, he made serious attacks on each of them, and, in a variety of ways, on himself. We had to keep him, the other children and ourselves safe, and sane. We had inadequate access to professional help, and our family train came perilously close to derailment. We came through with the help of all our children and extended family, some close friends, some colleagues who rode the storm with us, our determination not to renege on our commitment to any of our children, our own efforts to learn about and understand post-traumatic stress, and Liam's own courage and strength of character. He survived, and so did we.

Perhaps it was good for us all that we could not allow Liam's needs to dominate totally our lives at this time, although to the rest of the family that may often have seemed to be what was happening. We had to keep life as stable as we could for everyone else.

It was vital not to disrupt schooling, and important for each of the children still to have their own room. We were fortunate to find an affordable seven-bedroomed town house just a mile from Plainlands. By this time I was working as a social worker in an out-of-hours duty team, and Kate felt able to resume employment outside of home, as a social worker in a family placement team in the first instance. Four years later we virtually had an empty nest, and moved again within the local area to a four-bedroomed house with an adjoining flat. The flat housed Tom and Rich when they needed it over the next two years, and the house afforded us space to welcome back as visitors from time to time the rest of the family and their growing numbers of partners and children.

I believe that we have become a real extended family. My parents moved to our area in 1979, so our 15 children grew up with two sets of grandparents who accepted them totally as grandchildren. Our children see themselves as aunts and uncles to one another's children. We have attended nine weddings in the role of parents of the bride or groom, and are seen as grandparents by a growing number of children of the next generation. We have a regular annual family outing to the pantomime, with attendance numbers now above thirty; 26 of us shared a holiday in France in 2002, and there are hopes for a larger gathering in Greece in 2004. Kate and I continue to be available for parental advice and support – and increasingly many of our children look as well to their network of "brothers and sisters", recognising one another's varied expertise and experience within genuine bonds of commitment.

A few minutes after I wrote the last sentence, our phone rang. It was one of our young men, presumably in his lunch break at work. Here is the complete conversation:

Dad, I'm glad it's you, Mum wouldn't have a clue about this, you can settle an argument.

Hope so.

What's the name of Reading's football ground?

I know it used to be Elm Park, but they had a new stadium built a year or two back and it was named after somebody – the Majeski stadium or something . . .

But it used to be Elm Park, right?

Yes.

Great. Thanks Dad. Bye!

Men in their twenties whose early childhoods held no certainties still sometimes need to touch base for security, to know that there are people with whom they can dispense with all the formalities, to be able to say indirectly to their workmates that they have a dad too, who knows about football (and a mum who doesn't), to be seen to be "normal".

Professional development

As our children grew and developed, so did we. Kate and I both completed social work qualifications during the 1980s, in my case after completing a Diploma in Social Administration which taught me a great deal about the inequalities in society and enriched my understanding of the social context in which our family was located, individually and as a unit. Study helped me to be more objective, to become a more reflective practitioner, to find our relationships with our children endlessly fascinating rather than simply cause for alternating joy and sorrow, and in listening to carers talking about their difficulties with their children late at night I have tried to guide them towards a similarly objective stance. I became a Mental Health Act Approved Social Worker, and developed a better understanding

31

of the mental health issues which touched several of our children. The findings of the Office of National Statistics (ONS 2003) that 45 per cent of looked after children studied in their research had an identifiable mental health problem came as no surprise to me. Rightly, this report states (p. 21): 'The far higher rates of mental disorder among children looked after by local authorities than in private households is understandable if one looks at why the children were taken into care.'

Kate has written elsewhere (Cairns, 2002b) about some of the particular insights which our study and wider reading brought to us over the years, each one helping us not only to a clearer understanding ourselves of what was happening for our children, but also to an enhanced ability to explain to the children sometimes why they felt as they did, and to reassure them that they were not crazy, or evil, or emotionally grotesque, but simply people who were reacting quite predictably to huge pressures, from the effects of which they could recover and move on. We gained the confidence to inform their self-understanding, and sometimes their understanding of one another, and out of that shared knowledge grew empowerment and mutual support.

We learned to recognise how hard it was for children, who had rarely been given cause to trust anyone, not just to learn to trust us, but to form a concept of what trusting would be like. Children who had known physical abuse would cower in front of us with terrified eyes even if they weren't aware of a transgression; children who had been sexually abused would assume that we must either be expecting future sexual gratification or enjoying some perverted pleasure now; children would ask again and again what was about to happen because they had no reason to give any weight to what they had previously been told.

We learned how children's internal working models of the world are built on experience. Children who have lived with chaos, with unpredictable reactions, with broken promises, with the distortions of drug-dominated environments, build models of the world in which cause and effect, plans and consequences, play no part. They may feel unable to influence their surroundings, to understand events, to make meaningful choices. And, importantly, we learned how placing children in a new world of trust, and order, and safety, may not immediately be liberating for them. Rather, it may feel like being placed in a looking-glass world, a foreign, surreal world where all one's understanding of what it means to be a person disintegrates. Children whose world has become unrecognisable may try in all sorts of ways, consciously or otherwise, to re-create the old familiar chaos, to engender mistrust, to rediscover the pain of the known horrors, more bearable than the bewildering nightmare of disorientation. Just how disturbing is it for frogs to become princes? Such insights helped us to be realistic in our expectations of our children's ability to adjust quickly to their new circumstances, and to see the need for helping them gradually to find new stories, new metaphors, and new models to make sense of their new lives. And because of the number of children in our family, the new stories could be shared, their credibility enhanced by the sharing.

As time went on, we could explain this process in simple terms to our older children, helping them in turn to make sense of the perplexing behaviour of newer members of the family, bolstering their tolerance and involving them in the therapeutic process.

We learned about the crucial importance of early attachment, and how to compensate for poor attachment experience. We gained an understanding of the link between healthy attachment and the ability to manage stress, which helped us to understand the anxiety which several of our children experienced in the face of what might seem to be relatively minor stresses. Observing the interactions between other parents and children became almost an obsession for me, and I would notice how often adults confronted with a child experiencing stress will react in ways which increase rather than alleviate the stress, and then seem baffled when the child becomes inconsolable or uncontrollable.

Later in our time with our children we learned about trauma and its distorting effect on brain functioning. So much of our children's initially puzzling behaviour, their inability to name, express or even seemingly experience emotions, their hyperactivity, their inability to concentrate, their panics and nightmares, all made sense when we began to understand the effects of traumatic stress. This learning helped us to understand ourselves when we began to experience the effects of secondary post-traumatic stress disorder after prolonged exposure to the stress of those of our children who had suffered protracted abuse, and to acknowledge our gradual awareness of the pervasiveness of the networks to which they had fallen prey. Kate has documented some of this disturbing experience in *Surviving Paedophilia* (Cairns, 1999).

This growing understanding dovetailed with our awareness of some of our children's difficulties in managing impulses, which in turn linked to considerations of appropriate experience of shame and the dangers of failing to enable children to integrate that shame and experience rapid reincorporation into a mutually accepting relationship with us. The old maxim, "Never let the sun go down upon your wrath" contains a great deal of wisdom, and we learned that even a day is usually too long to allow a traumatised or poorly attached child to experience the alienation and isolation of shame, even if (perhaps especially if) that alienation feels comfortable to her.

Finally, recent developments in identifying factors which promote resilience (Gilligan, 2001) lent weight to what had been a largely intuitive part of our practice: a sense that the survival instinct is strong in us all, and that human beings have a remarkable capacity to adapt to injury and to overcome the effects of deprivation, given an environment which enables and enhances their development. Such an environment maximises the opportunities for children to experience positive feedback from the whole network of systems in which they find themselves. Our sense that this was the case lay behind our conviction that living in a larger-than-usual family group would be helpful for children with damaging early experiences, making possible a wider range of subsystems and potential compensatory experience within a framework of security and stability. It also lay behind the relative importance we gave to planning, creating and managing the overall home environment in which our children lived, rather than concentrating solely on specific interactions and interventions between ourselves and individual children. We tried constantly to fine-tune the experience of living in our household to the needs of the children, as we perceived them from day to day. No doubt gardeners would tell us that growing strong, healthy plants requires particular attention to be paid to the soil, especially if the seedlings have had to struggle.

3 Health
Developing awareness of our minds and bodies and respect for them

"Inherited" problems

For some social workers, the "health" dimension of the LAC Assessment and Action Records is basically an administrative checklist. Has the child had routine development checks from the health visitor, all the appropriate vaccinations at the right time, an annual medical examination? Does the child see the dentist regularly? Have there been any hospital attendances that might build up into a pattern causing some concern?

We need to take a more holistic view of children in state care. These children will often have been physically injured or neglected, with adverse effects to their long-term physical health. They will often have been abused in other ways, with potentially life-threatening effects on their sexual, emotional and mental health. The more we learned over the years, the more we realised that health problems relating to abusive treatment must be expected and looked for.

Most of our children came to us from other placements, not directly from home. They had been in care for several years. Nevertheless some brought with them what seemed to us to be glaringly obvious health problems, which should have been obvious to any carer.

By the time we had spent two hours with Lynn in our car it was apparent that she had a marked degree of hearing loss. Yet her previous carers and school assumed that she was 'wilful' and 'didn't listen'. The frequent pain in her ears had been dismissed as whingeing, malingering. The investigations and recurrent surgery which we initiated may have helped her to arrest the otherwise inevitable deterioration, but couldn't undo much of the damage to her ears. Martin arrived with us with grossly sunken arches to both feet which had caused him discomfort for years. We scoured the country for specialist shoes which would fit him properly, support his arches, and at the same time not make him the butt of cruel humour at school. Liam, we noticed, couldn't make a palm of either hand to count change, and had developed his own contorted compensatory technique. We had him examined and found there to be irreversible damage to tendons in his arms, probably the result of abusive treatment. It had never been recorded.

Karen provides a personal recollection. 'I had never had dental treatment prior to living in the family, and as a result ended up having to have braces fitted to my teeth. If this had not been done I would be living with a displaced bite and crooked teeth to this day. I used to complain about very bad headaches in my various children's homes or previous placements only to be told, "OK, Karen", but nothing happened. When I joined our family I was taken to the doctor and diagnosed with sinusitis.'

Physical problems are one thing – mental disorder is quite another. Even now, despite the statistics indicating the prevalence of mental health problems among looked after young people (ONS, 2003), appropriate services remain patchy and inadequately funded. The stigma that hangs over mental disorder doesn't help. Young people, carers, teachers and social workers alike prefer to ascribe problems to relationship dynamics, unco-operativeness, rebelliousness or malice rather than to recognise depression, stress, anxiety, reactive neuroses or even incipient psychosis. Drug abuse and self-harming behaviour are interpreted as bravado, attention-seeking behaviour, or simply naughtiness rather than being seen as they often are – self-medication for the effects of intolerable stress. Children pick up on this conspiracy of silence, this gap in comprehension. Better to be bad than mad.

Because of the associated stigma, I shall have to resort to anonymity here. Among our children there have been histories of eating disorders, of self-harming behaviour, of depression leading to suicide attempts, of stress-related psychotic episodes, of post-traumatic stress disorder in many forms, and of periods of uncontrolled manic behaviour falling short of the level which would result in compulsory hospital admission. We can relate the triggers for virtually all of these episodes to individual histories of childhood abuse.

Many of the episodes have continued to disrupt and complicate our children's adult lives, when doctors have been perhaps more predisposed to help and understand (especially doctors who have known and understood our children's care history). However, it has often been necessary for us to act as advocates for our adult children to doctors, to tell them what it is painful or impossible to recount about their childhood experience at a time of crisis. Often we have had to remind our adult children why they may be feeling as unwell as they do, sometimes in the face of scepticism from their partners or employers. It remains our task to hold the narrative and at times to help our children to share it in ways that others can understand. Our children's partners need to learn of the awful potential legacies of childhood abuse. So, as they grow older, may their children. One of our grandchildren was distressed and uncomprehending when her mother recently went through a period of depression linked to inappropriate medication for a thyroid condition – both conditions closely associated with childhood trauma. Kate explained to her as simply as she could, but she was unconvinced. Coincidentally the following week's biology lesson focused on the thyroid gland – now suddenly an expert on the subject, daughter acquired overnight sympathy and understanding for mother's difficulties, itself a powerful factor in mother's recovery.

Times of mental and emotional stress show up one of the strengths of our large family group. There is mutual understanding – all the family have seen it before, and many have experienced something similar themselves. There is a fund of goodwill – and because the group is large, everyone knows that the sense of responsibility (I hesitate to call it a burden) can be shared around, so that no one person needs to turn their back on the problem for fear of intolerable demands being made upon them. None of the children who grew up with us – unlike many of their peers in care – needs to experience isolation as an adult.

Health education

Several articles (e.g. Mather *et al*, 1997) have appeared in recent years about the particular difficulties experienced by young people in care or recently graduated from the care system in having access to information about health issues when they need it. Much is made about the young person having "nobody to talk to" in contrast with a young person growing up in the parental home whose preferred way of learning about health matters is a cosy chat with Mum. Health matters appear to be among those which young people in residential care see as falling into the gap between the remit of the residential care worker and that of the social worker. It was not so in our setting. "Mum" was there to be asked. We made no secret of issues about our own health and attempted to establish a climate where matters relating to health, sexuality, smoking, use of alcohol, etc. were ordinary topics of conversation. As our young people left home, an analysis of topics prompting a phone call home would feature health issues well up at the top of the list along with requests for culinary advice, lists of family birthdays, and loans of money!

I have fond memories of a schoolteacher who told my class never to believe anything we were told by anyone (even a schoolteacher) without checking it out with an independent source. He illustrated this by barking at us, 'Battle of Hastings, 1215!' – then immediately asking us the date of the Battle of Hastings and castigating those who obediently but incorrectly answered, '1215, sir'! Children who are having to learn to trust are less likely to believe or accept what we tell them. We always encouraged them to seek a reputable second opinion. In health matters we were fortunate in that Kate's mother was Head of Care at the school along the lane, and seen as an authority on health issues by the boys at the school, and therefore obviously, to our children at least, a recognised expert. They would often insist in involving her in treatment of minor injuries, and it was a short step from there to discussion of other health-related topics.

We had other very natural ways of including health education into our everyday life – the ways in which children have traditionally come to learn about health and sickness, and the cycle of life and death. Throughout our years with the children the household was full of animals leading eventful lives; additionally, many of our children were able to be involved in two of Kate's pregnancies and in the nurturing of our three home-grown children through infancy and beyond. There was also some family experience of terminal illness and death, not easy to deal with at the time since they stirred up some of the inevitable feelings of loss which the children brought with them when they joined us, but invaluable learning experiences, perhaps all the more so.

Children can learn so much from looking after animals. Most of ours – the dogs, the cats, the chickens, the donkeys – were in their various ways family pets, for which Kate and I took the bulk of the responsibility whilst encouraging the children to take an active part in looking after them. Others – Fred's ferrets and polecats, Josie's rabbits and guinea-pigs, Martin's goats, Sharon's budgie and duck, Dan and Rich's rats – were individual interests, their owners assuming the burden of housing them, caring for them, and separating them out from other members of the household menagerie which might either make life difficult for them or be eaten by them! They furnished constant opportunities for learning about hygiene, nutrition, exercise, appropriate stimulation, stress and anxiety, reproduction, antenatal and perinatal care, post-operative, intensive and palliative care, and – slightly anthropomorphic, this one, but we had the full range – personality disorder and associated behavioural idiosyncracies, often compressed into the space of conveniently short lifespans. We tried to make the most of opportunities to draw parallels between animal and human experience and behaviour when the comparisons weren't too far-fetched. Since several of our animals had come to us from deprived or damaging backgrounds – most of the cats from animal shelters, the chickens from a battery farm, the seven-year-old labrador from a shed where she had lived chained up for a year – their emotional and mental wellbeing was often an instructive cause for concern just as much as their physical health. Many of the lessons to be learned were about the possibility of change: the effects of a nutritious diet, of a warm, stable environment, of consistent kindness and of fresh air and exercise in improving quality of life were immediate and obvious. I was saddened on a recent visit to a small children's long-term residential unit recently to learn that staff had decided to turn down the young people's request for a house cat on the grounds of hygiene and the risk of ill-treatment of the cat. Somehow the enormous benefits to the children had been overlooked.

Sharing in the miracle of pregnancy and in the delights and demands of bringing up small children was just as valuable. The first cohort of children placed with us were able to observe and share in our preparations for the arrival of Tom and Rich, to be present when they were fed, to share in bathing them and Sal, to be aware of our responses to them, our stimulation of them, our attempts to ascribe meaning to their behaviour as they grew. They saw our mistakes – when Rich was sunburned through not being adequately covered for twenty minutes of a hot summer day, or when I secured Tom's nappy by pinning it directly to his abdomen – and the importance we placed on learning from them. They were party to our discussions about their development, to our decisions – and disagreements – about what to do for the best. They could join in, and exercise some caring responsibility – all children have a need to nurture, to care for others. Over twenty years later I have heard Sharon, Lynn, Josie and Fred each recall memories of our handling of our birth children in their early years, and consciously apply those memories to their dealings with their own children. Often there was a huge contrast with their patchy memories of their own childhoods.

Karen, in contrast, was close to our birth children in age: her only memories of parenting small children are of her own parents' neglectful and often abusive treatment of her younger siblings, and she has had to work hard to learn as theory to be applied to her own children what the former group had assimilated through experience and observation.

It is difficult in this chapter to stay within clear boundaries in discussing health. If you consider people holistically, as I learned to do increasingly as our family grew and developed, you cannot but see the concept of "health" spills over into considerations of identity, of behaviour and relationships, of self-care. Much of what you are reading in this chapter you will read again elsewhere in this book, only seen through a slightly different prism, or from a different perspective. The experience of loss, and the feelings associated with it, is a common factor in the experience of looked after children; the losses are particular, of people and of places, and it is hard for carers to recognise what each of these losses means for each child in their new situation, and for the child to feel that their experience is shared and understood.

Our stability as a family group over time enabled us to experience shared losses. An early and significant one for the family was the terminal illness and death from lung cancer of Kate's grandfather in 1980/1981. He and his wife had moved from the Midlands to be close to Kate's parents a year or two before. She had never fully accepted the children into her definition of "family", and consequently had remained on the fringe of their horizons – her sudden death from heart disease caused shock, but relatively little emotion. But the diagnosis at the same time of lung cancer in "Grandad Tom" had, I think, more effect. The children liked his Northern good humour – and were fascinated by his nose! As treatment for skin cancer several years before, half of his nose had been surgically removed, and was replaced by a very obviously plastic prosthesis which he glued on each morning. Good-naturedly and without the slightest embarrassment or irritation he would answer constant questions from the children about the nose, the skin cancer, its likely cause in decades of smoking, and could even be persuaded to demonstrate its removal and replacement! At the age of 82, he accepted his diagnosis of lung cancer with equanimity, and was able to be quite open about his impending death.

The children mourned his loss, and shared their mourning with us. And they learned about the long-term effects of smoking, about coping with physical disadvantage, about death, and how it can be faced with courage.

I don't remember how many of the children attended Grandad Tom's funeral: I do remember that most, by then grown-up, attended the funeral of my own father fifteen years later. I remember being aware of how they had learned to share their grieving and to comfort each other. And I am unlikely ever to forget the significance of the presence of Liam, who had been out of contact with us for two years, behaving dangerously and self-destructively in his own private hell, but who felt able to come and share with us all his grief for the substitute grandfather he had loved, which merged with his grief for his long-dead mother, and for himself. As I watched him hugging and being hugged by all our other children, I felt that this was the beginning of his journey back to emotional and mental health, as indeed it was.

There had been other deaths: a fifteen-year-old schoolfriend of Liam had died suddenly in 1992, the result of an unknown heart defect. Then, Liam had been unreachable in his grief. Soon afterwards, one of Tom's closest friends had died over several months from Hodgkin's disease. Towards the end, Tom was spending several hours with him daily, and receiving as much quiet support in his vigil from the family as they could muster. An awareness that "in the midst of life, there is death" can help young people, particularly those who have suffered loss in less stable periods of their lives, to identify and express their emotions in the safety of a supportive group, and to appreciate more keenly the significance of health.

Doctors and nurses

We share the responsibility for our children's health care and health education with others. Doctors, health visitors, school nurses, and teachers responsible for health education input at school are our colleagues in this task. They have a duty to co-operate with us: we have to ensure that they understand the nuances of the task we are sharing and have access to whatever information may help them.

The choice of a GP for a family of looked after children is almost as crucial as the choice of schools. It is important that the GP has an understanding of the likely health needs of looked after children. It must be someone who is prepared to work alongside the carers as colleagues, and who will value their opinion of what may be troubling the young person, and their advice on how best to handle him or her. Being touched and examined is a particularly sensitive issue for children who have suffered abuse, and sensitivity to this is required on the part of the GP. Diagnosis can demand patience. Insecurely attached or abused children may lack conscious awareness of their own bodies. Josie, as a young child, walked around for hours apparently oblivious to a huge piece of glass embedded in her foot; Lynn would be convinced that she had crippling pain in her knee, when the problem might be an ear infection; Kwesi, conversely, had as a child an amazingly low tolerance of any physical discomfort, unless acquired on a football field! They may exaggerate or minimise pain, or may appear to be inventing symptoms as they struggle to express in somatic terms what may be an emotional disorder.

It's hard to know how to go about finding a GP who meets these stringent criteria. Personal knowledge is the safest way, if carers know their local community. When we moved to Plainlands we were fortunate in being able to register with a local GP who had a particular interest and experience in children with troubled backgrounds. He was the medical officer of the special school where Kate's parents worked (soon to become the chair of its governing body). He both understood our children's difficulties and respected us through knowing us by repute. A gentle, quietly-spoken man, he said little so could never be seen to be patronising. He conducted examinations patiently and respectfully. When questions were to be asked, he directed straightforward ones to the children, which they appreciated, and more complex ones to us, which they also appreciated. When explanations were required, he would make them simply to child and carer together (sometimes indicating that Kate or I might care to talk to him in more detail on the phone later). If a child was really ill for a period of time, he would often drop in unannounced on his way to or from the surgery to check on his patient. It took some of our children some time to like him (his bow-tie, huge dark desk and ubiquitous pictures of steam-engines presented, in their various ways, barriers to intimate acquaintance), but they respected him, and trusted him as much as they could have trusted anybody.

Nevertheless, it took us some time to overcome some instances of deep-seated opposition to annual medical examinations. We could have handled this better. With hindsight, a possible solution is obvious. We should have recognised that most of the opposition was not to the process itself, but to the fact that singled out the child being examined as a child in care. After all, despite the widespread anxieties held by many people about visiting the dentist, we experienced nothing like the same opposition from our children to regular dental check-ups – indeed these were often appreciated as an indicator of our parental concern. We would book in three or four children at a time, along with Kate or myself. But the regulation insistence on annual medical examinations of children in care negated all our other efforts to enable our children to present themselves as "normal" members of the community, living in an ordinary house with a Mum and Dad and brothers and sisters, all of whom could use the same surname. They knew – and approved – that we had turned down the gift of a new minibus from a charity which would have come on condition that "Donated by X Charity" would be brightly painted on the side, preferring us to stick with our elderly, much less comfortable, but anonymous one, and use cars whenever we could. This was an identity issue, not a health issue at all. If Kate and I had insisted on a comprehensive medical check-up every year for ourselves, and for Sal, Tom and Rich, there might never have been a problem.

That GP has retired now. We are comfortable with his successor, but some of our children who have settled back in our area after time away are now registered with another local practice whose partners came to

know us all well as members of the community and professional colleagues over the years. They continue to be treated with great understanding by concerned doctors who are prepared to fight for them to get tightly
rationed resources in recognition of the health legacy of their childhoods.
I meet many doctors in the course of my own professional work, and note
with sadness that such understanding of the significance of an "in care"
history is far from universal. The public, media-fed perception of children
in care as punishment ('What have they done?') rather than as protection
('What has been done to them?') is still not uncommon even among
professionals.

We were fortunate in our school nurse, if not in our health visitor.
Fortunately the latter impinged little on the family. After Rich's birth she
informed us loudly (in the hearing of older children) that he would never
breast-feed, thrive, or reach educational milestones growing up in such a
large, chaotic household. (He did all of these, and Kate delighted in taking
him to the clinic for regular weighing and checking to prove it.) She
made clear her disapproval of any household containing more than two
children, the number she described as 'socially acceptable nowadays'.

The school nurse was more flexible, tolerant and insightful. She
became an ally both to us and to the children. They would go to her when
they were feeling low, or confused, or afraid, and she would see beyond
the spurious physical symptom (sometimes genuinely felt) presented as a
passport, administering the required amount of reassurance or
encouragement before making the right decision about helping them to
return to class or consulting us.

Recent studies of health education and looked after children have
pointed out that many looked after children miss out on health education
provided at school, simply because they are not at school. They may be
excluded, habitual truants, or simply not attending because they have
moved placement and are awaiting a school place in the new area. Regular
school attendance was high on our agenda, and our children will only
have missed school-provided health education because they were
genuinely ill on the day, not a common occurrence.

Food and drink

Friends and acquaintances have often asked us in bewilderment how we coped with the varied dietary preferences and fads of such a large family. On the whole, we didn't even try. Meals in our household were not run on democratic principles. Kate and I did the food shopping, and whilst we would listen to suggestions, the final decisions were very definitely ours. Mealtimes were social occasions, not battlegrounds, and it was table d'hôte, not á la carte. There was the food, and usually plenty of it; you could have as much as you liked while it was there, but there was nothing else, and we all stayed at the table until the meal was over. Appetite broadens and fussiness diminishes in such a setting. Peer pressure, yet again, is powerful.

Yet there were often big adjustments for children to make, and we had to recognise that our children's previous dietary experience was usually very different, and strike a reasonable balance. Karen remembers, 'Mum used to do a lot of home cooking which I had trouble coming to terms with after my frozen-produce-and-instant-mash diet at the children's home. This also became a bit of a worry for me when inviting friends to tea as the majority of them were used to frozen chips with burgers, etc.'

Our cooking was kept simple. If everything could be cooked in one big pot on our solid fuel range, then so much the better. We ate lots of home-concocted soups and stews. Jacket potatoes had obvious advantages over variants which needed more preparation. Big pies, straight from the pages of *Desperate Dan*, were commonplace. However, Kate was vegetarian throughout our time with the children, and usually at least one of the children would be showing solidarity with her for at least a few months, so we ate quite a lot of non-meat meals, or had a vegetarian option, or a meal which was nutritious and wholesome whether or not the meat was added. Neither of us is or was a brilliant or particularly keen cook, and several of the children overtook us in ability as they were growing up. But we did try to use wholesome ingredients, to avoid over-processed food, and to rate nutrition over fashion, and talked to the family about dietary balance and reading the list of ingredients with care. We could probably have done a Mastermind special subject on "E-numbers and their significance".

Our children were generally healthy when they were with us, and we openly made the connections with them between good health and diet. But here as in most areas of life, we tried to avoid rigidity, and the children knew that we had many friends who were much more fundamentalist than we were in their avoidance of a whole range of foods, for political as well as dietary reasons. Meals at one friend's house were avoided by the family, who described her vegan meals as tasting uniformly like baked doormat. We didn't forbid Macdonald's or KFC as an occasional "treat", tried to control rather than rule out sweets and snacks between meals, and to advocate rather than insist on fresh fruit as an alternative. And we tried to pass on the idea that food, like so many other aspects of life, could be an adventure, an area for new experiences. When we had visitors from other parts of the world who would bring ingredients and cook us something from their homeland, we would take the culinary journey with them.

We now see our children feeding their own families. Their choices are all different, their partners grew up with different expectations. The approaches they take to diet and health may not be the same as ours or one another's, but they are the result of considered and informed thought, not of ignorance.

Exercise needs a mention. Several of our children – mainly the boys – enjoyed sports at school, particularly football. But everybody took advantage of the large flat lawn behind the house, which became not only Wembley, but by turn Twickenham, Lord's, Wimbledon, Wentworth and wherever else the international venues for rounders and rally-o are, as the seasons passed. All that was needed was the provision of some basic equipment and good-natured tolerance around the incidence of balls meeting windows or plants. The ready availability of enough people to play and space to do it meant that little parental encouragement was necessary. Trees around the garden were ideal for climbing. The hill close by made a good place to walk the dog or go tobogganing in winter. The distances from school and other facilities were just right to encourage walking or cycling. In short, we didn't need to make the children take exercise – we were able to provide the space and freedom to do it, and it happened in an unregimented way.

Smoking and alcohol were also issues on which we tried to take a middle line, both responsible and pragmatic. Like many middle lines, its course changed over the years. Kate and I both smoked cigarettes as students and for a few years afterwards. Kate stopped when she was first pregnant, and hasn't smoked since, except for a few months in the mid-1990s when we felt under particular pressure. I became a pipe-smoker, and continued irregularly until about ten years ago. I still enjoy a very occasional cigar. Kate's father was still a "social smoker" when our first children were small; mine worked for all his working life in the tobacco industry and was partly paid in cigarettes. So outright condemnation of smoking would have appeared to our children highly hypocritical.

However, we talked to them of the dangers. We said we would discourage them from becoming smokers; we would not allow them to smoke in the house; if they did choose to smoke, we would not collude with it, and we requested them not to smoke in our sight. A visiting SSI inspector once looked out through Fred's bedroom window, which gave onto a tiny enclosed area of flat roof over a bay window below, and announced that it appeared to be someone's ashtray! Several of our children had, of course, been regular smokers before they came to us; others found smoking to be a calming prop when times were hard and emotions challenging; others again found that smoking gave them access to social groups from which exclusion would hurt. We learned to be tolerant and understanding. As the years went on (or perhaps when I gave up my pipe) our house became a virtual no-smoking zone for adults and children alike, and those of our children who still smoke go outside for a cigarette when they visit us. The smokers still outnumber the non-smokers, but we notice a general reduction in intake over the years, and continue to accept but discourage.

Our policy on alcohol was similar. We were, of course, officially running a children's home, however little that may have been apparent to our children, our neighbours, and often to ourselves. And I understand that contemporary regulations suggest that alcohol should not be stored in children's homes, that consumption of it in the home by older teenagers should be at most very occasional and closely supervised, and that there should always be at least one staff member who abstains entirely from alcohol. So much for our modest "cellars", then – usually no more than a couple of bottles of wine, a bottle of sherry, and maybe a six-pack of beer. And so much for our occasional shared glass or two of wine at the end of a long day when most of the children had gone to bed, or our modest Christmas and birthday celebrations.

We tried to demonstrate to our children by example that alcohol as a treat, in moderation, was fine for adults. As children reached their mid-teens we would occasionally invite them to share a drink with us on a special occasion. Alcohol in the house was not kept locked away, in accordance with our general policy of trust. The policy was very rarely abused. Josie and Mark's 1975 Christmas cocktail, featuring sherry, Coca-Cola and Andrews' Liver Salts, will long be remembered for its explosive properties, and Sharon's ill-fated attempt to take a bottle of sweet British sherry to a school bottle stall still lingers in her memory, since she drank virtually all of it on the way. By and large, we presented to our children a lifestyle in which alcohol played a minor role, and drunkenness was seen as neither clever nor desirable.

Illegal drugs

The use of illegal drugs was an issue of substance abuse which we had less frequent need to confront. For most of the 1970s and 1980s we had to contend with little more than occasional experimentation with solvents, which we dealt with as a serious and dangerous matter, but in a "more in sorrow than in anger" style, with the focus being more on the underlying malaise which had provoked the experiment. In the 1990s we had to work out how to view the relative seriousness of various different drugs – cannabis, amphetamines, heroin – and to come to terms with insidious links between drug use and grooming for sexual abuse, as well as the needs of children who had been born into the drug culture and experienced it in their early childhood.

We tried to read, to learn, to talk, and not to panic. So many other aspects of our children's behaviour – lying, aggression, stealing, smoking, and so on – were things that we or other children we had known had done as children. We had seen other parents address these things, and based our own favoured attitudes and approaches on the outcomes we had observed. But this was a foreign country, where we didn't know the language or understand the culture. And we were dropped into it without the benefit of an authoritative induction course.

It seemed right not to deviate from our philosophy of openness, trust and support, to talk about the dangers as objectively as we could, and avoid extreme positions. It seemed right to take a relatively relaxed position on cannabis – having stressed its illegality and the consequences of falling foul of the law for the sake of something so ultimately unimportant (if you're going to flout the law, do it for a noble cause like peace or the environment, not the right to smoke some weed or other) – whilst not denying our grave anxieties about meddling with "harder" drugs. It does seem to me that cannabis is on the way to becoming a common lifestyle accessory in our society similar to tobacco in the very recent past, and I am not convinced that this will be disastrous.

The harder drugs caused us a real problem because of their increased availability and our children's vulnerability, particularly those who, goodness knows, had cause enough to seek powerful self-medication to ease their pain, and yet fell lamentably short of adult capacity to weigh in the balance the unintended but life-destroying long-term consequences. I think we recognised that we could advise, educate, guide and encourage, but we could not enforce. If the advice and encouragement were not enough, we could only offer non-collusive support, in the knowledge that it might be needed, by the bucketful, well beyond the years of childhood.

Sexuality

And what, you ask, did we do about sex? You didn't mean what did *we* do, personally, and yet that has to be part of the answer. It took us a while to accept that the level of openness that Kate and I would have hoped to establish in the lives of our birth children in relation to nakedness and physical functions was impossible, and even potentially damaging, in a family such as ours. Our own sexual relationship had to be carried on discreetly, in a house where we were constantly, for years, alert to the unexpected cries or arrival in our bedroom or sitting-room in the early morning, late evening, or small hours of a distressed or frightened child. And yet our children, we felt, had to be aware of our strong physical relationship. They had to know that we were committed to each other and fulfilled in our relationship, for that gave them security.

Those who had been sexually abused by parents or carers had to know that each of us, as far as sex was concerned, was fully absorbed in the other. It was good for them, we felt, to notice us using terms of endearment to each other, or snatching a kiss or a cuddle, and it pleased them to see that we were happy (despite choosing to live with them, which others had found difficult enough!). I should also say that the strength of our relationship could be tested severely, through days sometimes marked by heated arguments, often in stage whispers, as we tried to resolve disagreements about how to resolve some child care problem that had arisen or how to allocate responsibilities between us. A firm resolve never to end a day physically detached, even when further discussion had to go on tomorrow, was a very necessary part of our life together.

As for the children, it was interesting to note that our insistence on defining ourselves as a family seemed to generate an almost complete "incest taboo" as they referred to each other as brothers and sisters. The experience of having small children in the house, who needed help at bathtime, was a wonderful prompt for natural questions about sex and childbirth which could be carried over into more general discussions at other times. Another advantage of the large family group was the huge range of acquaintance that they had – the sexual exploits or misfortunes of others were an easier lead-in to a general discussion, from which others would learn as well, than talking about oneself. We would talk openly about homosexuality – it is a sadness to me that Mark did not feel able to come out openly as gay until he was in his late twenties, but a source of pleasure that his homosexuality has been accepted without fuss by all the family.

We encouraged the bringing home of boyfriends and girlfriends, and expected them to remain in shared areas of the house, at least until beyond the age of consent, and even then, considerations of the susceptibilities of younger children would apply. Conversations about pre-marital sex were frequent, and the children will have been aware of my own transition over the years from a position of general disapproval to a more relaxed view. It is important, I have decided, to leave room in caring for children for your own views to change, and for the children to know that they have often been influential in those changes.

We did not, however, encourage sleepovers. This was undoubtedly due in some measure to the children's "in care" status, the degree of responsibility being placed on often unwitting parents of schoolfriends, and the difficulties of vetting and gaining permission. We preferred to take the decision ourselves, and be seen to take it ourselves, rather than shaking our children's sense of security by drawing attention to the fact that agreement to overnight stays had to be given by the local authority. But we had our own anxieties about the unknown night-time arrangements in many homes, and this was one way of reducing the chances of our children being exposed to further abuse.

We live in a social climate in which there is a growing suspicion of male carers. There can be no doubt that most of our children on joining us had a greater suspicion or even fear of me than of Kate, based presumably on gender expectations assimilated from their previous experiences. In most cases this fear took a long time to allay, and my own tendency towards impatience and irritability will not have helped, however I attempted to overcome it. But we felt strongly that it was very valuable for boys and girls alike to experience adult carers of both genders as both fully involved and sensitive, and to see our partnership as an equal and sharing one. I believe that that has made it more possible for our children to explore and define their own sexuality as neither victims nor aggressors. Sharon has recently remarked to me how she appreciated my apparent understanding of her initial discomfort if she found herself in a room alone with me, in that I would often come into a room where she was and find some reason to leave it immediately after briefly acknowledging her. The fact that most of our shared rooms had several exits also helped, as did our fastidiousness about respecting the privacy of our post-pubertal children in their bedrooms.

Mortality

Health is essentially about prolonging and preserving life. As I write, our children are all alive. I suspect that this may be an achievement in itself. We have long underestimated the long-term damage which childhood harm or neglect can cause – to the functioning of the brain and other vital organs, to the ability to recognise and assess risk, to self-esteem and motivation for self-care, to susceptibility to illness, addiction, accident, violence or self-harm. Growing up in care is not in itself dangerous, although the life events which precede it often are, but the experience can and often does perpetuate those earlier disadvantages. If I live to be averagely old – and I was born in 1949 – it would not be surprising if some of our children do not outlive me. I am sure that, had they remained in some of the murkier reaches of the care "system", some of them would not be alive now.

Key factors

- Being aware of the likely health-related consequences of earlier abuse or trauma.
- Considering possible health-related reasons for unusual behaviour.
- Remembering to take into account children's mental health needs.
- Explaining to children and other important people in their systems and networks the possible roots of their physical, mental and emotional difficulties.
- Using the strength of the group as a source of acceptance and support.
- Making health issues part of everyday family conversation.
- Making available varied sources of information.
- Encouraging children to care for pets and participate in looking after small children.
- Involving children in the miracles and emotions of birth and death.
- Exercising care in choosing a GP who will understand the needs of looked after children.
- Normalising routine medical procedures and check-ups as part of everyday life.
- Ensuring that children have access to a variety of people in whom they may confide about health matters.
- Providing a nutritious and varied diet without straying far outside cultural norms.
- Establishing mealtimes as enjoyable shared social occasions.
- Providing the space, freedom and equipment to encourage healthy exercise.
- Keeping open channels of communication to discuss health issues concerning diet, smoking, alcohol and other drugs, and sex.

- Leading by example, ideally one of tolerance and moderation.
- Recognising that you may be able to advise and encourage, but not to enforce.
- Acknowledging the particular stresses on looked after children which will influence their choices.

4 Education
Developing appreciation and
understanding of the world around us

Measurable outcomes

"Education, education, education". The 1997 election slogan still rings
hollow when we consider educational outcomes for children who grow
up within the care system. Ever since Mike Stein's work in the 1980s on
children "leaving care" (Stein and Carey, 1986) we have been aware that
the educational standards attained by looked after children at the point at
which they "leave care" are abysmal. The percentage gaining 5 GCSEs at
grades A – C remains obstinately in single figures despite having climbed
to over 50 per cent in the population as a whole. The numbers entering
higher education in their late teens are negligible (see Jackson (ed), 2001).

Perhaps these figures are not too surprising. Children in long-term
care are likely to have suffered severe emotional damage from their pre-
care experiences of poor attachment and the repeated trauma of abuse.
Their brains will have developed differently from children with secure
early attachments, safe environments and appropriate stimulation (Cairns,
2002a). They may have enormous difficulties with motivation,
concentration and retention, and may be too preoccupied with survival to
learn much in the arcane atmosphere of school. But if they are to survive
as coping people in adulthood, literate, numerate and able to make
connections within a reasonably accurate framework of knowledge, they
cannot be allowed to see learning as irrelevant and study skills as
unnecessary.

We may also have been measuring outcomes too early. People
increasingly continue to study and to gain qualifications throughout their
lives. Adults who have grown up in care and found it impossible to achieve
to their full potential during their childhood may and do discover their
ability to learn in later life, once blocks to learning have been successfully
overcome. Our family history suggests that placing enough importance
on education during childhood can help looked after children both to be

more successful at school and to return to education effectively later in life. It can also have huge effects on their health, self-esteem, social relationships, self-care skills, and so on, so education permeates every chapter in this book.

All of the children who grew up with us were able to attend mainstream primary and secondary school, and this met their need to see themselves as "normal". We did, however, negotiate for two of them, for different reasons, to move to a local Rudolf Steiner school for two or three years before reintegrating them into the local state schools. Another child, with a measured IQ of 147, had spent most of his school career before joining us in special schools or receiving (meaning "not receiving") "home tuition". Yet another had been referred to an expensive and prestigious therapeutic community home with education, and been turned down as "too difficult".

We made it an absolute condition of placement with us that each of these children would attend our local mainstream schools. Fortunately they joined us late in the development of the family, when we had already built up good relationships with these schools, whose staff were anxious to help.

Everybody took at least five, and usually a full eight or nine, GCE, CSE or GCSE exams in Year 11, and achieved a grade in all of them. Only four – and this included our three birth children – passed five or more at grade C or above at age 16+, but the majority had at least one or two at that level.

All but two of the children stayed in full-time education for at least one year beyond the age of sixteen. One of those two, as a mother of four in her late twenties, has completed an access course with very high grades and won a place to study at HNC level. The rest muster a clutch of BTEC, accountancy, and City and Guilds qualifications and an HND-equivalent qualification in agriculture, and there are three graduates, one of whom was one of our in-care children. Two of the men in their twenties continue to give consideration to returning to college or taking advantage of workplace training to gain more qualifications, having left school after one year in the sixth form. These outcomes may not seem glittering, but are far removed from the national picture. The post-16 successes would not have happened if the children had been "moved into independent living" at 16. The post-18 successes could not have happened without local authorities being prepared to continue financial sponsorship, including paying for a place at home with us outside term-time, which we might otherwise have had to fill with another child. The adult returners might well not have returned if they had not continued to benefit from the stimulation and motivation of remaining part of the family group, in regular supportive contact with each other.

There are also less measurable outcomes. There appears to be a positive and informed attitude among our children as parents towards the educational needs of their own children. Books are in evidence in most of their homes. They give careful thought to choosing their children's schools, and attend parents' evenings. They are not in awe of their children's teachers, or dismissive of them, but do appear to see them as partners in bringing up their children. Most of them reminisce with pleasure about their schooldays and with affection about their own teachers – at least, that is, their schooldays and teachers experienced after joining our family. For many of them, their earlier experiences, whether when living with birth parents or in other care settings, are remembered very differently.

Stability

Children find changing schools difficult, probably more difficult than most adults find moving house. Friends are new, teachers are new, uniforms are new, rules are new, written and unwritten. The National Curriculum notwithstanding, there will rarely be a seamless join in what is being taught. For children in care, placement breakdown often means a change of school as well as a change of home. Even if the new home is close enough to the old school to make it possible to continue at the same school, it is likely that the child will have to be taxied in from outside the catchment area to the detriment of social relationships and a sense of truly belonging to the school community. Parents of stable birth families will often make considerable sacrifices to avoid having to make their children change schools. Yet children in care will often experience several school moves for reasons of placement breakdown, bureaucratic expediency, or exclusion (often because of behaviour indicative of their need to be in care in the first place).

Our children experienced educational stability once they joined us. True, the first four children to join us had just over a term in primary school before moving with us to the house ten miles away which was to be their home for the rest of their childhood and enrolling at its local primary school. And there were other exceptions – the two whom we moved to Steiner school, and one who had a disrupted period at age 14-15 and left our care to return to her birth family's home area, returning to us nine months later and welcomed back to the local comprehensive. But largely our children's experience was exactly the same as that of virtually all our neighbours' children with whom they would walk to and from school – nearest local primary for those who joined us younger than 11, followed by the local comprehensive.

Indeed, the Steiner option would probably not have occurred to us had it not been the school attended – through parental choice – by the children of our immediate neighbours. But for a large, black, socially awkward and quite emotionally burdened six-year-old, it offered even greater peer group tolerance and less academic pressure while she settled with us; for an emotionally blocked potential school refuser who adopted the role of class clown as a coping mechanism, it provided an informal and sensitive setting and developed his undoubted artistic talent. Being able to share transport (the school was 12 miles away) with our neighbours and two other local families helped with logistics and a sense of it being a "normal" thing to do. Our children were always very sensitive to arrangements being made for them which appeared to be different from those made for "normal" children.

Only one of our children, Martin, came to live with us from an address within our county. At 13, Martin was reasonably settled in a comprehensive school about seven miles away from our house, and was anxious to stay there – so he did. In retrospect we should possibly have overridden the objections and moved him to our local school with the rest of the family, He might then have chosen to stay in the local sixth form rather than undertaking post-16 education at the FE College ten miles away, and might not, as an adult, particularly after his marriage at 21, have come to feel himself to be an outsider in the family, discriminated against and rejected by the others. He is now, in his early thirties, the only one of the children who grew up with us who has not been in touch for several years.

But there were other reasons for our decision not to insist on that change of school. We had tried in our "admissions policy" to build something like a "normal" family by avoiding having two children of the same age and gender who would therefore experience each other as direct competitors in the classroom. Martin was just two weeks older than Dan. When he joined us, Dan had been with us for over eight years, a placid, good-natured, well-adjusted and generally compliant person, respected in school by teachers and peers, already predicted to be capable of winning a university place. Martin was a more average achiever who had more difficulty with personal relationships. We felt that the competition of being in the same year group where Dan had already forged an identity would not be helpful for either of them. Teachers can make invidious comparisons. We could help them to get used to each other's presence in their lives and work out their relationship at home, but had minimal influence over events at school or within a shared peer-group. Moreover, Martin had a champion at his existing school in a committed and understanding Head of Year who took a close interest in him, and who, by chance, lived very near to us. There seemed to be compelling reasons to accede to his wish to stay where he was.

With these exceptions, then, our children attended two local schools. The primary school was less than a mile away from home, along, for the most part, quiet country lanes. It was a Church of England school of about a hundred and sixty pupils, one class per year except for a team teaching arrangement for upper infants/lower juniors where between 45 and 50 children were taught in a large space by two teachers. For 14 years we had between one and four children on roll there at any one time, and the Head and Deputy Head remained unchanged throughout that time. That consistency, most often found in rural areas, was valuable.

Children from this school, and from six or seven others in our town and surrounding villages, moved on to the local comprehensive. There was very little "creaming off". The nearest selective schools were in towns 10 and 15 miles away respectively, and the comprehensive, which had previously been a grammar school, enjoyed a good local reputation both among parents of high achievers and parents of children of more limited ability. It was a little farther away from home than the primary school, but still only just over a mile, and an easy walk by a choice of routes. Its headmaster had been in post since the school was formed as a comprehensive school in 1971, and the headship changed only once, in 1989, during the 20 years in which we had between one and six pupils there at any one time. Particularly in the first dozen years or so of this period, the staff were also a very stable group. Some of them had even taught Kate, for she had been a sixth-former there when it had been a grammar school in the 1960s.

Most of our children needed to use a lot of emotional energy throughout their childhoods coming to terms with the constant, perplexing and turbulent changes which had characterised their lives before coming to live with us. The stability of primary and comprehensive education in a small country town ensured that their subsequent schooling, at least, would take place in safe and predictable settings.

Choice of school

All this detail is important, because we didn't come across these schools by chance. These were precisely the sort of schools which we wanted to assist us in bringing up a family comprised mainly of children in care. We had chosen the community in which we would live in large measure for the sort of educational opportunity it would provide – stable, socially-mixed schools central to the life of their communities, where staff wanted to stay, and to which all the local children went, irrespective of ability. Our children would fit in, although we had some initial anxieties about those whose racial and cultural heritage were other than white British (cf. chapter on Identity).

The primary school had been founded in the 18th century, and the original house remained as the headmaster's house, with modern buildings and the inevitable "temporary" classrooms straggling down the hill behind it towards a stream. It was as if the kind, larger-than-life headmaster and his beaming, motherly wife kept a school in their back garden. Our children loved it. Directly in front stretched the village green, with two venerable oaks at either end and the war memorial in the middle. If it sounds chocolate-box and twee, it was all of that. But it was one of the many reasons why we set up our home where we did.

The school's atmosphere matched its setting. It was a happy school, with lots of music and singing. Teachers at the comprehensive reckoned that its pupils possibly arrived in Year 7 a little behind in literacy and numeracy compared with pupils from some of the other feeder primaries, but with a curiosity and interest in the world that could be captured by secondary school teachers, and a well-motivated approach to learning. Quite simply, they tended to enjoy school. And they tended to catch up and overtake their peers from other primaries very quickly. This was just what we felt our children needed. It was an uncompetitive school, but concerned that each of its children should make progress. It was small enough for no child to be lost or forgotten, but large enough not to be swamped by a family like ours and to ensure that, for the most part, our children would not be singled out because of their difficulties in some areas. Its catchment area included both local authority estates and imposing detached houses in rural acres, and was the sort of area where more people than usual tended to be a bit unconventional – in lifestyle, livelihood, family structure or outlook.

Our children needed this easy tolerance, and thrived on it. They liked the unthreatening buildings, the quiet, leafy surroundings, the informal atmosphere. They loved – on the whole – the walk to school in fine weather, rooting around in the stream, stroking the horses in a roadside field, kicking about the autumn leaves, or slithering down the hill in the snow, in those winters when we still had some. They still talk about it. To ensure that the journey to and from school was a relaxed one, we tried, not always successfully, to allow lots of time in the morning for a reasonably leisurely use of bathrooms and breakfast (Kate would often be singing and sorting out laundry on the upstairs landing shortly after 6 a.m., and I often found that the best time to do paperwork in my study), and not to have too many strict deadlines at the end of the school day.

The primary school was, as I have said, a Church school. We didn't choose it for that reason, and I am not a supporter of separate "faith" schools. However, it was not selective, and the ethos was certainly one of hard work on the part of the staff. Its religious education tended to present matters of opinion or belief as if they were fact, but this opened up some interesting discussions at home. Its regular services in the 14th-century parish church were an experience that our children would otherwise rarely have had. Perhaps they also helped our deracinated, emotionally bereft children to feel more of a sense of belonging to a community with a real sense of history. Or perhaps they just seemed scary and bewildering. The high, vaulted roof and profusion of statues and memorials, the archaic and confusing language of some of the hymns and inscriptions, the insistence on closed eyes and even kneeling for prayers, the cassocked vicar – all these were probably beyond the experience of most of our children, or may even have carried echoes of previous abusive situations. Certainly the church's profusion of memorials and well-stocked graveyard frequently seemed to throw up conversations about life and death which it was important for us not to ignore.

We only had to tell the vicar once, around our first Christmas in his parish, that we did not see ourselves, or our children, as suitable recipients of Church collections for local charitable causes. The primary school staff needed no such education.

We chose our children's secondary school by choosing not to choose. In moving our family to a town with just one, fully comprehensive, secondary school, we were ensuring that none of our children would suffer the stigma of being rejected by the school of their (or our) choice. Children in care have enough experience of rejection. We were also ensuring that they would largely be attending the same school as one another, lessening the scope for internal rivalry within the family and promoting shared experience and mutual support. In avoiding an area of selective schooling, we were ensuring that our "birth" and "in care" children would also attend the same school as one another. We guessed that children born to us were more likely to be selected for traditional grammar schools than children with more damaging early experiences would be. Removing potential barriers in the relationships between children born to foster- and adoptive parents and children placed with them does not, in my view, get enough attention. Birth children in such families may at times need a "safe haven" where they can escape from the pressures of acquired siblings who can be difficult to live with, but separate schooling is not the way to do it, for it can produce insidious notions of inferiority and superiority.

Having chosen a non-selective school, it has to be a good one. Our preference was for a school where many of the staff lived locally and had children who were pupils at the school (often difficult for those children, but a sign that the staff think highly of their own school and intend to stay). We wanted a school with some tradition of drama and music and sport, for we wanted less academically-able children to have the opportunity to express themselves in school in other ways. We felt it important that the head teacher believed it was important to know all the pupils individually. This one timetabled himself to teach each Year 7 group for one period a week so that he could get to know each of them at the start of their school career – and never forgot a name. He stood in the reception area most mornings and greeted individually as many of the arriving pupils as he could, a personal relationship which meant so much to our children who had had to behave outrageously in the past to be noticed by anybody. And we wanted a school that enjoyed a good reputation within its community, for we had no wish for our children's sense of themselves to be further tarnished by association.

We would not have gone to live where we did if the local schools had been less good. And if they had deteriorated significantly in quality while we were bringing up our family, we would have done our research and moved. It was as important an issue as that. Children spend so much of their time in school (or, should do, were it not for the contemporary scandal of exclusions) that considerations of where the children go to school needs to be a central part of the planning process for any new children's home. For new foster carers or adopters, choice of school should be a major concern, and moving house or even changing the schools of birth children should not be unthinkable. Caring for separated children in a family setting is not simply about grafting them onto an existing family – it is about making an existing household the right place for the newcomers to be.

Being involved with the school

There was a triangle of relationships to consider here. We had to build our own relationships with the school staff. We had to be aware of our children's relationships with their teachers, and do quite a lot of interpreting in both directions to keep them smooth. And we had to ensure that those relationships were helpful, and were perceived as helpful, to our children, and complemented our growing relationships with them.

Carers and teachers are colleagues in bringing up separated children. It was useful that I was working as a teacher in a local special school when we started our family, so I knew as professional colleagues some of our children's teachers. This helped to break the ice, for I knew as a teacher myself that there can be a reticence among teachers about relating to parents/carers, a suspicion of perceived "interference" unless it is on the school's terms, and often a professional reluctance to see them as authorities about their own children. Colleagues respect each other as equals, share ideas on equal terms, address each other by their first names. We tried to establish this sort of relationship with our children's teachers and other members of the school staff. It was a benefit to us that many of them lived very locally and that we would bump into them in all sorts of contexts outside school where we could oil the wheels of co-operation. And when talking to our children about their teachers we would refer to them by their full name – "John Cook" or "Helen Brown". It helped them to see their teachers as real people rather than distant authority figures.

We didn't leave the relationships to chance. A priority task early in the establishment of the family was getting to know key staff – heads, their deputies, teachers with pastoral care responsibilities. They needed to understand our family philosophy. They learned that, despite the disparate origins and legal status of our children, we and they wished to be seen as a family. We would ask them to be sensitive to the developing relationships our children had with us and with their birth families in terms of the vocabulary they used, the questions they asked, the assumptions they made. We made them aware of as much of our children's past histories as they felt able to assimilate, recognising that they would act as the repositories of this information in the school and share it with colleagues on a need-to-know basis. As we gradually learned more about how our children experienced their surroundings and how this directed their behaviour, we shared our findings or hypotheses with these colleagues. In particular, we had to interpret for them behaviour that arose out of panic or triggered fear, or inability to concentrate. We had to help them understand that our children were often experiencing the uncontrollable grief that follows loss, and that it could return after unsatisfactory contact with natural families, or further rejection by them. We made sure that they felt able to talk to us when they experienced or anticipated difficulties with our children, for teachers often fear a hostile response and rationalise decisions not to involve parents, whilst feeling that children's home staff just don't want to know.

During much of the family's secondary school years, their school's pastoral care was organised on a house system. Each house contained around 50 pupils from each school year. Siblings were normally placed in the same house. Our family was no exception, and the successive Heads of Barrett House became very influential people in the lives of our family. They came to hold a wealth of knowledge and information, and the children appreciated this acknowledgement of their "family" status.

Truanting rarely happened. It could never remain secret, given the closeness of family links with the school. We were uncompromising in our insistence on school attendance – Sharon remembers being "ill" in the morning, and being taken to school before lunchtime because she seemed to us to have "recovered". But mainly, as we helped our children to feel involved in school, they were happy to be there.

We had our own "early-warning system" at the comprehensive, in the shape of the receptionist/secretary. Strategically placed in the main foyer, overlooking the car park and next to the offices of senior staff, she missed little, and became adept at reading the signs of impending trouble. If it involved "one of ours", a telephone call advising us to contact a senior staff member often helped us to be involved in solving problems before they escalated. Herself the loving and loyal mother of a rebellious daughter who stretched the boundaries of school tolerance, she was also seen as "safe" by our children, who would turn to her if pressures were becoming too great.

In the context of these relationships we were often able to smooth the children's passage through an environment which early experience had led them to see as confusing or threatening. Compromises could be reached, about sanctions, uniforms or expectations, which made sense to our children without undermining the school's authority. We tried to avoid being confrontational, by being protective of our children whilst maintaining a dispassionate objectivity about their needs and abilities. We tried to explain rather than to defend.

The issue of uniform merits particular consideration. I go along with friends in Germany, who cannot imagine how or why British parents allow schools to make decisions about what their children will wear. My experi-ence of German schools suggests that older children will make choices about what to wear to school no more absurd than those made by their teachers when they are treated with a similar degree of respect as adults are. I find the British acceptance of the loss of self-expression and power to control their own bodies which we impose on older children by insisting on school uniform disturbing, and wonder if it is fanciful to postulate a link with our high level of teenage pregnancy.

Be that as it may, our local comprehensive insisted on school uniform. We made no secret to our children or their teachers of our general opposition to the concept of uniform, but equally made it clear that we could see no alternative to accepting it as a precondition of receiving the benefits of education in our area. We also shared in the joy felt by some of our children in the tangible evidence provided by the school uniform of their "normality". Honesty with children is always the best policy. Explaining why you will accept majority decisions within a group if the benefits of membership seem to outweigh the single issue helps to highlight and refine the subtleties of moral choice.

But sometimes we had to intervene. Forbidden to wear trousers to school, one of our girls who had previously been a frequent school refuser took much persuasion to go shopping for a grey skirt. Eventually she accepted a pleated, tent-like garment which brushed her ankles. Swathed in its folds, she set off to school only to be sent home with an ultimatum that she must wear a SHORTER skirt. The school skirt-length policy, no doubt the product of lengthy meetings, was mainly designed to outlaw skirts of eyebrow-raising shortness, but was explained by the Senior Mistress as being necessary to avoid extremes. In this case we were able to argue that our child had extreme needs, coming to terms as she was with awareness of an extreme degree of abuse. As her process of recovery from trauma continued, her need to cover up lessened, and peer pressure, to which we are all susceptible, prompted her to wear shorter skirts more readily, although she remained trousered by choice outside school until well into adulthood.

All schools should now have a designated teacher to monitor and co-ordinate the school's work with its looked after children. This will be a key person for all carers to get to know well. Just as we as carers moulded our home environment to meet our children's needs, so it is, I contend, the task of the LAC co-ordinator to ensure that the school recognises and meets the needs of the looked after child. He or she must be an advocate for the necessary flexibility, a repository of the necessary knowledge and understanding of each individual, and a rock to which parents and carers can cling in difficult times. It is a vitally important job, and carers need to know how well it is being done before the choice of school for a looked after child is finalised.

Creating a learning environment at home

'Do as I say, not as I do' never works. We felt that, if our children were going to take education seriously, they had to be aware that we took it seriously for ourselves. So Kate and I talked a lot with the family about our own schooldays and about the university where we met. We also continued to study as the family was growing up. Pressured though it was, I fitted into those years a Diploma in Social Administration, a CQSW, and a Certificate in Management Studies, while Kate also completed a CQSW and a National Institute for Social Work qualification in Social Work Education. And we tried to talk about what we were doing with the family, and to pass on some of our enthusiasm as well as our agonising when it got difficult. Some of our children found success hard; being praised for doing well at school jarred with their self-image. It was good for them to be able to congratulate us on success and to share our joy in achievement.

Our house was full of books. A well-filled bookcase, or several, was essential furniture in every room, every corridor, every landing. Deliberately, we mixed all the books up (finding a particular book often involved the whole family for several hours, with all sorts of serendipitous "discoveries" along the way!). We made little distinction between "our" books and "children's" books, and imposed no censorship. We read a lot ourselves, and it became a convention, if not a rule, of the household that to interrupt someone who was reading was almost as impolite and insensitive as to interrupt a conversation. Reading bedtime stories was an important activity for many years – sometimes with individuals in their bedrooms, sometimes communally by the living room fire all nestled on a huge corner sofa. Some of the older children enjoyed this opportunity to enjoy something they had missed as younger children. Usually we would do whole books over the course of several nights – I remember the Narnia saga and *Jacob Two-Two and the Hooded Fang* being particularly appreciated. We packed a book box when we went off on family holidays, plundered secondhand bookstalls, gratefully accepted gifts of book collections from older friends moving to smaller houses. Books were us.

Newspapers were important too. For many years we had two – a broadsheet and a tabloid – delivered every day, and encouraged passing them around the breakfast table and reading aloud from them. Kwesi, slow to read but with an early fanatical interest in sport, suddenly developed reading skills when he realised that the back pages of the newspapers were devoted entirely to sports news.

We could have done more to encourage more practical learning, although I shall return to that in the context of self-care skills (Chapter 8). A more practical father would have kept garage and sheds more fully stocked with bits of wood and metal and mechanical odds and ends, would have made more of the garden than an acre and a half of football field, lido, donkey pasture, scruffy orchard, site of secret dens and place to generally let off steam. But there was no shortage of practical skill and willingness to share it among neighbours, and at least three of our young people terrified their social workers with tales of underage tractor-driving on the adjacent farms. We did have our own whole menagerie of animals over the years, from which much was learned, and living alongside them brought other advantages in the development of sensitivity and responsibility.

Space to study and read quietly was important. I have visited many children's homes where the perceived need for staff to keep children under constant observation has engendered large open-plan communal areas as bleak as station concourses and not at all conducive to privacy. Being a lover of privacy myself, my study was always a sacrosanct place to which I could retreat, and although it housed all the children's files as well as things personal to me, we never gave it the institutional title of "office". Plainlands had three inter-connecting living rooms with comfortable sofas and armchairs in addition to the dining room, as well as armchairs in the hall and on the landing, so privacy was never difficult to find. A caravan in the garden was a real away-from-it all space, much loved particularly by Karen and Tom. Bedrooms all had a chair and a desk or table. And the house was full of cushions to suit those who preferred to sprawl on the floor to read or do homework.

Ah yes, homework! Once the children reached secondary school, we assumed that there would be homework and that it would be done. We tried to discourage its being done in front of the television, but otherwise didn't mind where it was done – some preferred their bedrooms, some the dining room table, some the kitchen while tea was being prepared, so that help could be sought every few seconds. Some liked to do it before tea, some after tea, some after going to bed. We tried not to dictate. We were willing to look over work done or make suggestions if asked, but chose not to insist on "checking", seeing that as part of the relationship between the children and their teachers, although sometimes we had to agree with a teacher to take on that task for a while if there had been problems. I am concerned by the contemporary assumption that parents must be intimately involved in every aspect of their children's schooling. Schools, in my view, educate children on behalf of society as a whole, not merely on behalf of their parents, and it is important for children to develop relationships with their teachers which are separate from and not somehow extensions of their relationships with their parents. We walked a careful tightrope between maintaining as carers a necessary close relationship with our children's teachers on the one hand, and maintaining a discreet and respectful distance from the minutiae of the child–teacher relationship.

We would offer help when a child was struggling with a particular subject (memories of hours wallowing with Josie in the unfathomable mysteries of vulgar fractions!) but would try not to impose it, and sometimes – one of the advantages of the big group – would suggest that one of the other children might equally be in a position to help. Of course that would boost the self-esteem of the child deemed to be "the expert", which had value in itself. Sometimes we would suggest approaching older friends or relatives outside the family – that too left the child in control of the situation, enhanced their network of relationships, and separated out education from parental authority.

Self-esteem is crucial to educational success, and we would try to boost individual self-esteem where we could see an opportunity (for a long time I was not good at recognising the opportunities.). For example, it was calm and practical eleven-year-old Josie whom Kate called for when she impaled her foot on a wicked four-inch nail protruding from a piece of wood. I increasingly called upon Mark's superior technical ability to solve problems with bicycles or cars; the developing culinary abilities of Josie and Martin were put to increasing and appreciated use; Dan's interest in maps meant that he often navigated on family trips and holidays. While Martin was keeping goats in the garden, we drank their milk with every appearance of appreciation.

Holidays and excursions were often planned with educational opportunities in mind. We avoided large holiday centres, partly a personal preference, partly a pragmatic decision based on questions of supervision of a large group. Until 1982 we took at least one, often more, British holiday each year, either swapping houses with some family brave enough to take the risk of having us invade their home, or renting a holiday house. So we explored rural and remote coastal areas of Yorkshire, Cambridgeshire, the Scottish Borders, the Lleyn peninsula, the South Hams of Devon. We would visit museums, farms, factories, castles, bird sanctuaries, coalmines. We would read and talk a lot about the area before we went. We would try to imagine with the children what it would be like to live there, in the present and the past. We worked our family minibus hard! We took a narrowboat holiday through the canals of the Midlands and learned about the Industrial Revolution. We borrowed a house in suburban Surrey and used it as a base to explore London, with a lot of prior discussion of what sights to visit. From 1982 on we developed the confidence to go further afield, always to places reachable in the minibus within a few hours of the coast – France, Denmark, Germany, Sweden, Ireland. Always again the house-swap or the rented house off the main tourist trail. Always trying to find opportunities to spend time with local people, to find out how it was to live there. In central Jutland the children made friends with local children who took them to their school. In Paris, in Dublin and Belfast, we toured the salubrious and less favoured (sometimes notorious) residential areas, and brought the television news alive. In the Harz Mountains of Germany, in 1989, we stood on the borderstones marking the Iron Curtain and looked into the unblinking eyes of East German border guards where the road petered out – and marvelled when the Berlin Wall fell just two months later. In Sweden we stayed in a friend's father's deserted wooden house in the middle of a vast forest, imagining how my friend's childhood must have been, and keeping our eyes peeled for elk – we also visited the local school and saw its beautifully set breakfast-tables, its carpeted classrooms with teacher's study off each one, and heard the head teacher say, 'We would not expect children to be less comfortable in school than they might be at home'.

But trips and holidays occupy very few days of a year. We also wanted to bring the world into our home. We joined SERVAS, a peace-promoting organisation whose international membership join as hosts or travellers. The hosts' contact details are published in a directory, and travellers can contact them and ask to stay for one or two nights as they travel the world, in exchange for being willing to talk to their hosts about their homeland and perhaps cook a meal from their home tradition. A succession of interesting people visited us and enthralled our children – we have particular memories of an Israeli woman who told us how her family had smuggled her out of Germany as a schoolgirl in 1938 before falling victims in the holocaust themselves; an Australian coalmine owner who traced his ancestry – and appearance – to the same Durham village as Kate's grandparents; a German couple, the woman heavily pregnant, who were looking forward to giving birth on the beach of a Greek island, and sent us a postcard a month or two later to announce the happy event. These visitors extended our children's horizons and opened their eyes to reality. Their stories prompted discussion, perhaps none more than that of another Israeli, a young teacher on his first trip outside Israel who during three months of travelling had renounced his earlier views and was now convinced that for a society to achieve internal order it was essential for it to be at war. Children in care rarely have this sort of experience, and are the poorer for it. It was a shame that in order to provide it for them we were often sailing close to the wind regarding regulations around police checks on overnight visitors.

We tried to bring other helpful influences into the house. Having become Quakers ourselves, we often hosted Meetings for Worship and discussion groups at Plainlands. Most of the adults in the Meeting were skilled in relating to our children in a natural, unpatronising way. They expected to be addressed by their first names, and listened with respect to our children's views. They encouraged our children to question, to reflect, to value themselves and their own experience. Their own inquiring spirit was infectious. Children need access to people like this in settings other than school.

Arising out of this connection came our own interest in peace organisations, which also met in our house, meetings occasionally attended, out of curiosity, by some of our children. And we would go on demonstrations as a family, parading through London with thousands of others, the children enjoying the music and the sense of power in stopping the traffic on Piccadilly or Waterloo Bridge.

The importance of this in terms of the children's education wasn't the "cause" itself. It was our drawing the children into our adult world, making the links with what they would watch on the television news, involving them directly in a wider society than they had previously experienced, opening their eyes to wider issues, providing more and more context for what they would learn in school. For children, particularly, who have suffered attachment deprivation or the distortion of traumatic experience, the content of school lessons is often far removed from their primary, self-protective concerns. We tried, through the medium of experiences and activities natural to us, to open minds closed by neglect and assault, to enable them to begin to look outward rather than inward, to develop imagination and empathy, without which learning cannot take place.

Artistic activities were also important, and again, example and opportunity were important. No skilled pianist, I bought an ancient piano on which I would plonk for no-one's enjoyment but my own. I took up clarinet lessons, briefly and ignominiously. I joined a choir. Kate sang constantly as she went about the house – it helped the children to know where she was, but also made music a part of daily life. We learned carols together to go and sing at the doors of friends and neighbours on Christmas Eve. The largest living room in the middle of the house – no TV, which was in a smaller adjoining room, just cosy chairs, cushions, books and a real coal or log fire – also housed "our" stereo. There Kate and I would often sit in the evenings, listening to our choice of music, reading, but welcoming company. And the music bug began to bite.

Several of the children joined the school brass band, and practised raucously at home. Karen took this furthest, eventually touring Germany and Austria with a local youth brass consort, and now believes that it was the sight of our musical instruments on her introductory visit, and a conversation with Mark about his cornet-playing that first made her want to join the family. John and Fred requested a drumkit, which was installed in the attic and then in a garden shed. Sal took up the flute, Karen had a brief and painful skirmish with the violin. Gradually, some of our classical music came to be appreciated and identified (I remember someone suddenly and totally unexpectedly being enraptured by the trumpet solo in a Shostakovich piano concerto), and analysis and choice of contemporary music became more thoughtful and discriminating. The children "discovered" that my mother (my parents came to live near us in 1979) had once been a piano teacher, and some of them began to visit her for rudimentary lessons and weekly spoiling with boiled sweets.

Our town has a thriving amateur dramatic society, and had for many years a successful junior section which staged an annual play or musical running for several nights. We frequently went to these performances as a family, and were pleased that some of our children eventually wanted to join the society. Karen and Martin, as well as our birth children, appeared in several productions and gained enormously in confidence as a result. As with music, this carried over into school and involvement with drama groups there, helping them to feel more part of the school community. Even Dan, normally quiet and self-effacing, was eventually bitten by the drama bug and took on a sizeable part in a school play, on the basis, perhaps, that anything the others could do he could do as well – living in groups can be positively contagious.

School trips were important, both because they cemented the children into the school community and (usually) because of their actual content. We encouraged our children to take part, even if the cost seemed prohibitive at first, and tried to say yes *before* entering into discussions about extra funding, if that was needed. This was also true of foreign exchanges, when we were insistent that our children should be allowed to take the same "risk" as other children in the community that their hosts might, despite all the school checks, pose a threat to them. We would not allow a distinction to be drawn between looked after children and others. As a result, our children had some valuable experiences, and the experience of having other children visit us from abroad was a further exercise in developing empathy and increasingly a source of pride in showing off "our" family. Indeed, the apparently obligatory bilingual party/riot on our lawn for the whole exchange group was often the highlight of the exchange visit.

It is difficult to see how conventional children's homes, with their ever-changing staff who leave their own lives in their own homes when they come to "work", could provide the richness of educational back-up experience that we were able to – difficult but not impossible if staff were encouraged and prepared to share more of themselves with the children in their care. Foster carers and adoptive parents can do all this if they have sufficient physical space and financial resources – and they should have. Carers in small family groups, however, may lose the knock-on effect of one child's enthusiasm sparking off another, the benefit of cross-fertilisation. Too often the presence of several looked after children to-gether is seen as contaminating, whereas with careful sowing of the seed and managing of the harvest, the yield can be remarkable.

The importance of conversation should not be underestimated. Too often I notice that carers talk to children and young people only about what they perceive to be the children's concerns and interests. This widens no horizons. The evening meal with us was as far as possible a fixed point in our family day. We would gather around a large table, even though it became rather cramped when we had visitors. We would expect the meal not to be too rushed, and we would talk. Sometimes Kate and I would start a conversation between ourselves on some subject far removed from the family's everyday concerns, and the children would gradually join in. Much of our input on personal and sexual relationships started off in this way. Politics, philosophy, religion, conservation, literature all had their place. I can clearly remember a discussion about Heisenberg's Uncertainty Principle. Our expectation was that, despite the numbers, there would only be one conversation around the table, that individual sensitivities would be respected, and that nobody would leave the dining room/kitchen area until the meal was finished (and that included the washing-up). So discussions would develop on a whole range of topics, trivial or abstruse. Friends of our more able children particularly loved to join us for meals because they loved the unpredictability, range, and often hilarity of the conversational torrent.

Television was, of course, an issue, but never, I think, a major one. We controlled it quite tightly. One of our three connecting living rooms – but not the main living area – housed the TV set and plenty of comfortable chairs. Any one of the children who wanted to watch a particular programme or programmes was expected to come and ask us, and permission was sometimes refused if we felt that the programme was totally unsuitable or that that particular child was in danger of becoming a "telly addict". A child who wanted to watch four or five programmes consecutively over an evening would be encouraged to exercise some further choice. There was an expectation that TV programmes should be watched with concentration rather than being just a background noise, and that conversation in that room during a programme should be largely about matters arising from it. After all, there were plenty of other rooms to which people could go if they wanted to talk about something else or do something else.

We had various ways of negotiating disputes about conflicting choices, and had a black-and-white set somewhere else in the house (I can't now remember where, so it can't have been used often!) for situations where there were serious requests for two conflicting programmes. "Soaps" were strongly discouraged as being too addictive and therefore time-consuming, and we made little use of video. We didn't allow individual children to have their own sets in bedrooms until they were well into mid-teens, and that only long after it became a social norm, and we insisted that children could not gather in bedrooms to watch TV. The children developed a wide enough range of acquaintances to recognise that some other families were more restrictive than we were, to the extent in some cases of banning television altogether.

Music was treated rather differently. We encouraged the children to use radios or hi-fi equipment in their rooms from quite early on, provided that volume was controlled so as not to interfere with anyone else. The stereo equipment in the main living area was "ours", and we reserved the right to decide how and when it was used.

So quickly has society moved on that I have not mentioned computers. They have only become an integral part of our lives since our children grew up. I can only guess at how we might try to exploit their educational possibilities if we were still caring directly for children now. My guess is that to have several in the house would be essential. And that we would be expecting local authorities to recognise the financial implications for ensuring that their looked after children could enjoy at least the same educational advantages where they live as do the children of their own managers. How could anything less be justified?

Reviewing progress

It is unrealistic to expect looked after children to match, in their academic achievement at any age up to 18, the achievements of their peers in stable birth families. The disruption of their earlier lives, the damage caused by neglect and abuse to their brain development and ability to concentrate, the distress following grief and loss, the inability to construct a coherent framework of perceived reality in which to assemble new learning – all these militate against accumulation of exam passes, keystage attainments and so on. But this is not a counsel of despair.

When we review at regular intervals the educational progress of any child, but particularly a looked after child, we need to consider how the child is developing an ability to learn. Is the child developing curiosity about the world outside him/herself, and being enabled to explore it? Is the child experiencing stability and reintegration of a fragmented life, and so increasingly able to concentrate and find meaning? Is the child becoming able to experience joy and wonder, to notice the beauty of the dewdrops on the spider's web or the petrol in the puddle, to call others to come and see the bluetit's nest, to catch breath at the song of the skylark, to experiment with new tastes, new sounds, new activities? Is the child learning to trust other people, other children and adults from whom he or she might learn? Is school a place where the child feels welcomed, respected, safe? Is the child being helped to develop a realistic and positive self-image over time, to have faith to link cause and effect, to see a future and their own place in it, and thereby be able to begin to set personal goals and plot a path towards the achievement of realistic ambition?

These were the questions which we tried increasingly to ask and answer at statutory reviews. It was important that others felt they were relevant questions. We tried to have some control, depending on the likely effect on the individual child, about whether someone would attend from school, and if so, who it would be. Some of our children welcomed the presence of a trusted teacher. Others preferred not to discuss possibly painful aspects of their lives in front of a teacher and leave that piece of mediation to us and to our judgement. This kind of delicate balance was ever-changing, and we felt that it was important that we as parents/carers, and not the local authority social workers who could not develop the same personal relationships or maintain the same regular contact, could make decisions about school matters. Similarly, it was important that teachers were clear that it was to us, and not to a distant social worker, that they should turn to discuss the children. And it was important to the children that, as far as possible, we could make decisions about school matters as autonomously and immediately as could the parents of their non-looked-after peers.

Finally – when we would consider the educational progress of Kwesi, to take one extreme example, every six months, we would often have to answer a qualified "no" to many of the questions above. Kwesi was determined to become a professional footballer, and little else in life held any interest for him. A leading professional club spotted him at the age of ten, and for the next six years our family life seemed to revolve around ferrying him once or twice weekly to matches and training sessions 30 miles away, and then a hundred miles away at the club's headquarters. Older family members helped out with transport. Fred virtually became Kwesi's personal coach. Sometimes because of other family commitments we transported him by taxi at huge expense. Constantly we – and others, social workers, teachers – questioned whether we should rein him in, restrict the football, try to compel him to widen his interests, concentrate on his schoolwork. We didn't, and I think if we had done so the consequent resentment would have closed down progress anyway. Moreover, the football club did make it clear to boys that they encouraged them not to neglect schoolwork. Kwesi did achieve ten reasonable GCSEs and stayed on at school post-16 only because of the one month difference between the Football Association year and the school year. He completed a Leisure Studies course that he could build around his sports interests, before weathering rejection by his club of six years and getting a contract with another, less-favoured club, a hundred miles away in the opposite direction.

His professional football career lasted two years. As part of the huge army of professional footballers who are deemed not to have made the grade at 18, he came back to our area, moved into a flat with one of our older foster sons, and started a succession of dead-end jobs whilst playing football semi-professionally. But five years later, having recognised his own potential, he has a responsible job in financial services and is studying for further qualifications, while playing football for pleasure rather than reward, and enhancing his income as a popular club disc-jockey. A reluctant participant as a child in discussion of anything but sport, he now revels in the cut and thrust of debate on any subject, especially with older brothers. I now feel that the combination of our family life and the teamwork and discipline of professional sport worked together to give him a base of security and self-confidence from which he is continuing to learn, grow, and discover the wider world.

Key factors

- Keeping the long-term perspective – building a framework for lifelong learning and learning for life.
- Using mainstream, local non-selective schooling where possible.
- Maintaining stability in placement and school settings.
- Avoiding competition and competitiveness whilst encouraging co-operation in learning.
- Choosing schools with care, with emphasis on a happy, tolerant atmosphere.
- Ensuring that the journey to and from school is stress-free.
- Getting to know school staff well and becoming a trusted part of the school community.
- Negotiating with teachers to avoid or mitigate inappropriate sanctions or exclusions.
- Helping teachers to understand the children's experience.
- Making books, computers and anything else that enhances learning readily and profusely available.
- Ensuring that there are always quiet, peaceful areas in the living environment.
- Modelling reading, thinking and learning with enjoyment.

- Encouraging children to take responsibility for their own learning whilst making extra help available.
- Providing varied, stimulating leisure experiences and ensuring that children meet a variety of interesting people.
- Exercising some reasonable control over access to television.
- Extending horizons through wide-ranging conversation and discussion.
- Challenging children to form and develop opinions, and respecting them as they do.
- Facilitating the development of the necessary building-blocks for learning – concentration, curiosity, wonder, imagination, empathy.
- Enabling each child to identify and develop individual interests which may enhance self-confidence and increase "connectedness".
- Assuring each child that there will be no financial barrier to achieving educational ambition.

5 Identity
Developing a sense of where we came from, who we are, and who we are becoming

Identity and growth

I change, therefore I am. If I don't change and move on, I stagnate.

The 1995 Report to the Department of Health on the development of the LAC materials to assess outcomes in child care comments on how many workers and carers assumed that the section on "identity" was concerned only with issues of ethnicity (Ward (ed.) 1995, pp. 76–78). Although this misconception was addressed and corrected, it illustrates a widely held notion that "identity" is something given and immutable. In this world view, to accept one's identity is to be "well-adjusted"; to be uncomfortable with it, to seek to change it, or to move easily between several perceptions of oneself is therefore to be maladjusted or disturbed.

My understanding of identity and its importance is different. I see a sense of identity as being a clear self-understanding. Only a few parts of that are fixed. Having a sense of my identity means knowing, under-standing and accepting my origins, the early and later influences that were brought to bear on me, and how they have contributed, and continue to contribute, to making me the person I have become so far. It means recognising how other people see and have seen me. It means being aware of the various systems of which I am and have been a part, and my place and role in them. It means self-awareness about my own personality, my strengths and weaknesses, likes and dislikes, past and current stances on issues of religion, morality, politics. It means having preferences, being able to make choices. It means being able to locate and describe myself as a social being. And so long as I remain thinking and feeling, acting on and being acted on by my relationships and my environment, much of it has the capacity for constant change. Perhaps the more secure I feel in my identity, the more able I am to change it.

For many of our children this was not the case when they began to live with us, and then it was sometimes a long time before a clear identity began to form. Some of the barriers we expected; others were more of a struggle for us to recognise, and another struggle for the children to overcome. Attachment disorders had left some with an inability to make trusting or differentiated relationships. The trauma of repeated physical and sexual abuse, often unacknowledged, had left some with distorted brain function, unable to concentrate on anything other than self-preservation, unable to experience wonder or joy. Neglect had deprived some of the experience of choice and the language to express it. Emotional deprivation, sometimes downright cruelty, had left some with no capacity for naming their own feelings or recognising the feelings of others. Some were virtually paralysed by fear, or grief; others fizzed with undirected rage. (See Cairns, 2002 for a fuller exposition of how these damaging early experiences may affect our development of coherent identity.)

To help our children to recognise and develop their identity, and then to make choices about the person they would become, we had to move with each of them through three stages: stabilisation, integration, and adaptation. None of these happens overnight; each needs continuous reinforcement. Stabilisation is about feeling safe, trusting and trusted. Integration is about putting together a true personal story that we can recall and tell without distortion or suppression, and without falling prey all over again to feelings which damaged us in the past. It is also about beginning to make connections again with the real world of other people, and finding new horizons. Adaptation is about moving on to build a dynamic picture of oneself with a past survived and processed, a present where choices can be made freely, and a future full of potential.

Stabilisation

I have a great deal for which to be grateful to my parents, the community in which I grew up, and the schools I attended. But from quite early in my childhood I was conscious of an oppressiveness in the rectitude, competitiveness, and overwhelming concern about the good opinion of others, and felt that I would only begin to find my identity outside Northern Ireland, which is the only place I know where people are likely to hang their curtains with the pattern facing out to the street. In contrast, my first impression of the industrial Midland community where Kate's extended family lived was of a welcoming warm bath of a place, where people would be accepted good-humouredly whether or not they had three noses, a score of illegitimate children, and a propensity for public raucousness on a Saturday night. It was important to us that our children found their home with us warm, welcoming and accepting.

Children joining us, we felt, had to feel individually cherished. Fred, who was almost 15 when he came, appreciated being taken out on a personal shopping trip to buy new clothes, and being allowed to burn the most hated of his old ones. Several others, notably Sharon and Liam, clung to the clothes they brought until long after they fitted or hung together. Our children needed each day to have a pattern, but a pattern flexible to their needs. So mealtimes – breakfast, lunch on non-school days, tea (these always eaten all together as a family), and most important, supper just before going to bed, took on a symbolic importance, even if the times at which they happened varied. Bedtimes weren't decided by the clock, but by apparent individual needs from day to day. Mark was for years totally incapable of going to bed without "supper", even if he had come in late from an outing which had ended with a large meal. They needed their own space (although we weren't able to manage single bedrooms for everybody until we created three more by way of a loft conversion in the early 1980s) furnished individually, their own pictures, their own cupboards for clothes and toys, and not too much insistence from us about tidiness. Some were able to exercise some choice in designing their personal environment, others needed a lot of direction, but to take time to build it was important either way. This was to be home, a place where they could relax and be safe as well as they were able, without feeling too much burden of expectation or threat of unmeetable demands.

Bedtime rituals were very necessary and couldn't be rushed. Always individual, but almost invariably including a story, a drink, "tucking in", a period of shared quiet as the lights were dimmed (not extinguished), a lullaby, perhaps some quiet music, an expression of appreciation – praise for something done – or, a favourite of mine, 'You're Dad's favourite six-year-old' or nine-year-old, or whatever. Without knowing anything about hypnosis, I learned the advantages of lowering and slowing my voice and adjusting my intonation as I reached the end of the final story, softened the lights, turned down the volume of any music. We tried to keep "loud" images out of bedrooms – Superman duvet covers and Arsenal wallpaper were avoided.

For many children it is frightening to have one's own space and the choice of what to do in it. Some needed to know that they could always be with one or both of us. Kwesi, who was fortunately a small four-year-old, spent much of his first six months with us being carried around on Kate's hip. Our bedroom door was usually slightly ajar so that we were accessible to quell night fears, and for younger children our bed could be a safe haven. Mark, who was perhaps the most lost of our children on arrival, having lived in a convent nursery from a few weeks old, had a cot-like bed in a corner of our room in which he spent the greater part of the nights of his eighth year. Several others needed to be sat with until they fell asleep during their early months with us.

Stability was also about people. The "staff" consisted of Kate and me, and in the early years a much-loved cleaner who took on a grandmotherly role, and one or two teenage neighbours who "helped out", becoming big-sister-type role models. We also employed a kindly elderly gardener for a year or so to help us bring the garden into shape. Although we often craved more time away together from the constant demands of family, we were aware that a constant succession of different people in the house would be unsettling when children were in their first few weeks or months with us. We would cut down on adult visitors, and only use our parents as "babysitters". Living nearby as they did, Kate's parents also took on the role of comforters on those occasions when children were feeling out of sorts with us.

Using the environment as a tool to establish cosiness helped. At the outset we covered up (sacrilege!) the lovely oak floors of Plainlands with the best carpets we could afford, to muffle sound. We bought warm, thick curtains to keep out the cold and the night. We had central heating, but the open fires in our living rooms symbolised warmth, even contained behind huge fireguards. Many of the children tell me now that our real fires, and the solid fuel range in the kitchen, conveyed to them a primitive and powerful sense of security. Plants, cushions, fabric, mobiles, rounded objects of all sorts, all served to smooth away hard angles and make the house more womb-like. We avoided harsh lighting, preferring to use lamps to create pools of light for activities within more restful, dimmer spaces. And how many children seemed able to relax only when on a settee clutching one huge cushion and surrounded by half a dozen more! We chose colours with care, for warmth and calm.

In daylight, and especially in summer, the curtains were pulled wide open and the house was filled with light. Doors to the garden stayed open. We preferred lots of vacuuming to fussy rules about changing footwear. We usually found that children joining us (unless already teenagers) had no desire to stray far, rarely even venturing to the boundaries of the garden, coming back to find us regularly for reassurance. Keeping an eye on them was discreet and not intrusive; they were welcome to join us in whatever we were doing, greeted with a smile, invited to talk if they wanted. Kate and I would talk a lot (I wasn't very good at this, but I could see its importance) – mainly undemanding talk, describing what we were doing and why we were doing it and how we felt, with a minimum of questions, but prepared to listen actively if that was required. And all the while we would be assessing opportunities for closer, trust-engendering contact – a hurt knee that needed a "magic touch" to make it better, hair to be brushed, a chocolate-coated mouth to be wiped, lightly and gently, never forcing unwelcome touch unless necessary for physical restraint, and then keeping the voice soft and soothing, the ambience calm. At least, that was what we tried to do. We didn't succeed every time. We couldn't always control our own emotions, our own anxieties But we would try to talk about those emotions, passing on, we hoped, a vocabulary to children whose emotional language was often less developed even than their spoken one.

Learning to trust us had to go alongside being trusted. The openness of the household helped. Money wasn't locked away – if it went missing we talked to everybody about the importance of being able to trust each other. It often reappeared. But the important bits of trust were about trusting children to do something, rather than to not do something. So we would involve them in simple tasks with us – fetching things, passing up the clothes pegs while we hung out the laundry, making paper sticks for the fire, keeping an eye on the baby. Kate once popped out of the bathroom for a clean towel while Lynn was helping to bath Sal, then only a few months old, to be greeted on her return with 'Look, Mum, Sally's swimming!' We tried to be genuine but not effusive with praise, and clear but gentle with criticism, but didn't always succeed.

Pets were good – we always had cats, robustly independent but often prepared to be a cross between a cushion and a hot-water-bottle. Our first experience with a dog – a border collie – was not a success, its increasingly wild behaviour eventually attributable to a brain tumour, but a later elderly labrador was a long-suffering purveyor of comfort. Other animals, requiring more care, were best left to more established family members, but children found their presence, their survival (usually) despite vulnerability, reassuring.

From the outset we told our children repeatedly that they had come to be with us for good – if that was what they wanted. Nothing in my experience has prepared me for caring for children temporarily, that is, in a situation where everyone knows from the outset that the placement is likely to end and the child to return to their birth family or to some more permanent situation. Such a child is always a visitor. I find the prospect of sharing my home with a visitor, of any age, for months or even years, impossible to contemplate. For a child, the prospect of being a visitor in someone else's home for huge spans of time in childhood must be intolerable. Our children knew – or at least we wanted them to know – that they had arrived somewhere that could be home, if they wanted it to be. But – although the subtleties of this may often have been lost on them at the outset – they were not tied into the deal as in adoption. Our offer was unconditional: they could break the contract but we could not. As the first children to join us grew older, they were able to confirm the truth of this to newcomers.

We analysed carefully the reaction of our family and friends to the task we were undertaking. For the most part they accepted gladly our insistence that children joining us should be seen and related to as fully part of the family. But if they weren't able to we had to explain to them gently but firmly that our future contact with them would be limited. The same was true of neighbours, except that here we had to undo the potential damage of the snippet in the local paper, read and remembered by so many people, about the planning application for change of use of Plainlands from private house to residential home, and stress that this was a designation for administrative convenience only – in reality it was our family home. We would note carefully each child's reaction to new people who became part of their lives, encouraging contact with people who seemed to have a relaxing, trust-enhancing effect, and discouraging people who seemed to initiate unsettling, fearful, or inhibiting reactions.

It was to children who came to us from children's homes (the majority) that symbols of fully belonging were most important. We were insistent throughout that our house had no internal locks except in bathrooms, and Kate and I didn't jingle as we went through carrying large bunches of keys. Sharon insists that it was primarily the absence of locks and keys that made her begin to feel both that she could trust us and that we might even trust her. Learning how to respect one another's privacy was something we all had to do over time, and exercising restraint about the chocolate biscuits in the larder isn't just a difficulty for the children. Food in a household is shared, not individual property; children who help themselves unreasonably should not be accused of stealing. Their fault is merely one of failing to discuss how and when the food that belongs to everybody might be shared.

Anybody could and did answer the front door, or the telephone. We called the children our family and introduced them to people as such. We sought out and took advantage of opportunities to introduce the children to other people who lived harmoniously in arrangements which were not nuclear families, demonstrating a wider range of self-chosen communities. A potter friend made for everybody a ceramic plaque with their name on for their bedroom door – including for Kate and me. Ours said "Mum" and "Dad", for that is what we encouraged the children to call us, and I shall return to the significance of that. Our surname was available for use too. Sometimes several surnames would be used interchangeably for a while through the period of stabilisation – this may seem paradoxical, but it was important that all options were available so that a choice, when eventually made, was genuine and thereby significant. Dan was clear about his options from day one. Knowing that he had had a placement for adoption which had broken down just before the final making of the order, and that the adoptive parents had changed all of his names, we asked him what he was called. "My name is", he began importantly, and went on to list four given names and five surnames in correct chronological order, ending with "Cairns"!

Integration

An adoptive family could have taken the beguilingly simple decision to encourage the children to relax into their rural idyll and let the past drift away. Most of our children were, after all, placed by fairly distant local authorities and had minimal direct contact with their birth families. But our past does not leave us alone. When we observed in our children seemingly irrational fears, inexplicable behaviours, apparent blocks to feeling, relating, learning, we realised that the past was here with us, often experienced as an insidious, persistent intruder. To make progress we had to welcome it in, embrace it and disarm it.

The social work network was the main conduit for the past. For the first 12 years we had a consistent relationship with a local social worker and her team manager who supervised all the placements made with us on behalf of the children's various local authorities. She visited the family at statutory intervals as well as giving us informal supervision and helping us to make sense of the puzzles with which the children and their behaviour presented us. She linked with the caseholding social workers in the "home" local authorities who attended reviews, acted as the repository of the past, and attempted to maintain contact with birth families and mediate that to the children and ourselves. On the whole, all these workers saw their role as assisting us to make the placements work. An important part of that assistance was ensuring that we and the children had access to information. Since the information was often about parents' past and present shortcomings, it was not always welcomed by the children, and the best of the distant social workers understood their importance as scapegoats, as messengers who could be shot, and often were!

After 1987 we had a more direct relationship with social workers from the children's various "home" authorities. They often wanted to work more directly with the children, and there were times when we felt that our knowledge and understanding of the children and their needs were undervalued. Some of them found it difficult to cope with the children's negative feelings towards them, and were surprised by the strength of them, not understanding that this was part of the children's integration of their past, which the social worker often embodied. They could also be surprised at what would happen if they allowed the children to set the agenda and the pace. Frequently a relationship of mutual mistrust would be transformed by a timely and appropriate response to the child's recognition (or ours), that *today* was the right point in the integration process to push for contact with Mum, to trace the Scottish grandparents, to think about revisiting the convent in Dublin or the nursery in Southampton, to allow the fearfully-buried memories of the abusive residential school to emerge.

We never wanted to take upon ourselves the sensitive task of exploring our children's past experiences with them, but sometimes we had to. We preferred to be the now, the safe place to which they could return, geographically or figuratively, after brave voyages into the turbulent waters of early neglect and trauma. It wasn't always possible to persuade others that guiding these journeys might be *their* job. We were prepared to weather the storms that often followed the return – the rages, the despair, the self-hatred, the howling at grief. And we did our best to soak up the behaviour that accompanied them – the aggression, the self-harm, the destructiveness, the rejection of those parts of a present identity that jarred with the past. We tried to explain, as we began to understand it, how past traumas can distort the way we see situations, ourselves and other people in the present. We tried to reassure our children that they were neither bad nor mad to react so violently to the dysfunction in their lives and disjunction in their perceptions.

It can be hard to appreciate how difficult it is to unlearn what we have come to believe. That our parents cared for us, when in reality they were selling our infant bodies. That our parents wanted the best for us, when they left us with drug addicts for days at a time. That our previous foster carers were good, kind people, even though they got us up every day before dawn (unlike their own child) to work on their smallholding, and excluded us from family celebrations. That we deserved the beatings, the imprisonments in locked cupboards, the abuse when we fell asleep at midnight, left to look after three younger siblings at the age of six. That we are incapable of learning, incapable of loving, incapable of laughing.

Children of ours had to unlearn all of these perceptions, which had become part of their identity. At times it was like ripping up the very foundations of their being. They railed against it, and it was our task to help them through, with firmness but without punishment, with understanding but without sentimentality.

It was sometimes difficult to hold children and young people through this process of integration. Karen would scream and kick for hours on end when powerful memories of her family were triggered or when she was beset by her sense of responsibility for her younger siblings, left in an abusive home. Kate would hold her, trying to ignore her own shins turning to shades of black and blue and avoiding the biting teeth, leading Karen, still screaming, to the bottom of the garden so that I could settle the rest of the family and get them peacefully to bed while Karen continued her onslaught. Eventually she would subside, the screams would turn to sobs, the sobs to explanations and apologies, and we would feel that a painful and necessary process had advanced a little further.

More than once, both Karen and Liam left us when the pain became too great, the security we could offer too inadequate, or the situation too dangerous for the other children to tolerate. We worked hard to convince local authorities that this was not a "placement breakdown", but a necessary short-term separation for work to be done which couldn't safely or adequately be done at home with us. Each time, they returned to us, and today see themselves and are seen by others as full members of our family. I fear that, if our doors had been closed to them after they first left us, neither would have survived. Incomplete integration would have finished them through self-harm or recklessness.

These were among the more extreme scenarios – but virtually all our children would of necessity work through periods when coming to terms with the past was more pressing, more demanding of their attention, than anything else. A visit, or planned visit, to or from parents was often the catalyst. Or, as was the case with several, an unsuccessful attempt to persuade parents to agree to a visit. But it was important to be honest with the children. Lynn and Mark had been told that they were in care because their mother was disabled and couldn't look after them. As they grew older, they realised that other children had disabled parents who had help with caring for their children. They realised that they had a father who had deserted mother, formed a new family, and didn't want to know. They realised that they had grandparents who had also withdrawn. They recognised that the convent where they were placed as infants had treated them cruelly and neglectfully. This information all had to be weighed and processed, and all produced reactions in behaviour which we had to identify and explain to them and to others. Eventually, in their teens, contact with mother was established. The children met a woman who appeared to be totally wrapped up in her own needs. The relationship staggered on for a while mainly because of the children's generosity of spirit, but they were able to talk about it. They reached a point – Lynn quickly, Mark more gradually – of feeling that they had no need for this person in their lives, and moving on. And yet, there was grieving to be done.

When work of this sort was going on, children could be infuriating to live with – they would lose all sense of time, abandon tasks half completed, seem unable to concentrate on anything, snap and grumble and react impulsively and with often uncharacteristic aggression. If carers do not understand what is happening, or fail to communicate their understanding to the children, and react critically or punitively, the relationship can be terminally damaged, or the child left unable to work through the process. Imagine how we, as adults, come to terms with the ending of a relationship, being passed over for promotion, or being duped by a dishonest builder, let alone with losing a parent. Sometimes it seems that the expectations of carers and social workers for already damaged children to modify and control their emotional reactions far exceed their expectations of themselves.

Integration of past and present was not always a story of gloom and disappointment. Josie and Dan were both adamant for many years that they did not want to have any direct contact with their mother. She intruded into their lives at unpredictable intervals by making drunken telephone calls to us and sobbing to Kate, for hours if we would let her, about how life continued to treat her badly. But no birthday or Christmas passed without Josie and Dan receiving a tastefully-wrapped present and card signed only "K". We learned that K had been a partner of their mother while the children were very young, and had visited them in the children's home where they lived. He demanded nothing – we never knew where he lived. But he represented a kind of caring.

As Josie and Dan entered their teens, we felt that it would be good for them to have some family contact. Their father was untraceable, but we knew that their mother had relatives of Russian-Jewish origin in Scotland, and felt that it would be helpful for them to have links with these roots. We pressed the local authority social worker hard to trace them. He found an aunt and uncle, with whom Josie and Dan in due course enjoyed several holidays, and they in turn took them, after careful preparation, to meet their grandparents and learning-disabled half-brother in another part of Scotland. Although Josie and Dan had never lived in Scotland or met these relatives previously, it helped them to a more complete understanding of themselves.

Fred's mother cared too. Impoverished and prematurely aged by mental illness and alcohol dependency, she loved the son she had placed in care before his first birthday. When he was moved from London to a foster placement in Bristol, she moved to a bedsit in Weston-Super-Mare, from where she could arrange to meet him occasionally in a Bristol café. She knew that to demand more would have been too difficult an intrusion into his life. When he came to us at 14, she moved to Worcester, and having come to our house once to assure herself that he was in a good place, never came again. But she still set up occasional brief meetings in Gloucester, and few Saturdays went past without a little packet arriving in the post, containing a toothbrush, a pack of paper handkerchiefs, or a comb, and a carefully written slip of paper with the words 'Love, Mum'. I think we were able to help him to appreciate these weekly tokens. When Fred was 19, working and living on a nearby farm and roaring irregularly in and out of our lives, we heard that his mother was dying of cancer in a Worcester hospital. We were able to take him to her deathbed, to the funeral, to clear out her few sad possessions from her bedsit. It meant a lot to him that he could do those things with us, and that there was a family to whom he could now fully commit himself. Indeed, it was at this point that he felt empowered to make a rapid decision to return to college, to study more determinedly than he had ever done before, and to take the first steps towards what has become a very successful and fulfilling business career. Sharon, too, has stated that, although living with for us for seven years had helped her to see herself 'as a person, not a thing', it was only on moving out at 17 to a residential job that she could allow herself to accept that she really 'belonged' with us, because she realised that she could come back, that she was still one of 'the family'.

Of course, it was not unusual for the children to take out on us (through aggression, verbal abuse, damage of property) negative feelings which were really about earlier experiences of care or family life. We tried never to initiate criticism, real or apparent, of birth families or previous carers, but to find ways of urging the children gently to consider who or what they were *really* angry with. We would try neither to defend the adults they were angry with, nor to agree wholeheartedly with the children's critical comments when they did work out the true origins of their anger, but to acknowledge the feelings: 'That must have made you feel really useless/hurt/sad/rejected'. That can lead on fairly naturally to agreement that the situation is different now, and discussion of how we as carers might help in dealing with the inconvenient emotional legacy – which carries us into adaptation.

Adaptation

These three stages of identity-building don't, we found, divide up neatly like a modular study programme with a certificate of completion at the end of each semester. They overlap considerably. The presence of several children at different stages of discovery of their own identity was, we found, motivational for all of them, and they were regularly learning from one another's experience, or consolidating their own learning through observing and supporting others going through experiences similar to those they had already encountered. We would never have considered introducing anything so structured as formal groupwork, but spontaneous conversations often arose (maybe seeded by us just occasionally!) in which one family member's recently-acquired insight would strike a chord with another. The intensity of living and working with just one seriously damaged child must sometimes be unbearable, most of all for the child themselves, who understandably must feel constantly under the spotlight.

I have often used the analogy of a web. In a small household, say, four people, the structure of the web of relationships holding them all together has only six strands. When one of these strands is temporarily broken, or under intense pressure, the whole structure is immediately unstable, and the individual(s) at the end of the broken strand feels immediately insecure. In a household of 12 mutually supportive people, the web has 66 strands. Several can break without noticeably impairing the stability of the structure. Support and caring are still experienced by those who are temporarily vulnerable. And that applies to the adults as much as the children, for without the support of our other children when one or two were in the depths of emotional torture, we would have crumbled. Knowing that we needed them to be in there for us was a far weightier boost to self-esteem and positive identity than spurious praise for having put away the saucepans.

Our more recently-arrived children had the opportunity of watching those who had been with us longer reach the stage where they could quite often recall their past reasonably accurately without re-experiencing the bad feelings associated with it, or be confronted without warning by sudden triggers or memories without being thrown immediately into emotional disarray. Then the fun could really start, introducing all sorts of new experiences as tasters to encourage new activities, new relationships, new ambitions, anything that might help individual family members to find personal fulfilment, and positive endings to sentences beginning 'I am . . .' and 'I enjoy . . .' I have looked at this in more detail in Chapter 4 under the heading of education. Carers can't do too much of this, provided that activities aren't forced upon children and young people like a perpetual assault course.

I think now that we – certainly I – should have done even more, not only with and for the children, but with and for ourselves, for it is important to model constantly the joy of new discovery, of finding new skills, of being more adventurous. A Quaker advice is to 'live adventurously'. Those of us who are responsible nowadays for children or vulnerable adults are obsessed with obviating risk, and building bland environments which lack risk and stimulation in equal measure. For Fred, a city boy coming to us at 14 with a sense of identity more intact than many, the thrill of going out with mates in the early hours of the morning armed with ferrets and lamps to hunt rabbits opened up vast new horizons. Josie, just beginning to read confidently at almost 13, wanted to travel on her own by train to a weekend residential gathering in Cardiff, and I agreed on the basis that there was no change of trains, and she would be met at Cardiff Station. Arriving at the station just on time, I put her on the train standing at the expected platform, to realise only as it moved off that it was in fact the Plymouth train, 20 minutes late! While I made frantic phone calls to deal with the scenario of her alighting in confusion in Taunton or Plymouth, Josie calmly realised the mistake almost as quickly as I did, got off in Bristol, ambled up to a porter and was directed to the Cardiff express, arriving in Cardiff before the intended (delayed) direct train! I like to think that this was the kick-start to a passion for independent globetrotting that took her to virtually every continent in her early twenties. Driving her door-to-door down the M4 would not have had as positive an effect.

Identity is enhanced by autonomy. While our children were still finding stabilisation with us, we felt we had to give them a sense of a supportive framework in which we, as carers, removed the burden of a lot of decision-making at a micro-level. As each child moved through integration towards adaptation, we handed decision-making power back (a relief for me, since I hate making decisions for others, and prefer the independence of cats to the devoted obedience of dogs!). Bedtimes and coming-home times were a prime example. Just as, if Kate or I was going out, we would tell each other (and the children) when to expect us back, and be open to negotiation if this was felt to be unreasonable, we expected our children to say when they intended to arrive home rather than have an arbitrary time imposed on them. We modelled the behaviour we expected from them. Disagreements were probably much less common than if we had set limits, and indeed the times agreed were often very reasonable indeed! Times could be revised later by phone, and lifts requested – and often, but not always agreed, because we sometimes had an agenda of our own, as we made clear. As for bedtimes, our attempts to enhance emotional awareness and empathy worked well on Sharon, who was the oldest (and bossiest!) of the children at home for the first seven years of our extended family. She would regularly usher the others upstairs at around 9.30, saying, 'Let's give Mum and Dad some time to themselves', and this accommodating behaviour could sometimes be prompted by my turning down the lights and opening a bottle of wine while Kate changed into 'something more comfortable', without either of us saying a word. For our children, learning to be themselves went along with becoming aware of others.

Their growing sensitivity to one another's feelings amazed and delighted us, and still does.

Becoming aware of each other, in a protective sense, happened quite quickly. At the outset, our first group of children decided that they all wanted to use our surname at junior school to avoid awkward questions from other children (although on the whole they were keen to explain their 'true' situation to friends) and 'feel like a proper family'. One of their teachers told us a few years later that if any one of them was having a hard time from other children in the playground, Cairnses would appear from all quarters of the school site to assist their beleaguered 'sibling'. Sometimes this developing family identity would be questioned by people who felt that it was damaging to their 'true' family identity. We felt strongly that this was not the case, for several reasons.

Our children had been placed with us with a plan of permanence – separated often by considerable distance from, and having only occasional contact with families of origin, they needed to have the choice of forging a family identity with us. We worked hard to keep alive those family contacts that our children wanted, and to ensure that they had as much information as possible about their birth families as they were able to integrate. Most people find comfort from being able to talk about "we" – many children in care become increasingly self-absorbed as they can only realistically think of "I". It was the children's wish, checked with them frequently.

There were two exceptions to this latter point. I have largely excluded Alan from "the family" as described in this book. He stayed with us for less than a year, and left to go into a large residential institution largely at his own choice. Ideally he should not have been placed with us, and we should have recognised this. Sharing was very difficult for him, and he was very strongly enmeshed with his own dysfunctional family, and found being part of our group emotionally intolerable, since the need of the others for a new family to identify with ran counter to his own needs and feelings. A couple of years later, at 16, he joined another family as a supported lodger, and came to identify with them strongly as a young man, having worked through more feelings about his own family. We still hear from him from time to time, and he regards us all with affection, as we do him.

Pete also came to us late, at almost 15, the youngest of four brothers who had grown up in care together in a family group children's home which was closing down. The older brothers had moved on to independent living, and their relationship was close, if not always healthy, since, as we later discovered, there had been considerable paedophile activity centering on the children's home. But they were Pete's family, and it was always likely that he would return to them, and his home county, after a few years. Not liking being "different", he flirted with calling himself Cairns, but it never felt right, and we were pleased when he made the decision to stick with his family name. We hear from him too – it seems as if the years away from his birth family helped him to move beyond his original identity of the bullied little brother and to establish himself as his own person within the family network.

As for the rest, we offered each of them as they reached the age of 18 the cost of a deed poll if they should want to change their name officially. I believe they all did – certainly all of them continued to call themselves Cairns, and three of the girls married as Cairns before assuming their husbands' names in accordance with convention. Fred chose to hyphenate Cairns with his own surname. Dan confirmed the final selection he had made informally of the splendid list of names at his disposal, as discussed earlier, becoming officially known by the first name given him by his (briefly) adoptive parents, his original first name, and then Cairns. Just as adoptive parents often tell their children that they are special because they were chosen, our children told us that they were choosing each other and us as their family.

Karen recalls a landmark point, quite soon after joining us, on her first visit to the library with me and some of the other children. 'Brian asked me if I wanted to join the library, which I was really pleased about, and I jumped at the opportunity. He then asked me "Do you want to be M—— or Cairns on your membership card?" I was amazed – for the first time in my life I had been given a choice about something. I felt immediately part of the family and decided to be a Cairns.' Significantly, Karen had not made the transition to calling me 'Dad' – she still felt uncomfortable around men. This decision was about joining the group, and was a powerful symbol whilst being totally informal and revocable.

Allowing the children to call us 'Mum' and 'Dad' was a choice made for the same reasons. We would remind the children that we were not replacing their birth parents, but explain that we felt it was fine to have more than one person for whom you used each of those special names. We pointed out that Kate and I both called each other's parents 'Mum' and 'Dad' as well as our own. As divorce and stepfamilies became commoner they were able to see how some of their friends had two 'Mums' or two 'Dads' or both. We wouldn't have minded first names, but we felt that 'Mum' and 'Dad' offered more security. Now that they are adult, it is our "home-grown" children who will often call us by our first names, not our "imports". And as for the next generation – my suggestion that our children's children might call me 'Brian' rather than 'Grandad' has been roundly rejected.

We maintained clear boundaries in our family, to enhance the sense of "we-ness". The simple indicators of this were significant. Any member of the family might answer the doorbell, or the telephone. Family members could come in without ringing the doorbell – others were not expected nor invited to, although the door was never locked during the day. Where there were exceptions, they were agreed among us all. We expected that non-family visitors – professional or personal, child or adult – would be formally introduced to other family members by whoever they had come to see.

We developed rituals – ways of celebrating Christmas, Easter, Hallowe'en – which became our sacrosanct family traditions from one year to the next. One of our practices which most surprised visitors was our silent joining of hands around the table for a few moments at the start of meals, before somebody – anybody – would say simply, 'Enjoy your meal, everybody'. This was actually suggested by Sharon, who had noted it with approval in the 1970s television series, *The Waltons*, and was taken up with enthusiasm. Kate and I liked it because it made a formal beginning to the meal, it was less false for the children than saying "grace", but helpful because it can take a long time to serve out 12 helpings! We abandoned this in the 1990s when the family had reduced to three or four teenagers at home – a decision reached in response, perhaps, to teenage self-consciousness when there were no longer young children to be protective towards, to a belated recognition of the difficulty it might pose for those struggling with the legacy of sexual abuse, or to a sense of embarrassment as the effect of intimacy changed in the smaller group. It had been a powerful uniting force, and is sometimes still suggested and re-enacted when we all meet for a family get-together.

We have been asked if there were tensions or jealousies within the family arising out of perceived "differences" between our foster children and our birth children, perhaps due to "class" or due to the foster children's awareness that Sal, Tom and Rich had always belonged to the family and always would.

I see the idea of "class" as being nowadays an over-generalised attempt to categorise the huge range of assumptions, attitudes, beliefs and values that inform the day-to-day lives of families in our society. Most children become aware from quite an early age that these vary remarkably from family to family, and become more or less critical of the general ethos established by their parents. Our foster children were quite remarkable in the diversity of their previous family backgrounds and experiences, and numerous enough for the differences to be quite clear within the subgroup of foster children. The children closest in age to our birth-children – Karen, Pete and Liam – were the most likely to make direct comparisons between their own experience and early socialisation and that of Sal, Tom and Rich. When they were feeling stressed or frightened, their distress was likely to be projected onto our home-grown three, as both Rich and Karen describe elsewhere from opposite sides of the question. But I don't believe that "class" was an issue in itself. "Difference" often was, and here the size of the group was a valuable lesson in the "differentness" of everyone's experience. The difficulties of "differentness" could never be realistically over-simplified into being the odd one out in an otherwise socially homogenous group.

As adults, the children have found their own niches in very different areas of the "class structure" from one another. Interestingly, many of them may seem to inhabit very broadly similar areas to those to which their parents may have seen themselves as belonging. But none of them could be seen as belonging to a socially excluded "underclass", for which so many children growing up in care seem sadly destined. As for the issue of belonging, I cannot understate the importance for our children of knowing that we were offering them "a family for life".

Sometimes there were regrets that they had not come to us sooner, about the absence of "baby photographs" or shared early childhood experiences. Sometimes later arrivals in the family would be party to conversations about family events, incidents or holidays which had taken place before they joined us, and say wistfully, 'I wish I'd been there'. It may have helped that our birth children had no recollection of some events remembered and enjoyed by our older foster children. Perhaps the most salient comment was made by Liam, in the depths of his distress and confusion in his mid-teens: 'I should have come to you when I was little. I just got lost along the way.'

In May 2002 we had a family holiday in France. Nine of our children were there, with partners, children, and in two cases, parents-in-law, as well as Kate's parents and my widowed mother. We rented a chateau for the week, going off as couples, nuclear families, or ad hoc groups to do our own thing during the days, meeting up for riotous shared meals at night. It was a celebration of identity, individual and group. Those who didn't or couldn't come were those who have established their present identity more separately, or who were prevented by ill health, children's commitments or financial pressures, and they were missed. There are already plans for us to do it again in 2004.

The three Rs: "Race", religion and responsibility

Having redefined identity for the looked after child as *not* being primarily about "race", I must nevertheless look at how our children have come to understand their racial origins. Kate and I are white. My Northern Irish origins allows me conveniently to claim membership of an often vilified minority (the Irish), and indeed our shared Irishness, despite being on opposite sides of the Great Religious Divide, was a major factor in my being able to build a relationship with Karen, who was born into an aggressively Irish Dublin family. Our three birth children, Sal, Tom and Rich, are white. Of the others, Josie and Dan are of mixed heritage (mother Scottish Russian Jewish, father Guyanese Afro-Caribbean); Kwesi is African (mother from Uganda, father from Ghana) and lived with an aunt in Uganda in the troubled period just after the rule of Idi Amin; and Martin's grandmother was Chinese.

We would not have gone out of our way to seek these placements with us, feeling that, other things being equal, it would have been easier for all these four of our children to grow up in a family with at least one parent who reflected the "minority ethnic" part of their inheritance, and to be living somewhere less predominantly white than our area of rural Gloucestershire. But ours was a tolerant community, on the whole; we had more than one child from a racial minority, and the placing local authorities felt in each case that we represented the best option they had. I don't feel that the four people concerned look back now and feel that they made the wrong decision.

I hope we did the right things. We made efforts to deal appropriately and without fuss with hair and skin care (through perpetual tantrums from Kwesi who didn't want his tight curls to be treated differently from anybody else's). We talked about colonial history, slavery and emancipation. We were pleased when several of the few other children from minority ethnic groups who lived in the area became friends of various members of the family and regular visitors. We confronted racism wherever we came across it, and tried to take opportunities for the children to meet people from different cultures. We worked around the untraceability of all the non-white parents, with the exception of Kwesi's mother, who had insisted that Kwesi should be placed with a white family. We felt numb when, as we walked together through a picturesque German town in 1989, racist abuse was hurled at Kwesi from a carful of neo-Nazis, and relieved when the children made good friendships with white children whose families seemed devoid of prejudice.

At school, their white siblings staunchly waved the anti-racist flag, and I remember no racism within the family. It was good for them to grow up in a racially mixed household, learning at first hand the nonsense of racial prejudices. Kwesi overcame some difficulties at school by excelling at sport (itself a racial stereotype, perhaps, but a genuine talent which I recognised when I first met him at the age of four and he drop-kicked a football into my hands from about 30 feet!). Dan melted opponents by a combination of natural calmness and ready wit – his put-downs could be original and scathing, but never malicious, and gained him a general popularity. Josie and Martin perhaps suffered more: Josie's size and relative inarticulateness as a child meant that she sometimes needed to rely on physical strength to intimidate those who would taunt her, and Martin's Chinese appearance had been the subject of unkind and racist comments from his previous foster family, leaving him ill-equipped when he joined us at 13 to learn new coping strategies. For him, drama proved to be the route to self-acceptance and self-confidence.

After Kwesi had been with us over four years, a change of policy in his home local authority meant that the new social worker there made plans to find a new placement for him with black carers. Kwesi was terrified. He felt at home with us and had no wish to move, and thought (possibly correctly) that he would be placed with an African-Caribbean family, from whom he felt much more different, without being able to explain why. We defended his remaining with us on the grounds that this had been the original plan and therefore we had made serious promises to him; that our household, at least, was a "mixed race" household; that he was now well settled and stabilised with us, having little contact with his black relatives (their wish), and that proper matching of his cultural origins would be extremely difficult if not impossible. Our threat of taking wardship proceedings eventually won the day. Thereafter, for some years, Kwesi developed a tendency to construe criticisms of his conduct from us as racist discrimination (he found our philosophy of considering individual circumstances rather than applying rigid rules hard to understand for a long time). I felt that he may have been extrapolating into the domestic setting some of the attitudes he was encountering in playing as an associate schoolboy footballer with a leading professional club, which had signed him up at the age of ten, and remains one of the "whitest" in the Premiership, but for many years he saw the world of professional football entirely through rose-coloured spectacles and would tolerate no apparent criticism of it. Our eventual solution was to request an independent visitor for him, and to suggest a young man known to us professionally, a black residential care worker in a local children's home who knew and well understood the differences between our family model and the ethos of the home where he worked. This was very successful, and Vince and Kwesi had some good times together. With hindsight, there could have been great advantages in seeking a carefully-chosen independent visitor for each of the children.

In recent years, Josie has chosen to settle in a town with large and diverse black populations and to join a church where almost all the members are African-Caribbean. She seems able to move across the racial communities in the town with ease, perhaps more so than people who have only lived in one, and has friends of varied ethnic groups and cultures. Her passion for travel, before she became a parent, has helped her to see herself as a citizen of the world. Dan has chosen to live in a small country town, virtually exclusively white, where he feels totally at home, commuting to a white-collar job over 20 miles away. Kwesi is now proud to be black and adopts black fashions and hairstyles. He shares a flat in a racially mixed area with a white friend and works as a DJ at weekends in a largely white club. Some may say that Dan and Kwesi have lost their roots. I feel that they have simply moved on, as I have done. They have gained adaptability, tolerance and social connectedness. They have been enabled to have and to make choices. And the rest of us in their family have gained these things too from being their parents and brothers and sisters.

The Children Act requires local authorities responsible for children in their care to give due consideration 'to the child's religious persuasion'. I am not persuaded that it is at all common for children and young people entering care to have given much thought to religious issues, and am sceptical about the likelihood of religious views they may express being more than the results of indoctrination or socialisation, for or against, accidental or deliberate. But the child's view of religion is part of the culture that he or she brings to the placement, and as such needs to be handled respectfully. Karen came from an Irish Catholic family, with a fear of being "cut off" from her religion. We arranged for a local Catholic family to take her to church – knowing that the opportunity was there for her was enough, and she only exercised the choice once or twice. Lynn and Mark, however, had come from a convent nursery with little understanding of Catholic values or doctrines, but a real fear of priests and the general accoutrements of dark Catholic churches. We felt that it was important for them to see that religious practice could be more joyful.

When we started the family, Kate and I were becoming disillusioned with the established churches, but wanted our children to have experience of being part of a church community. For several years we combined affiliation to two such communities. Sometimes we attended Quaker meetings, which met mainly in members' homes; sometimes the local Methodist church, where Kate's parents were heavily involved. The former offered an enquiring approach to spiritual truth in an atmosphere of tolerance and social concern; the latter offered the comfort of certainty and a strong community link to our own town. The differences between the two caused the children to ask many questions, particularly since their Church of England Primary School provided yet another slant. Until the children were old enough, one by one, to stay at home alone if they chose to, they would come with us wherever we were going on a Sunday, although now and then someone might decide to accompany grandparents separately. Increasingly decision-making was broadened to include the children. Over time we gradually moved away from the Methodists, as both the children and we adults felt more "at home" with the Quakers.

I think our general approach was right. The children had access to a wide range of people who had a sense of the divine and the spiritual, but used very different language and practice to express it. Their church connections gave them a network of relationships with many fundamentally decent and some quite remarkable adults who respected them and gained their respect. They learned questioning, but not cynicism. In adult life, possibly only Mark, Josie, Sal and Rich maintained any connections, however tenuous, with organised religion, but all are capable of a sense of awe and wonder, and a recognition that spiritual matters cannot be dismissed as irrelevant to human life. And they are each developing a thoughtful moral code which they exercise in their relationships, in their choice of livelihood, in their approach to caring for their own children and considering national and international issues, and one which is both respectful and dynamic.

This leads me to responsibility. In encouraging the children to take responsibility for themselves, we hoped that this would be a step towards enabling them to take responsibility for others. The measure of that is discussed in the chapter on emotional and behavioural development (Chapter 8). But I want to note here a tendency among parents and carers of younger children which saddens and disturbs me – the tendency to forbid children from doing what they want to do for apparently arbitrary reasons ('Don't walk on the grass, come here and hold my hand'; 'Don't stand in that man's way' – when the child has just as much right to be where they are as the man in question; 'You can't pack your schoolbag until you've had your bath' – or vice versa, according to parental whim). We felt strongly that other than for therapeutic reasons, such as addressing attachment problems, we should respect our children's right to make minute-by-minute choices wherever possible, recognising their status as autonomous beings. If the choice made by the child is harmful or greatly inconvenient to someone else, it can be stopped and the reasons explained. If the choice appears mildly inconvenient to someone else, that can be pointed out without an unnecessary exercise of authority. The Children Act requires courts to make no order unless absolutely necessary. We tried to follow a similar approach as parents to our children.

The same is true of taking risks. We believed that it is not required of parents – even those who are taking on the task on behalf of the state – to eliminate risk to their children. Children must learn to recognise risk, to assess it, to make decisions. They must set themselves challenges. We would try to emulate the bank (in the advertisement) that liked to say yes, rather than wrapping children in a protective but potentially stifling cocoon. A request to do something independently – to walk home alone from Cubs rather than be collected, say – should be welcomed as an indication of growing self-reliance, and reasons found to concur, having checked out the child's appropriate awareness of traffic danger points and "stranger danger". If the risk really seems too great, then a negotiated compromise, we found, was more constructive than an outright 'no'. Somebody older could meet the child at a halfway point, perhaps, or nowadays a mobile phone provided in case of unforeseen problems.

An extension of this was our children's perception of our autonomy in relation to them. Our local authority social workers were generally very prepared to delegate to us the freedom to make decisions regarding our children and inform them afterwards. They rarely disagreed, although there were exceptions. I had taken Sharon, then a ward of court, to visit my parents when they still lived in Belfast, without thinking until afterwards that I had taken her outside the jurisdiction of the law of England and Wales. The following year I booked a plane ticket for John to come with me, and informed his local authority – which then refused on the grounds that Belfast was an unsafe place to go. I argued in vain that hundreds of children in care live in Belfast permanently.

This was damaging. Our children needed the security of feeling that Kate and I were ultimately in charge; social workers provided a right of appeal on serious matters rather than an authority to which we always had to defer before making decisions about visits to friends, holidays, school trips and related expenditure, etc. None of us thrive if we feel like puppets on a string. Only when we are assured of our own autonomy and exercising our own independence can we voluntarily enter the more fulfilling relationships of interdependence.

Key factors

- Recognising that most aspects of our identity are not static and that looked after children will need much help and encouragement to develop their own identity.
- Offering unconditional lifetime family membership.
- Offering each child a real choice in establishing an identity in which they can feel comfortable and true to themselves.
- Allowing children the maximum control possible over what name(s) they choose to call themselves.
- Enabling stabilisation in the present, integration of the past, and adaptation to current and anticipated circumstances.
- Establishing recognisable but flexible routines and acceptable individual and family rituals.
- Assisting children to recognise and identify their own emotions.
- Encouraging self-expression in personal space.
- Establishing clear boundaries around personal and family space.
- Using the physical environment to create an atmosphere of calm, comfort and safety.
- Finding opportunities for acceptable physical contact.
- Minimising arbitrary rules and physical barriers.
- Finding opportunities for developing mutual trust and a sense of self-worth.
- Recognising children's frequent need to identify themselves as part of a group.

- Using the strengths of the group – in modelling, supporting, caring, indicating acceptable behaviour.
- Encouraging contact between children and a range of respectful adults who may be helpful role models or offer moral or spiritual insight.
- Helping children to identify a spiritual dimension to life without imposing religious conformity.
- Encouraging contact with birth family at a level that the children can sustain, whilst being aware of their changing needs and wishes.
- Retaining autonomy through assertive negotiation of clear roles and responsibilities with social workers.
- Trying never to say no when it is possible to say yes.

6 Family and social relationships
Developing tools for conviviality at home and beyond

Which relationships?

Much material will be found in other chapters which could easily be repeated under this title. In particular, I see many overlaps between much of the content of this chapter and that of the previous chapter on identity, since it is our perception of ourselves which prompts and guides the relationships we form.

In statutory reviews of looked after children, it is likely that, under this heading, most time will be spent in considering how well the damaged relationships within the child's birth family are being rebuilt. In our case, children were placed with us as an alternative to adoption – a judgement had already been made that there was little or no likelihood of the child ever living with a birth parent again. Whilst taking care to minimise further harm befalling the children, we tried to maintain links with our children's birth families, and these relationships are the subject of the first part of this chapter.

But we were also consciously and deliberately building for our children a substitute or additional family to which they could feel that they belonged. That family comprised not only our household but also our extended family, and the development of that web of relationships was very important. For this to feel real to the children our family had to be seen as a genuine family in the community in which we lived and still live. So the second part of this chapter looks at how we tried to form ourselves into something that could be recognised and experienced as a family, and to find a place for that within our extended family in which our children could feel comfortable.

Within our household were various natural subgroups – Kate and I as a couple and four sets of natural siblings, including our three birth children. A later chapter looks briefly at how we have developed as a couple through our experience of looking after children and stretching the boundaries of our family. Our birth children, Sal, Tom and Rich, as the three people who had least choice about being part of this unusual family group, also deserve a separate chapter to themselves. The third section of this chapter looks at other sub-groups within the family, as well as ad hoc groupings which had temporary significance. It could also be argued that sub-groups might be made of those who shared majority or minority ethnic status, or gender, and I shall consider this.

Finally, we all had and have our place in society as individuals, starting from various points along the spectrum of social exclusion. How we have each to a greater or lesser extent developed these individual social relationships forms the final section of this chapter.

Relationships with birth families

Studies of young people leaving care have consistently suggested that the majority gravitate back into the orbit of their birth family, even if the problems and difficulties which necessitate their being "looked after" have not fundamentally altered. In some cases this will be the natural thing to happen, especially if the family had not placed the child in "significant harm" or if major positive changes have taken place in a previously dysfunctional family group. But for many care leavers, the return to the bosom of the family happens because there is nowhere else to go or to be, no one else to relate to. The foster placement or children's home can no longer be "home".

But all our children were placed with us with a plan for permanence. There was no expectation that their family could offer them a supportive kinship group in the future. Moreover, we offered an alternative lifelong family relationship with us – with Kate and myself acting as parents and with our other children as siblings. That did not mean that we ignored the maintenance of relationships, where possible, between our children and their birth families, but such relationships were within the context of the permanency plan. In Chapter 5 I have written of how we tried to facilitate Fred's ongoing relationship with his mother, urged the local authority to act on Lynn and Mark's wish to resume contact with their mother after a gap of many years, and enabled Josie and Dan to meet their relatives.

These were all relationships which had a positive impact on our shared family life at home, and formed no threat to our carefully maintained boundaries. The adults concerned were supportive of the placements and had no wish to jeopardise their success.

There were other relationships which presented greater difficulties. Sharon and John had been removed from their parents after 19 previous periods of accommodation resulting from neglect or emotional/physical abuse. The parents were not happy about the plan for permanence with us and expressed a wish to remain in contact. John was keen, Sharon less so. Sharon was highly critical of her parents, John less so. The parents' few visits to Plainlands were uncomfortable for everyone. Kate and I struggled to find a role for ourselves, a way of relating to them. We could find little in common. The other children disliked them. They related to Sharon and John, and to the others, in ways that we found unacceptable. It appeared to us that they used blatant emotional strategies to try to undermine their children's developing relationship with us. We were relieved when they stopped coming, and wondered how far their intrusion into the world which Sharon and John shared with us contributed to John's continued ambivalence towards us and the family, and the ever-deepening rift between Sharon and John in adolescence and adulthood. Sharon's view now is that no contact should have been allowed, and indeed she says she felt let down by us at the time for allowing it to happen.

The experience of these visits made me question the wisdom of expecting long-term carers to host contact visits from birth parents within the placement. I felt that this collision of their two worlds with their very different experiences was too difficult an experience for the children to manage, and not necessary. Moreover, the experience was disruptive and uncomfortable for the rest of our family. It was almost certainly uncomfortable for the birth parents as well, since it will have been the *differences* between our home and theirs that will have struck them most forcefully, not the similarities. The potential positives could have been achieved in other ways. The social worker could have arranged for contact between Sharon and John and their parents to take place on neutral territory. Occasional meetings between Kate and myself and Sharon and John's parents could have been arranged if they had wanted this to happen.

On the other hand, at Sharon's repeated request, we persuaded her local authority to facilitate contact between her and an older sister who had been taken into permanent care several years earlier. We had reservations, because the sister was presenting (experiencing?) considerable problems in a city children's home and behaving dangerously, and we feared that the relationship would be destabilising to Sharon. Our fears were unjustified. The renewed contact appeared to have a positive influence on both girls, and they now live within a few miles of each other and enjoy a mutually supportive relationship.

Some children carried into their lives with us a heavy and inappropriate burden of perceived responsibility for parents or siblings. For some years Kwesi saw his mother rather as a wayward, rather irresponsible sister whose decisions were sometimes outside her own control, and would berate us for seeming indifference to her needs – if we could care for him, why couldn't we care for her too? He found ways of excusing her inconsistency, her unreliability about making and keeping appointments to see him, whether at Plainlands or in London, or her inability to remember birthdays, and blamed these shortcomings on others. His image of her was overturned in his early teens when she told him on the phone that she didn't want to see him any more because he had been rude to her, and he realised that she was working as a carer for children in a residential home, without apparently having any plan to care for him. Over the intervening years the task, carried out by the social worker but supported by ourselves, had been gently to maintain realism in his perception of his relationship with his mother, rather than colluding with him in building unrealistic expectations. We have never allowed him to forget his mother's courage in retrieving him from great danger and likely death in Uganda at the age of three.

The mother of Josie and Dan would often phone us tearfully, late at night, possibly drunk, pleading to be allowed to speak to her children. The local authority had decided, wisely, to respect the children's wishes that they wanted no contact, and we were able to resist her pleas while attempting to calm her expressed fears for their welfare. Dan has maintained consistently that he wants no involvement with her. Josie, however, renewed contact with her as a young adult, moved to the same town, and attempted to support her in her many needs, but after the birth of her son felt that her mother's influence on her child as grandmother would be damaging, and discontinued the relationship.

Karen, as the eldest and most able child in her birth family, had a keen sense of responsibility for her younger siblings, who had remained in the family home, and wildly vacillating feelings about her birth parents. When she saw her parents as "good", she wanted to be back with them, and she needed to feel that they were "good" to ease her concerns for the younger children. When she saw them as "bad", she had an almost irresistible urge to be at home to protect the younger children. It was not easy to persuade her to allow others – social workers – to carry the responsibility for her siblings, especially as we thought it likely that significant abuse was continuing. It was also not easy to explain why we felt unable to offer a home to her eldest sister when she was eventually accommodated as a teenager. As an adult, Karen continued to find the pull of her birth family hard to resist, even when their abusive behaviour threatened her own children and the stability of her own family life. We have had to consider with her how some demands are incompatible. We would have been unable to keep her safe as a child if very clear boundaries had not been placed on her contacts with her birth family, however much we acknowledged her concern for the younger children. Similarly, as an adult and a parent, she could not have exercised her primary responsibility to protect and nurture her own children if she had continued to allow her birth family to have access to them.

Now, Karen says, 'I truly believe that I hated Sal and Tom. Sal was so perfect with her blond hair and her slim figure – she never did anything wrong; Tom knew it all and would correct you if you used a word in the wrong context. The problem for me was that I lived with these two people who were the same age as my own sister and brother, but were also different from them in every way. Why should I like these two people who had it all and knew it all? They did not need me, whereas my own sister and brother at home needed me to help them and protect them from harm. The worst moment for me was one day when I was playing with Sal and her best friend Liz up in Sal's bedroom. I left the room to go to the toilet, and when I got back I decided to listen at the bedroom door to see if they were saying anything about me. I heard Liz say to Sal, "She swears so much – shall I tell my mum?" at which point I lurched into the room and shouted at them both, "I don't care who you bloody tell, I ain't staying in this shithole anyway with you snobs". This was the first time that I really questioned my position in this new family. Where I was before, everybody swore and it was accepted, although deep down I always wanted to be in a family where people were more like this – "normal". But how could I live somewhere when I did not fit in very well? Today it's a totally different story – if anything, I feel even closer to Sal and Tom than other members of the family, and they are really more important to me than my own natural siblings who have had a great habit of letting me down over the years.' These tensions might have been impossible to contain and eventually resolve in a much smaller group.

The final decisions about contact with birth families rest with the social workers and the courts. We clarified our own role as a combination of: supplying information about the child's needs and experience, as we observed them, to inform the risk assessment and decision-making process; enabling the child to express their feelings about their birth family by non-judgmental active listening and emotional education; and protecting the welfare of the children entrusted to us, especially within the boundaries of our own home. After all, if we felt that exposure to friends or acquaintances of ours visiting our home was damaging to any of our children or to the environment we were building for them, we would discourage the friends from returning. The same would be true of friends of the children if their presence had a damaging effect on others. We felt that this should apply equally to some of our children's birth families. If present or potential benefit for the children could be seen in facilitating continuing contact, we would do as much as we could to make it possible. If contact appeared only to perpetuate damage already done to the children, we felt that it should be minimised. The welfare of each of the children was paramount, and there seemed to us to be no place for an ideological approach that did not take account of the dynamics of each individual relationship.

Relationships within our family

A couple who have become very close friends of ours live in a large village remotely situated in West Wales. Neither of them is Welsh, and neither of them has relatives living closer than a day's journey. They are childless; they fostered one child who left them at the age of 16 and now lives in North-East England. They have made many friends in the village where they live and are actively involved in supporting several of these friends through bereavement, illness and other personal crises. They talk of this network as their "village family", and live within it as part of an interdependent, mutually supportive community.

This is something like the vision we had for our family, although geographical proximity would become less important, we hoped, than the emotional ties. With their birth families largely absent from their lives, we hoped that the children could build within our family an alternative network which they could belong to beyond childhood into their adult lives. We encouraged them to relate to one another as siblings and to share one another's joys and pains. For most of them, that has been the case, and they speak of 'the family', rather than of 'Kate and Brian' or 'Mum and Dad' as being the powerful positive influence in their lives. It helped that our birth children grew up having experienced no other way of living and were not a pre-formed group which had to accept a huge expansion. And it helped enormously that most of our own relatives were prepared to share our vision and to become grandparents and aunts and uncles to all of our children without making distinctions that were readily apparent.

In practice, this meant a lot of sharing. While personal possessions were important and had to be respected, we tried to miss no opportunity to encourage everyone in the family to make their belongings available to others, and to give and receive shared presents. Several of our children found this very difficult. Mark was one such, at first. One year at Christmas we gave him a huge box of chocolates on the firm and straight-faced condition that he was not allowed to share them with anyone else. It worked – disobedience trumped egocentricity! Sharing of experience was important too. Taking several children together to buy new shoes for school doesn't have to be an "institutional" experience, and therefore to be avoided. It can be fun. I believe that the larger families of previous generations or other contemporary cultures learned and benefited a great deal from such experience, which works provided that each individual is respected within the group. So bullying and victimisation within the family group could not be tolerated, and the strength of the group had to be harnessed to protect potential victims.

In our own social dealings Kate and I refused to make distinctions between our foster children and our birth children. Chatting to an acquaintance on the high street, we might say 'Must dash – got to pick my son up from football', whether the son concerned was a birth child or a foster child. If asked by a new acquaintance how many children we had, we would say – and still do say – '15', and offer no further explanation unless asked. If it was necessary to make a distinction, we would sometimes talk of 'home-grown' and 'imported' children. People would often ask us 'How are your children?' and we would perversely talk about all of them even if it was apparent, perhaps through a slight emphasis on 'your' that the questioner was asking about the birth children. The children took their lead from us, and for the most part took an impish pleasure in answering 'Eight', or 'Fourteen', or whatever the number was at the time, to the casual question, 'How many brothers and sisters do you have?' And the family grades in GCSE French oral exams probably dropped as a result of examiner disbelief in the accuracy of the answers given to 'Combien de frères avez-vous?' or 'Combien de chambres y a-t-il dans votre maison?'

Birthdays and celebrations

All "special days" can be difficult for separated children. There may be painful memories of Christmasses and birthdays in previous settings where everything went horribly wrong, where children were forgotten or ignored, or where the day was marked by violence or abuse. There may be stress and uncertainty around the role which birth families will or will not play, or about being the centre of attention. The first Christmas or birthday in a new placement needs careful preparation and explanation of what will happen, with a manageable level of choice for the child.

We went for a combination of "specialness" and simplicity. Christmas gradually fell into a familiar annual pattern. Having plenty to do on Christmas Eve seemed important. So it was not until then that we would share putting up the Christmas tree, festooning the house totally tastelessly with decorations, scouring the garden for holly and mistletoe, wrapping the presents, and doing quite a lot of the "special" food shopping. Late afternoon and evening saw us do a carol-singing tour of local friends and relatives in whose houses we would eat and drink prodigiously. On our return the older children might go off with friends for an hour or two, but the younger ones would bring a stack of Grandad's largest socks from down the lane and place each one on a chair in the main living-room, one for each member of the household and any visitors, with a cartoon drawing of its temporary owner pinned to it to aid Father Christmas's recognition.

On Christmas morning the door at the top of the staircase (as insisted on by the fire officer) became useful. It became traditional that our bedroom (nearest to that door) would be besieged with increasing urgency until we would give in, the family would assemble at the head of the stairs, I would go down to switch on Christmas tree lights and seasonal music, and then summon the others who would descend on the assembled treasures. We didn't make a distinction between presents from "Santa" and from ourselves, and as the children grew older their presents to us and to one another would often have been put on or next to the "stockings" before they had gone to bed. Presents from and to non-household-members remained under the tree until later in the day.

We ensured that stockings contained plenty of things to eat, including the traditional fruit, so we had no breakfast as such, keeping the kitchen clear for more important food preparation. In the early years we would drive off mid-morning to "Mince-Pie Meeting", a Quaker gathering which was much loved (children visiting now as adults still like to go), involving fifty minutes or so of vaguely seasonal readings or stories brought by participants and shared around a roaring fire, followed by the eponymous mince pies and hot spicy punch. In later years this gathering happened at our house, and there could be up to fifty people around our hearth.

Christmas dinner happened in mid-afternoon, when we were joined by Kate's parents, sister and great-aunt. We would put together as many tables as necessary. It features the usual ingredients – crackers and silly hats, turkey and trimmings, and a ceremonial extinguishing of lights as brandy was poured on the pudding and it was set aflame.

After dinner we would gather to share out the presents under the Christmas tree, and in later years were often joined by some of our grown-up children who may have eaten in their own homes or with their partners' families, and who would also bring and receive presents. Gifts from birth families were mixed in with the rest under the tree, and in the general good-natured mayhem comparisons or disappointments were minimised. So the room would disappear under boxes and wrapping paper, and we would try with moderate success to ensure that the right people were thanked for the right present and that nothing was trampled underfoot and smashed before it could be enjoyed. After that the day was totally unstructured, and people would disperse through the house playing games, reading new books, or watching television. Food and drink were readily available if required, but we had no more formal meals. It was a pattern for Christmas Day which developed over the years, was flexible enough to meet the family's changing composition and maturity, and seemed to work.

Birthdays developed a pattern too. We were fortunate in that most of the family had sping or summer birthdays, which usually allowed for outdoor celebration and exuberance. Presents and cards would be stacked on the breakfast table for the birthday person, and there was a convention that the whole household, or as near to it as we could get, would assemble for their opening amidst the cereal and toast. Kate's parents would arrive in the middle of this with their presents. The pattern was the same whether the birthday was that of foster child, birth child, Kate or myself.

Each child was offered the opportunity to choose a birthday celebration, which could involve all or none of the rest of the family. It might be a gathering of friends or an outing: ice-skating and swimming trips, football and cricket matches, seaside trips and Chinese restaurants were all popular. Often the "birthday treat" would not be on the actual birthday, and then a family birthday tea with cake, closest friends and grandparents would happen anyway. With seven birthdays between 17 July and 12 August, we were often away for birthdays, and the birthday treat would become something we might have done anyway, like a visit to Legoland, but none the less enjoyable for that. Our children rarely asked for extravagant parties – although Kate was organising games on the lawn for Sharon's eleven-year-old friends while going into labour with Tom!

Another regular family event was Hallowe'en, perfectly timed for building a huge bonfire of garden rubbish, to which we added pumpkin lanterns, bobbing for apples, occasional fireworks, cardboard masks and skeletons and ghostly mayhem in the garden. Similarly, Easter had its traditions of dyed hard-boiled eggs, garden treasure-hunts, and the game of "sharps and blunts" from which one robust "super-egg" would emerge victorious as an "eighty-niner", having smashed the shells of eighty-nine others.

Contacts and relationships with our extended families were encouraged. Apart from our parents visiting frequently and being involved in birthday and Christmas celebrations, we tried to ensure that other relatives visiting them also got to spend some time with as many of us as could be gathered. Valuable relationships evolved. Kate's younger sister, single and childless, joined us on holidays and became a trusted and respected aunt. An uncle in the Midlands often hosted reunions of Kate's extended family, and we made great efforts to attend these, family weddings and so on, despite the logistical difficulties of doing so. A single foster child might have found such social occasions intimidating; ours enjoyed the simultaneous advantages of having one another around to provide security whilst taking the opportunity to be accepted by a tolerant and welcoming wider network. The presence of the other children reduced stress, so made stress reactions in the form of disruptive or anti-social behaviour less likely. Kate and I would explain beforehand as far as we could what form we expected the event to take and where we could be found, and then tried to be as relaxed as we could rather than giving a long list of behavioural do's and don'ts. For the most part, all the children would regularly rise to the occasion. We found that availability was the key – never to become so engrossed with other adults as to be unavailable for a child in difficulty, always to have some part of our attention focussed on how the children were coping and to be ready to intervene, comfort, distract, advise or occupy. Our role on these occasions was to be unobtrusive facilitators of valuable learning experience for the children, and to know and respond when saturation point was being reached – in other words, to subsume our own preferences to the children's needs from moment to moment.

If there was ever a difficulty in the midst of our foster children about the fact that we were "paid to look after them", I was not aware of it. We were totally open about family finances and accounting (see Chapter 9). All the children were very clear that we could not have afforded our reasonably comfortable lifestyle for such a large group of people had it not been for the allowances being paid by the various local authorities. They knew that the "salary" element of our income from local authorities was used largely to buy "extras", to fund trips and holidays for us all, to ensure that we were well enough protected financially to know that if one of us died or became seriously ill we could afford enough additional help to keep the household together, and to save for the time when we would need to buy ourselves a house. The foster children could see that the birth children were not having more money spent on them than they, as foster children, were. The birth children came to recognise that our accommodation and lifestyle probably exceeded in comfort and scope what we would have been able to afford if we had had three children and one-and-a-half teaching or local government salaries. And they all came to know that we would continue to give all of them financial support in adulthood if they needed it and we could afford it, whilst at the same time expecting and assuming that they would accept the responsibility of managing their own financial affairs wisely.

Subgroups and groupings

The three sibling pairs who were the first children to be placed in our family in the 1970s were very different from one another, and have remained so. Ostensibly similar – in each case an older sister and a brother less than two years younger – their relationships had already developed along different lines when they joined us, and continued to do so. None of these readymade sibling groups ever became a "power bloc" raised against the rest of the family or in rivalry to another sibling pair.

The relationship between Sharon and John (who came to us from a violent family home) was volatile when they came to us, and worsened, and there is now no contact between them. At least in our busy household there were other young people for each of them to relate to. Lynn had been protective of Mark when they were together in the children's home, and remains so, defending him if others feel he has been unreliable or insensitive. In our household she was able, with our encouragement, to relinquish to others her self-appointed role of protecting Mark and concentrate more on her own life. As a small child, Dan was wary of Josie and unimpressed by some of the extremes of her behaviour under stress, and yet they remained quietly supportive of each other whilst developing their lives very differently. A clear bond of mutual affection still exists. Looking back on the childhoods which each of these children enjoyed with us, I feel that it was good for them to grow up with a sibling, a link to their shared past – and even better for them to grow up within a larger group of children in which they could expand their experience of sibling relationships and effectively dilute what could have become a damaging intensity and a disabling exclusivity. For Karen, on the other hand, whose parents had induced something approaching a siege mentality in their children – 'us against the world' – it was the right decision to separate her from sibling relationships in which she could well have become hopelessly enmeshed to the exclusion of everybody else.

Other relationships became important among the children, some long-lasting, some transient but important. Sal and Dan were very close from primary school onwards – a typical big brother–little sister relationship which forged a strong link between the older group of foster children and the younger group which included our birth children. Interest groups formed that spanned boundaries of gender, age or origin – the brass instrument players, the amateur actors, the footballers, the animal-lovers.

Within social work we are becoming increasingly aware that fostering is offered by families, not individuals. We therefore pay more attention to the roles and needs of the birth children in the family (cf. Chapter 11). In a family group such as ours, individual fostered children are also "children who foster" – providers as well as recipients of a service. This is good, both for them and for the adult carers.

We tried to be aware of the ebb and flow of relationships among our children. We recognised that, when individual children were experiencing difficulties and felt alienated from Kate and me, it would often be their relationship with other children in the group, birth children or foster children, that would become their lifeline, the link that held them within the family and kept lines of communication open. We frequently suggested changes of bedroom (usually only if we already knew that they would be acceptable) that put particular children closer to each other as "neighbours" if they seemed to be drawing something particularly valuable from the relationship. Once we had converted the Plainlands attic to make three additional bedrooms, we paid particular attention to which three children would share that rather more self-contained space. Interestingly, none of our children had the same bedroom throughout our time at Plainlands – only Kate and I stayed in the same place. Perhaps that was a valuable symbol: we represented stability, fixed points around which our children had freedom to change and grow. An awareness that we were constantly changing and growing too might not always have been helpful, even though a capacity for flexibility and adaptability undoubtedly was.

As the family grew, the spread of ages became enormously helpful. Children need to get to know well people of all ages. The generation gap can become real and insuperable when children have contact with no-one of an age between that of their own immediate peers and their parents or carers. In the early days of our family, our teenage "nannies" helped to fill the gap (although there are only 15 years between Kate and our oldest child, Sharon) between the older children and ourselves. For our younger children, it was their older "siblings" who filled the gap, providing role models (positive and negative), and often mentors whose advice could be followed more easily than ours. The debt which Kwesi acknowledges in this respect to Fred in learning how to relate socially has already been mentioned. He also learned much from Dan and Josie about how to manage being a black person in a largely white community, and from Mark about the responsibilities of sharing a rented flat. As a young adult, Liam found a home with Sharon and her family for several months when he was particularly needy, as did Karen for a brief period in her troubled teens. The chronology of some of these examples shows how amazing they are. Kwesi is 13 years younger than Fred; when he joined us as a four-year-old, Fred had already left school, and within a few months had gone away to college. Karen came to live with us in 1989, six years *after* Sharon had moved on to live independently, though one of the first family occasions she shared was to come with us all to Sharon's first wedding. Our older children were remarkable in their willingness to accept as part of their growing family network children with whom they had never lived under our roof.

Most of the younger children can list practical skills which they learned from the older children rather than from Kate or me, and can reflect on criticism from older siblings which they took to heart but would have rejected if we had been the source. In households where there are several fostered children, it is not only the birth children who become "children who foster", for all children, including those who are themselves fostered, who have new foster children come to live with them are contributing to the task of integrating them and helping them and one another to grow. And the next generation of children enjoys a rich variety of input from cousins, uncles and aunts, which the older ones among them already enjoy and appreciate.

Relationships beyond the family

The first aspect of this to strike me is what we did *not* do. Two guiding principles for us over the years were to avoid, as far as possible, any way of organising our life together that seemed institutional, and to reduce stress for our children. So in accordance with these principles we did not, on the whole, involve ourselves or the children in activities which underlined their situation of being "children in care". The voluntary organisation under whose auspices we worked set up opportunities for its families, like ours, to meet together, and we did not take up those opportunities, although we were glad to meet the other foster carers separately on other occasions. We preferred our children to make their social contacts with other children in less "artificial" ways than in a gathering of "recipients of charity", where the children would be all too aware that the adults' shared topic of conversation was likely to be them, the children, and where the one common factor was being in care. We also did not push our children to go on the annual holidays for children of the organisation led by its staff and trustees – whilst allowing any to go who wished to. Far better, we felt, for them to go, as they did, on camps and trips and holidays with school or other community groups, where the majority of their companions were not looked after children.

Even so, we noticed that our children found it stressful to spend time socially as a family with other families, particularly if they were not foster families. For a variety of reasons there would, with a very few exceptions, seem to be an awkward mismatch when we tried to develop friendships with other parents and bring the families together. Parents of smaller families found it hard to understand our group dynamics and see how we functioned and maintained order. They seemed either to be totally involved with their children or totally oblivious to them, not understanding that it might be possible to be aware and attentive at a distance. Sometimes they would speak about their children in front of them in ways which seemed to us disrespectful, and expect us to do the same. Their children often found it difficult to manage the amount of space and freedom to which our children had become accustomed, or found it overwhelming to feel that they had to relate to so many very different people all at the same time. We found it easier to develop friendships with single or childless people, or with people of a slightly different generation whose children were older than ours. And we had to recognise that foster carers, carrying sometimes as they do the contagious traumas which their children bring, are not always the easiest of companions for other adults. I return to this issue in Chapter 11.

We came to recognise too that, for a long time, several of our children lacked the necessary social skills to be able to relate as host to any child who turned up at Plainlands accompanying their parent who was a friend of ours, or as guest in the homes of adults whom we visited. These were skills which took years of stabilisation, integration and adaptation to learn, and social situations which required them were stressful for many of the children. That is not to say that they lacked the ability to make friendships with other children, although inevitably some found this more difficult than others. But often they had the knack of seeking out good friends – sometimes unlikely friends – who were able to tolerate their idiosyncrasies, and these would often be young people who, for whatever reason, hovered on the boundaries of social exclusion themselves. It is often the unusual children who are the most sensitive.

Of course, the friendships made were sometimes not the friendships that pleased us to see. Looked after children often seek out children who seem to be "like me", and they are, not surprisingly, the children who are themselves struggling with the legacy of poor early attachment or neglecting or abusive parents. We would try to put safe boundaries around these friendships without attempting to stop them altogether, and to talk with the children as non-judgementally as we could about the difficulties that the friends might be getting into. Since we were largely successful in helping our children to be aware of their own problems and to work at resolving them, they would often become dissatisfied with friends who were not making a similar effort, or be able to exert a helpful influence on troubled friends who lacked support at home. It was again a question of ongoing risk assessment: is this relationship putting our child at risk? If so, how can the risk be minimised? And if that cannot be done, what realistic steps can we take to protect our child? Driving the relationship underground was not likely to be helpful, but that was a lesson that it took us some years to learn.

Fundamental to the children's ability to gain acceptance and make positive friendships was their "membership" of our local community. School was central to this. It seemed essential to bring John and Josie back into the local school community after a period at the Steiner school some distance away had helped them to accept being in school and to begin learning. With hindsight, Martin may have done better to transfer to Year 10 in our local school than to stay, as he did, and by his own choice, at the comprehensive in the next town. Being in school meant that the children knew everybody there was to know. All the children in town knew somebody in the family; as did most of the shopkeepers, most of the parents, most of the people who made the town tick. It was impossible to walk down the main street without meeting somebody who would say hello. We had connections with the churches, connections with the youth organisations, connections through my work as teacher and social worker, connections through our parents who had their own networks in the town, and those connections, those interlocking systems, grew as the years went on. The shared use of our surname tied the children in to all these systems. Moreover, our gate stood symbolically open, for although gates may be helpful for keeping small children in, they send a very effective message to the rest of the world to keep its distance, and we knew that our children needed that community beyond our gate to know them and help them to become included in it.

We owe a particular debt to our neighbours – to the quiet, methodical family whose property was carved out of Plainlands' original garden, and who treated our idiosyncrasies with tolerance and our children with courtesy; to the farming family whose land surrounded ours and who introduced several of our boys to work on the farm; to a neighbour who grazed his sheep in our orchard; and others who offered the children lifts to school or simply treated them with friendliness and courtesy. All these people helped all our children to become part of the community, and as I have suggested elsewhere, the development of a wide range of social relationships with adults of all ages beyond the confines of the house where they live is as vital to children's growing sense of identity and belonging as is the development of relationships and friendships with their peers. It is important, too, that they are enabled to make many of these relationships as themselves rather than as the adjuncts of their parents or carers. We were pleased if some of our children got to know some of our neighbours better than we did ourselves. It is unfortunate if a well-meaning concern for children's safety makes it less possible for them to make social contacts which help them to feel valued with the vast majority of adults who are decent and benevolent. For children whose early experience of adults has been very different, it is all the more important for them to be encouraged to find out for themselves that the world is not uniformly hostile.

Another helpful experience for our children as they reached their teens was the experience of part-time work. The role of our local farmer as a work provider is already recorded, and paper rounds and babysitting gave a valuable taste of responsibility and being trusted to others in the family. Social workers sometimes raised concerns about looked after children being 'put out to work'. We defended the children's right to do what many of their most responsible and successful peers were doing and enjoying. The advantages in terms of self-image, self-esteem, learning skills, social inclusion and managing time and money seemed to us to be overwhelming. Our task as carers was to be aware of what could go wrong, to look discreetly for warning signs, and to intervene before damage was irreversible, since sometimes late-developing moral codes had not totally caught up with the demands of employment.

When we started our family, some people were concerned about the fact that we had no ready-made support network of our own in the community where we would be leaving, having moved from Yorkshire to Gloucestershire. True, Kate was returning to the town where she had lived eight years previously before going away to university – but her former friends had all gone. Kate's parents' networks and standing in the town were useful and meant that there were people who were disposed to see us and our family favourably – but with hindsight it seems to be that most people got to know us as the family we had become without the difficulty of having to forget what we were before. They got to know us as a family unit. We had to feel our way gradually, just as our children did. Finding our place in a new community was a task for all of us to share, and there was no danger of Kate or me underestimating how hard this might be for the children, because it wasn't easy for us. As with so many aspects of how we chose to live together, we had to risk some vulnerability in order to succeed.

Key factors

- Encouraging our children to relate to one another as siblings and to expect a lifelong mutually supportive relationship.
- Recognising the significance of relationships with birth parents, but being realistic about their limitations and the risks that they may pose.
- Actively looking for opportunities to facilitate helpful relationships with other birth family members.
- Understanding when children feel an inappropriate level of responsibility for other family members and helping them to let go.
- Giving children a wide range of models of successful relationships within a family context.
- Helping our own extended families to understand our children's place in our life and to include them naturally in wider family activities.
- Reducing contact with any of our own extended family who found it hard to accept our children as family members.
- Refusing to make distinctions between birth children and looked after children both in practice and in conversation with others.
- Recognising and using the strength of the family group to add richness to shared experience, to provide mutual support and to address problems.
- Developing our own friendships among people who could relate easily to our family.

- Avoiding placing our children in unnecessarily stressful social situations.
- Explaining in advance expectations in unfamiliar social situations and being on hand to alleviate stress or help children to withdraw appropriately.
- Planning shared and individual celebrations which become a recognisable pattern whilst retaining enough flexibility to meet individual needs, sensibilities and choices.
- Being aware of potentially helpful relationships between individual children and facilitating their development.
- Encouraging older children to take responsibility for younger children.
- Encouraging children to make a wide range of friendships and social contacts with people of all ages.
- Discouraging children from making "child in care" a central part of their identity.
- Trusting as far as possible the children's own choice of friends whilst helping them to recognise the social difficulties that some of their friends may experience.
- Welcoming children's friends into the house whilst expecting them to relate appropriately to all of the family.
- Seeking opportunities to be involved in the local community both individually and as a family.
- Helping teenage children to seek and maintain suitable part-time work as well as involvement in school-based and community activities.
- Accepting the social vulnerability which can accompany being part of a foster family, and working at overcoming it in ways that meet the needs of everyone in the family.

7 Social presentation
Developing the confidence to claim social inclusion

Inclusion

In May 2002, I sat outside the converted stable which was our French holiday home for a week, and looked across the lawns of the château at a large cross-section of our family, their partners, in-laws and children, playing and relaxing around the pool and volleyball court. I was interested to see whether I thought that a stranger would guess that any of them had grown up "in care", and if so, which ones. Obvious differences in skin colour, I decided, might offer the stranger a clue, but it would not, of course, be definitive. Certainly I could not discern any traits of behaviour, patterns of relationship or styles of dress or personal appearance that the stranger might have picked up as indicative. Even when I mentally added into the scenario those of our family who were not with us in France, the result remained the same. And yet, when they joined us, the majority of our children had something indefinable but unmistakeable about them that marked them out from their peers, an aura of deprivation. Scrubbed up and dressed in new clothes, they had looked gauche and incongruous.

I am sure that the concept of social exclusion sheds light on the change that had taken place over the years. When they came to us, many of our children were primarily aware of being and feeling "different", outside what appeared to be the norms of society. We had invited them unconditionally to be an integral part of our family, indeed, to contribute to the evolution of our family. And the mainstream schools which they attended, the friends they made (who were, almost without exception, not "in care"), and the small town community in which we all lived, had welcomed us, and them, as integral parts of their systems. As the children became able to accept those invitations – and in some cases that took a long time, well into adulthood – they stopped feeling excluded, and identified more and more with the values and behaviours of the majority systems to which they now felt they had a right to belong.

Fred and Karen have specifically told me of the amazement of people they meet who learn that they grew up "in care". Their experience is shared, I know, by many of our other foster children.

However inextricably linked with other aspects of development social presentation may be, there are some elements to which we did give specific attention as our children were growing up. Different approaches might have produced different results. I shall look briefly at questions of dress, of personal style (personal hygiene, hair, piercings, make-up), and of verbal self-presentation.

Dress

What could the children have observed from us? Most of them had little admiration for our preferences in dress! They first knew me as a tweedy schoolteacher with a penchant for gaudy ties, whose concession to informality at home was to open my collar and swap woolly jacket for woolly jumper. Kate's preferred style for most of the family years was defined by the children as "hippyish": lots of loose, comfortable cotton, bright colours, a dizzying variety of hemlines, but often long dresses, tight jeans or patterned leggings for variety, "sensible" shoes or sandals. Both of us bought a lot of clothes from charity shops, partly for reasons of economy, partly because we approved of recycling. Neither of us paid much attention to fashion or designer labels, although we did like good quality clothes, and we rarely went out specifically to shop for clothes for ourselves, preferring just to buy something when it took our fancy.

However, we did think it important to look appropriately dressed for social, particularly formal, occasions, and for work away from our home. As social workers we tried to dress in ways that reflected a positive image of our employers whilst not putting up unnecessary and unhelpful barriers between ourselves and people whom we were trying to help or influence. We would compliment each other on our appearance, and would tell each other if we thought that styles or colours clashed, or something didn't look quite right. We would often buy each other presents from charity shops: a family story often repeated with predictable hilarity involves my bringing home in triumph a summer dress which I thought would look just right on Kate – she had worn it for several years and taken it to Oxfam the previous week! Several of the children have become as adults and parents shrewd bargain-hunters in charity shops and car-boot sales, and thank us for the example. So from us our children may have learned that clothes are functional but can be fun, that they don't need to cost a fortune, and that it can be important at times to consider the image they are presenting to people who may appear to be very different from oneself.

We were aware that clothing might have had very different meanings to our children. They might be linked to experiences of sexual abuse – either provocative because that was what one had learned to be, or deliberately unattractive to put off potential unwelcome advances. They might be a way to shut out a threatening world, a cocoon in which to hide. They might be, particularly in the early stages of placement, important symbols of the past, only to be set aside when one was really sure that the placement had become home. Having come to us in the summer, Liam spent much of his first summer holiday with us a few weeks later huddled in a huge, thick, black hooded jumper, while the Brittany sun beat down at a steady 35 degrees.

As with so many other aspects of our children, we had to learn each child, and allow them the space to be themselves. Buying clothes for the children was often a very different exercise from buying clothes for ourselves, involving infinite patience. We set budget limits; we vetoed apparently extreme choices while we were paying (this relaxed when each of the children felt able with our agreement to progress to managing a quarterly clothing allowance themselves); we balanced our own dislike of heavily-advertised "fashion" items against the children's need to become or remain socially acceptable to their peers; we explained what we saw as the tyranny of advertising and all-powerful multinationals. We encouraged them to think about what statement particular items of clothing might be making about them to their friends, their friends' parents, their teachers, their potential Saturday employers, and that was effective as long as we could keep them socially connected. We forged a relationship with the manager of our local shoeshop, who came to know all our children's needs in terms of comfort and fit, and what would or would not be acceptable to us, and would greet our children politely and often by name when he met them in the street. We bettered this relationship for a few years when Sal took a Saturday and holiday job in the shop that sold school uniforms! We would use the charity shops occasionally for the children too, and buy them occasional presents of something fun to wear, not making a fuss if the gift was rejected, as it sometimes was. And of course, compliments were always important, and far more valuable, as I came eventually to understand, than criticisms.

I have mentioned school uniform. In general, I disapprove of it as an unwarranted intrusion into individual autonomy, a denial of self-expression, and an unacceptable means of imposing authority. There were times when rigid adherence to arbitrary principles of uniformity led to conflict between us as carers and the school, particularly in areas which touched on the sensitivities of children who had been sexually abused. But there were also ways in which uniform helped many of our children. It gave them a visible symbol of belonging – to a school community, to the local community of which the school was an important part, and to the group of similar-age children within the family. It gave them a legitimate way of looking conventionally "smart" without undermining their integrity or causing them embarrassment. And it gave them a harmless vehicle for acts of minor rebellion to which they knew, eventually, that we would feel sympathetic even though we had to advise conformity.

The laundry system in the family was a vital part of education about self-presentation. We were as insistent as we could be about clothing being changed and laundered regularly, making a distinction between general bedroom mess (largely acceptable) and heaps of dirty clothing (largely unacceptable). Laundry baskets were profusely available. Washing, drying and ironing were constant activities – ironing became, and remains, one of my favourite household tasks. Children knew that a favourite garment put out to be washed wouldn't be lost forever in a tangled heap in the laundry room, but would be back with them, clean and well-presented, within a couple of days. Kate's regular early morning task was sorting out clean laundry and placing little piles outside each bedroom door as she woke the family. Anything needing repair would be noticed and dealt with. As the children reached late adolescence we tried to ensure that they each understood how our communal laundry process worked, and were themselves able to move it on a stage if they felt like being helpful.

Looking at the children now as adults, I see a group of people who dress appropriately for the various aspects of their lifestyles. They look comfortable in what they wear. Their style frightens neither horses nor elderly ladies. Those whose work requires formality in dress carry it off with understated panache; they have learned the rules, and come to an accommodation with conformity which is not, I think, enslavement. Their lives are not dominated by the ever-changing demands of fashion. And Lynn will still burst in on a Sunday afternoon with a trophy in black silk or white linen, crying, 'Mum, look what I found in the car boot sale, it will look great on you and was only 50p!'

Personal style

Here again the children, when they bothered to think about it, will have learned from us a fairly broad tolerance. It was never our habit to make critical or disparaging remarks about other people's appearance, and we avoided doing so more and more rigorously as the years went by. For ourselves, we avoided extremes in our own personal appearance, although the children have never known me without a beard, they have never seen Kate use make-up, and those who were around in the late 1970s will have been well aware of our dislike of punk fashions in hairstyles and indiscriminate body piercings.

Our line was usually to look at these issues from the pragmatic standpoint of health and the perceptions of others. Handwashing before eating food was always requested, but not insisted upon unless the grime was obvious. Regular washing, we said, was a good way to keep unpleasant infections and unattractive skin complaints at bay. Hot baths and showers were never rationed. Kate and I both liked to have a bath or a shower every day, and we assumed that many of the children would be of the same mind. I recall fewer difficulties around encouraging recalcitrant washers than there were around urging slow bathers to be aware of the impatient queue outside the bathroom door! We had three bathrooms, each including a toilet, and a further toilet beyond the kitchen, not by modern standards a surplus. We didn't segregate by age or gender; everybody tended to use most frequently the bathroom nearest to their own bedroom, where their toothbrush would be kept, except for one bedroom which had its own washbasin. Aware that bathrooms, like bedrooms, might have particular traumatic associations for abused or traumatised children, we tried to avoid any institutional-looking features, and to ensure that they always smelt fresh and inviting, but we could probably have done more to make them attractive places to be with more attention to soft surfaces, pictures on the walls, and so on, as we did with other areas of the house. We learned over time the importance of a range of soaps and shampoos and bath salts and bubble baths to make bathing as relaxing and enjoyable an experience as time would allow. Privacy in the bathroom was encouraged as soon as a child requested it or seemed able to manage without help.

Hairstyles, which seemed to occupy a disproportionate amount of time and energy on the part of schoolteachers, never seemed to be a huge problem. Length never greatly bothered us: where there were no obvious boundaries to be tested, there was little point in extremes. John and Rich, over a decade apart, went through "grunge" phases when washing hair became an issue, as it did with Kwesi at a younger stage when he resented having to have his tight curls carefully combed and oiled. Occasional experiments with colour produced raised eyebrows and genuine concern about school's reaction and its consequences. We reserved greater concern for those few occasions when we felt that a chosen hairstyle indicated a desire to attach to a social group with anti-social values – skinheads, for example, at the time of the emergence of the neo-Nazis – and we would share these concerns with the children, in what we hoped was a spirit of debate.

We were less tolerant about piercings, although of course if one of the children had gone off and had a stud through a lip or a ring through an eyebrow there would have been little that we could have done. But we did feel that this should be an adult decision, so held out against agreeing to ears or anything else being pierced until children reached their mid-teens, citing examples of piercings that had gone wrong. Of course, one or two of the children came to us with piercings already in place, and I found that difficult, without ever quite being able to identify or explain why, other than that I saw it as some kind of child mutilation.

I think it would bother me less now. Perhaps we were inconsistent; Kate, after all, has pierced ears and likes long, dangly earrings, which I find attractive. We are often a puzzle to ourselves. But it was an issue on which we had strong feelings, and maybe it enabled the children to better appreciate our more relaxed attitude to other things.

There were, however, lively family discussions around image and self-image, the urge to self-harm and the desire to self-destruct, conformity and rebellion, acceptance and rejection of society's values, and so on. Such discussions often arose out of a comment about someone's style choices, inside or outside the family. There were usually enough of us for nobody to feel totally isolated in their view, for individuals to sit back and listen if they didn't want to expose themselves by committing to a particular argument, and for others to develop in their own self-awareness. As so often, the number and variety of people sitting around our supper-table lent balance to many conversations which were seminal in forming and refining opinions and identities.

Sal told me recently that she was glad to have older sisters who taught her about make-up, because Mum didn't have a clue! That about sums it up – unless it looked really bizarre, I didn't notice it, and if it did look really bizarre, all our family were surrounded by people much more knowledgeable than Kate or me, who would dispense advice, often unbidden. I think our ignorance was really quite touching.

Verbal self-presentation

With few exceptions, our children were fairly inarticulate when they arrived, especially when they found themselves in conversation with adults. Those who had lived in foster placements for some time had developed more social skills and a wider vocabulary than those who came from deprived and/or abusive birth families or from children's homes. It appeared that those who found conversation – or simply asking for something in a shop – most difficult were those who had least experience of being listened to in a non-threatening way. They expected that adults would have little interest in what they were saying, or would be interested only to criticise, correct or ridicule.

Adults often go instinctively in one of two ways when children are talking to them. Some will scarcely acknowledge the child at all. These adults avoid active listening, and their posture and body movements indicate neither attention nor interest. They make little response, neither carrying the conversation further, picking up the mood, nor inviting the child to continue. They will look away, remain expressionless, or use a "closing-down" statement or intonation that suggests that they have more important or stimulating things to do than listen further. Others will beam on the child a blinding torch of attention and exaggerated interest that can make the child feel acutely exposed, like a performer in a freak show. Either response is likely to be damaging to further efforts to converse on the part of the child – and I suspect that most of us have often been guilty of both.

When children have experienced poor early attachment with a parent or carer, their attempts to engage adults in dialogue will reflect their early difficulties in obtaining the desired response from that carer. Their anxiety about responses which they cannot predict may alert the unsuspecting adult to a difficulty, which is likely to push them towards one of the extreme responses. The adult either wants to avoid being drawn into a potentially difficult interaction, so avoids engagement, or over-reacts to the anxiety by becoming gushing and false. Or perhaps the child will have learned that it is better not to talk to adults at all, so remains withdrawn, or, if communication seems unavoidable, adopts a tone of belligerence to repel the perceived threat. Again the unwary adult is pushed into an extreme reaction.

It was a hard lesson for me to learn that it was important to talk with my children with the level of attention that felt comfortable to them at first, and then gradually help them to move towards socially acceptable norms. I found withdrawn children easy – they seemed to be like me. I had been a fairly solitary child, content with my own company, tending to see adults as people who got bored from time to time and unreasonably wanted me to entertain them. I found it difficult to be with children who were constantly demanding my attention and yet didn't seem to have anything interesting to say or share with me. I had to learn how to dig out appropriate channels of communication to each child, to realise that it was important for that communication to take place, to help the child to feel at ease with me, neither dismissed nor pressured. Learning was slow, and I am still not good at it. Fortunately Kate is. I like to feel that several of the children have learned from me how to be comfortable with shared silence.

It was helpful to introduce to the children other adults or older young people who enjoyed their company and who had the gift of being able to talk with them easily, unselfconsciously and respectfully; people who weren't always in a hurry, who were as happy to listen as to talk, who knew how to make them feel that they mattered, not because they were unusual, but because everybody matters. These are people who are not afraid of children, mistrustful of children, or dismissive of children. They are also not exploitative of children, and it is our job as carers to assure ourselves of that. They do not seek to impose the power that their age and experience have given them. They naturally look children in the eye, and their smiles are not forced. They are neither clowns nor "the life and soul of the party", and are probably not people who claim to "like children". They simply like people and find people interesting. Children will learn to trust them.

Key factors

- Aiming to have children included in as many broadly-based social and community groups as possible.
- Modelling a relaxed, autonomous, non-consumerist attitude to matters of clothing and personal style.
- Respecting individual preferences and not judging by appearances.
- Helping children to understand appropriateness in terms of the feelings of others and the social consequences of deciding to set aside social expectations.
- Recognising the effects of children's damaging experiences on their choices of clothing and perceived self-image.
- Getting to know local retailers as a family.
- Supporting the school, with qualifications, on school uniform issues.
- Laundering and caring for children's clothing carefully and efficiently.
- Encouraging frequent bathing as a pleasurable and relaxing activity in a comforting environment.
- Tolerating self-expression in matters of personal appearance whilst advising against extremes.

- Facilitating discussion about image and self-presentation in a non-judgemental context.
- Learning how to give attention appropriately to each child.
- Enabling each child to make safe and rewarding relationships with adults who enjoy their company.
- Learning how to listen and respond to each child respectfully and without condescension.

8 Emotional and behavioural development
Developing the ability to understand and manage feelings and impulses

Recognising the difficulties

Moyers and Mason (Ward (ed) 1995, pp. 79–83), in their brief attempt to identify standards and styles of parenting in the wider community and link them to the seven dimensions of development considered in the Looked After Children Assessment and Action Records, made the unsurprising discovery that some children experience and present emotional and behavioural problems even when there appear to have been no potentially damaging experiences in their childhood or family environment. Interestingly, they noted that it was difficult for their parents to find appropriate help. Pathways to professional help were not clear, systems and approaches varied alarmingly and capriciously, and it was hard or impossible to have the means to exercise informed choice about the sort of help that might, eventually, be offered. Most worryingly, the authors noted that looked after children, whose experiences were much more likely to have had major effects on their emotional and behavioural development, were not greatly helped by the direct involvement in their lives of social services departments, which, on the face of it, should have acted as an informed gateway to appropriate and skilled sources of help. There seemed to be a prevailing view that the "service" being offered, of placement in foster family or residential home, was sufficiently therapeutic, and that "tender loving care" was the only compensatory input required.

When we began our family in our mid-twenties, we thought that being a parent wasn't too difficult. Children, we observed, usually grew up fine. Just as we learn naturally to walk and to speak our native tongue (with a few exceptions), so we are cleverly programmed to learn how to relate to others, to acquire new skills and knowledge, and to form a moral code which is more or less acceptable to the people around us. Basically, our view has not changed. But we have learned the crucial importance in that process of the early miracle of attunement between parent and infant in the context of a stable and benign environment. We have learned how much damage can be done to the child's ability to develop naturally if that attunement does not happen, or if the child's security is threatened or destroyed by natural disaster, personal trauma, unexpected loss or serious illness which compromise those essential first relationships. Most of the children who came to us were disadvantaged to a greater or lesser extent by elements of their previous circumstances which effectively impaired their ability to develop as social beings. They would not "grow up fine", unless we could identify the barriers which life had already placed in their path, and find ways of helping them to remove those barriers or find a new way round.

Some of these great emotional and behavioural needs could and possibly should have been addressed professionally, by people other than us, sooner or more thoroughly than they were. Lack of appropriate services, and of some professional (and financial) will to involve them, was certainly a factor. The voluntary organisation which provided our home, and was involved in negotiating our placements, certainly subscribed to the "Love is all you need" philosophy. A further factor militating against the use of "outside" professional assistance, and an important one, was the children's own overwhelming desire to see themselves, and our family, as "normal", greater even than the desire of most children to conform to the lifestyles and expectations of their peers, since they had experienced the stigmatising "differentness" of institutional life.

We tried to take a long-term view. Our aim was not targeted and time-limited, with an expectation that we could undo the effects of previous harm in a few months. Rather we trusted that the passage of time and the provision of a committed, loving, healing environment and a mutually supportive family group would assist the children's natural resilience in making it possible for them to become coping adults in their twenties and thirties, as they now largely are. The professional help of others would play its part: social work supervision was essential, pushing us to keep asking questions of ourselves and to reaffirm our commitment to the children, and directing us to the published wisdom of others. But the onus would be genuinely on us, the carers, to work out what forms the loving and the healing should take for each child in order to address their particular needs, and the commitment had to be complete – simply, we would not reject.

It occurs to me that, despite new government initiatives on child and adolescent mental health, the commendable efforts of Sure Start, and so on, there are never likely to be "enough" resources in the shape of qualified social pedagogues, play therapists and drama therapists and art therapists and music therapists, emotional literacy experts and psychologists and psychiatrists, to meet the needs of all the children and young people whose emotions are in a mess. And if that is true in the UK, how much more must it be true of countries which have been slower to develop child care services, or which are struggling with huge numbers of children damaged by war and social dislocation, in the former Yugoslavia or other Eastern bloc states, or Iraq, or Zimbabwe . . . The vast bulk of the restorative, therapeutic work will always have to be done, in as safe and non-stigmatising a way as possible, by the direct carers, using their own commitment, insight, and informed reflection, and constructing a physical and emotional environment which grounds, complements and facilitates their work.

Punishment (or the lack of it)

Let me get this one out of the way now – we decided quite early on that we could and should not be punitive. Punishment now deserves no place in a philosophy of child care, and is not essential for discipline, which is fundamental. This was a hard shift for me to make. I had grown up in a society where it was taken for granted that the "discipline" of children required punishment, often corporal, to reinforce it. I taught in schools for ten years, seven of them whilst already caring for looked after children, in which systems of more or less arbitrary sanctions were a main plank of the maintenance of an outward order, and were backed up by a widely practised though officially denied regime of physical punishment used mainly by male staff against boys to assert their place in a pecking order based on physical strength. I never felt comfortable with it, and yet it took some years for me to be wholly convinced that there were effective alternatives, not only to corporal punishment, ritualised or spontaneous, but also to any system which relies on fear, deprivation or emotional damage to alter the behaviour of the already frightened, deprived, or emotionally damaged.

Children's Home Regulations required us to keep a "punishment book" (later renamed "sanctions book" as the barbarous implications of "punishment" began to sink in a little) along with records of arrivals and departures, daily menus, and so on. So we possessed a little red notebook with the word "Punishment" boldly written on the front. It remained empty. Sometimes we were questioned by a visiting inspector about its pristine pages. We would explain that we had rejected the values and implications of punishment. 'So what,' he would persist, 'do you do when one of the children does something naughty?' And we would explain at some length how we might see how the rest of the group dealt with the situation before deciding whether to intervene ourselves; how we would consider whether intervention was appropriate anyway on this occasion, in the context of the child's overall needs and difficulties, and the other pressures weighing on the child on that particular day; how we would of course intervene immediately if there was a risk of someone being directly or indirectly hurt; how we might decide to address the situation in a general discussion with the whole family, or to talk to the child individually, pointing out, sometimes with a fine show of anger, the consequences of the offending behaviour in terms of personal relationships, trust, inconvenience to self or others, family finances, or whatever, depending on the child's understanding and level of moral development. The consequence might simply be: 'I don't think it was right to do that, and I'm not going to let you.' Or it might be gloriously non-specific: 'There will be consequences', or 'There will be blood on the moon' were two suitably solemn favourites. If we were expressing anger, we would try not to feel it (I used to find this very difficult!), or to acknowledge that its rightful object was not the child but the whole tangled history of ignorance, error, abuse and institutional inadequacy which had distorted the child's feelings, thoughts and reactions. If we found the whole scenario actually quite funny, we would try to keep an appropriately straight face (Kate used to find this very difficult!). And all the time we would be trying to work out today's bit of the puzzle – what was going on in this child's brain to prompt that particular piece of behaviour, and what can we learn from it about how we might change the child's experience now?

One inspector listened to an explanation like this for some time before saying, 'And *then* what would you do?' It was as if no such encounter could be effective or complete if it did not end with some symbolic exercise of parental domination. He tried to prompt us. 'Withdrawal of privileges?' If the offence has been the smashing of a golf ball through the sitting-room window, then the withdrawal of the privilege of being allowed to hit a golfball towards the house rather than away from it would certainly follow – but as a logical consequence, not a punishment. 'Deprivation of pocket money?' In the above example, there would certainly be an impact on the family budget, and it might be reasonable for the child to recognise this and redress the balance a bit by having a little less next month – but that, too, would be a logical consequence, not a punishment. 'Grounding?' What would be the connection to the original incident? What purpose would be served by reducing opportunities for stimulation and social relationships? 'Confiscation?' How does this help a child to develop concepts of personal property, of sharing and of trust, and how would it fit into the value system of a house without locks and keys?

Eventually we agreed that we might need to spend quite a long time talking through the consequences of the behaviour, that the child might actually find this quite uncomfortable, that there might have to be a fairly robust insistence, on our part, that the conversation continued until reaching what we felt was a satisfactory conclusion. The inspector took the view that the discussion should then be recorded in the punishment book. We refused to regard discussion, even discussion in which one party was a reluctant participant, as punishment!

Dan's comments are interesting: 'I remember various discussions following misdemeanours or bad behaviour. This protracted discussion of why what you did was wrong was, for a child, somewhat gruelling. Such discussions left me feeling uneasy and more than a little shamefaced. To me this was more effective than the "groundings" that friends suffered. I was made to think about and confront the awkwardness that resulted from my transgressions. This meant that I was sorry about what I had done and in no hurry to go down the same path again. Friends would say, "I got grounded – what happened to you?" I would say, "I just got a lecture," to which they would reply, "How did you get away with that?" I didn't feel I had "got away with" anything, and it seemed to me that in asking that question, the implication was that they had learned a lot less about the error of their ways.'

There can be no doubt that the British have a punitive attitude towards children. As an out-of-hours social worker I find myself talking to parents – and foster carers – who are at their wits' end with the children in their care, having handed out punishment after punishment only to find to their amazement that the behaviour to which they object continues unabated and the channels of communication with the children have totally broken down. There can appear to be an expectation that children come into the world with a moral code already formed, and an assumption that their behaviour is the result of rational choices, uninfluenced by fear, stress, emotion or environment. It was increasingly our view that our children's behaviour was almost always an understandable, even reasonable, response to situations *as they perceived them*, or a virtually inevitable response given the distorted picture of the world with which their experiences had left them. Punishment would change nothing and could add to the very stresses or confusions which had prompted the inappropriate or unacceptable behaviour in the first place.

Sometimes our responses to anti-social behaviour would have seemed to outsiders to be more like rewards. Mark has reminded me of how we responded to his eight-year-old destructiveness of toys, his own and those of other children. Putting together the chronic material deprivation of his early years with his manual dexterity and ability to think three-dimen-sionally, in stark contrast to his difficulties with words, we bought him an Airfix model and set him to work, on the dining-room table. When the model was completed we gave him another, and another. Soon he had "toys" which he had taken pride in making for himself and new "toys" to give to other people. He had the admiration of others for his skill in making them, and a new interest which he maintained for years. His destructiveness diminished remarkably.

We employed tangible "rewards" for "good" behaviour less and less as time went on, and avoided arcane systems of "privileges", to be awarded or withdrawn as a result of jumping or failing to jump through particular behavioural hoops. Reward "systems" are difficult and time-consuming to administrate, and the scope for perceived "unfairness" is huge. "Privileges" seem to me to involve an arbitrary restriction of what we allow children to do, in order that we can keep something in reserve to offer as a "privilege", and this seems a manipulative and dishonest way of relating to people. We became increasingly convinced of the value of openness with our children about our disciplinary approach, and this precluded deviousness and artificiality. The rewards of pro-social behaviour, we held, should be intangible – reduction in stress, improved relationships, an increasing sense of involvement and participation. These are of far more lasting importance than a chocolate bar, a new toy, an extra half-hour in front of the TV or twenty gold stars on a chart. So these intangibles were the rewards we held out, the gains we tried to measure and demonstrate to the children. If we did use material rewards from time to time, we would try to present them as merely symbolic of the "real" rewards, and to choose something that could be shared by us all rather than one individual.

Modelling

As with so many aspects of our children's development, we had to look first at ourselves. Examining my own reactions to unexpected stresses or situations, my fears, petulance, outbursts of anger, embarrassment, envy, indolence, desire to do others down – the list is endless – and recognising that they were different from Kate's, prompted by different things, and often related to aspects of my childhood, helped me to see how much we are all the products of our environment and experience, and gave me clues to the puzzles set by each of our children. Our relationship – our marriage – had to be strong to bear this sort of constant analysis whilst keeping it focussed and preventing it from becoming self-absorbed navel-gazing. It was exhausting, but necessary.

Then we had to be open with the children. For many of them, their earlier childhoods had been spent, like meerkats on guard duty, scanning the near horizon for the slightest sign – the smell of alcohol, the bang of a door, the smudged make-up, the glint of an eye – that could be an early warning of violence or abuse. They knew when something was wrong. So when our reactions to each other or to them were inappropriate, we would try to acknowledge it, to explain, to apologise. Sharon remembers her incredulity on an early occasion when I felt I had treated her unfairly, and sought her out to apologise with a box of chocolates. Adults apologise far too rarely to children, as if to do so were to lose face, rather than gain respect.

Children, particularly those whose experience has taught them not to trust, are good at recognising hypocrisy. So the behaviour of the adults who are caring for them needs to have an internal moral consistency. It is no good trying to teach that stealing is unacceptable if you are bringing home stationery from work or boasting about fiddling your expenses or tax allowances. Telling children not to make cruel comments to their classmates is meaningless if the crushing put-down is one of your ways of dealing with errors or incompetence. How often have we heard parents lay into children with a string of expletives for "swearing"? A simple example is around time-keeping. If Kate or I were going out, we would tell the other (and the children) when we expected to return. If we were going to be later than expected, we would phone. How much easier that made it to have the same expectation of the children.

We have here the beginning of the approach we endeavoured to take to helping our children to recognise the socially unacceptable aspects of their behaviour and to modify them. It involved recognising the emotional content of behaviour, including our own, particularly anti-social behaviour, and responding to it in ways which helped us to understand so that we could help one another to learn about ourselves and be more in control. It involved trying to bring "Do as I say" and "Do as I do" as closely together as we could. It involved seeing inappropriate behaviour as a puzzle to be solved rather than as a challenge to authority, eliminating any vestige of punitive retribution from the response, even when the emotion aroused by the behaviour was predominantly anger. It was, for me, as for many people who live and work with damaged people, the most difficult, and yet the most rewarding aspect of our life together.

I suggest that this emotionally-literate, child-centred approach to parenting mirrors the approach of many thoughtful and committed parents to the children born to them. It is made easier for them by their knowledge of the history which they have shared directly with their children, and by the likelihood that many aspects of personality will be shared. During the crucial early stages of the child's life the miracle of attunement will have taken place, as parent and child learn to respond to cues from each other in predictable ways that become almost instinctive to both.

Dealing with problems of attachment and post-traumatic disorders

Those who care for looked after children, and adoptive parents, start without these advantages. Over and above the sensitive and respectful approach outlined above, they have to take account of emotions and learned or reactive behaviour which seem to make no sense in this new environment which they are offering the children. Kate deals much more fully elsewhere (Cairns, K, 2002a) with behaviours associated with early attachment deficits and unresolved trauma, which I believe account for a great deal of the apparently puzzling behaviour often observed among children with disrupted lives, and which, if not responded to therapeutically by carers, may continue into adult life as "personality disorder" and a propensity to crime and/or self-harm. I shall look only briefly at how we gradually tried to bring to bear our gradually increasing understanding of attachment and trauma issues on our shared life in the family.

Attachment
Several of our children had experienced poor patterns of early attachment with parents. Some parents had been rejecting, some abusive, some unpredictable. In each case the child had developed survival styles of behaviour which were designed in infancy to manipulate, modify or control the unsatisfying, sometimes potentially dangerous response of the parent, and these behaviours persisted. A common response is for adults to label these behaviours "attention-seeking", a disparaging, dismissive term. In the earlier stages of the child's membership of the family, we tried to recognise such behaviour, annoying though it might be, as indicating a genuine need for attention, a need to build the attachment and attunement with us that had been lacking in earlier relationships. Our aim would be to respond with all the gentleness and

patience we could muster. This was not always easy and I didn't always succeed, for I often found such behaviour exasperating and had to react rationally rather than intuitively. We aimed to set boundaries which could be clearly understood, were not seen as punitive, and which could easily be changed as our relationship with the child developed. One of us might insist that the child, rather than being excluded from our company for anti-social behaviour, should stay physically close to us for some time, in a relaxed atmosphere of stress-free chat or silence, and with the underlying message that we were content to be in the child's company. But this too could become stressful for children who had learned to find adults a frightening puzzle, so couldn't be overused. Sometimes the way for a child to learn to be at our ease with our adult company was through being comfortable with the rest of the household, learning to be at ease with the animals, with older children, with younger children, or alone in the next room with an open door between. Each child had their own approach path.

Most inappropriate behaviour is a reaction to stress. We underestimate constantly the level of stress experienced by many children most of the time as they try to predict and regulate the behaviour of the adults on whom they must depend. They are burdened children. As adults, most of us know about stress. We can identify and learn our own physiological, emotional, behavioural reactions to stress, and those of the people closest to us. If we have good relationships with partners and close friends, if they don't place unrealistic expectations on us, if we can relax in their company, we will seek them out. If those relationships are uncertain, or if we are unsure about how they will react to us, we may avoid them, or find that they raise our stress levels rather than lowering them. If we are to help our children to reduce stress, we need them to learn that we can relieve their stress rather than increase it.

Our imaginations often had to work overtime to understand the stresses that our children were experiencing from day to day and to respond appropriately. Interestingly, it helped that we were a large group. We weren't tempted to extrapolate from ourselves – 'If I were behaving like this, I would be feeling . . .' – because the fact that our various experiences and temperaments differed so much from one another was always evident. And very often one of the children would have a better intuitive understanding of why one child was behaving in a particular way than we had, and could throw light on the mystery. We would often go through the "various hypotheses" approach – 'I think you might have hidden the TV remote control because . . .' – until we saw some spark of recognition. Certainly there is rarely any point in asking the child 'Why did you . . . ?' Either the child genuinely doesn't know, or is dissociating from the behaviour, or lacks the emotional vocabulary to express the feelings, or feels too stupid to say, and would rather be seen as "bad" than (terrifyingly) mad, or is simply feeling extremely confused. We came to believe strongly that it was *our* job, as carers, to take the lead in helping children to explain their own behaviour to themselves, and to reassure them that their behaviour was understandable, before explaining that the consequences of inappropriate behaviour could be unpleasant for themselves, for others, or for both, and to offer help in making desired changes.

We learned not to take our children's behaviour personally. It is not easy to do this when you are being kicked or punched or sworn at, or when you are having your home or possessions destroyed. It is particularly difficult when such behaviour is being meted out to other innocent parties – your birth children, your friends, perhaps. An awareness of transference helped us sometimes to realise that we were often a convenient substitute or symbol for the person or scenario against whom or which the rage was "really" directed. We found it helpful to ask ourselves at which stage of the child's development today's particular display of behaviour was stuck at (all ages up to two are common), and to remind ourselves that this demonstrated a point at which the attachment process had failed. (Have you ever tried to put words to the rages of a furious – or terrified – nonverbal infant? Wouldn't they often look like 'f@&**** sh%%*** b++##** c&@*'? They are coming from a primitive, survival-seeking part of the brain which has not yet developed the intricacies of social intercourse in polite company.) Poorly attached children (or young people, or adults) are thinking with a different brain. In their uncontrolled behaviour we can glimpse some of the horrors of their earliest experiences. Like stroke survivors, we can help them over the years to use their brains differently, to learn better impulse control, to be more self-aware. But to behave in ways acceptable to others may always require an effort rather than being the natural result of firm, reciprocated early attachment. It may always feel like going from London to Birmingham via Edinburgh. One of our children recently said to me that his job, which involves a lot of direct work and problem-solving with customers, was particularly interesting and challenging because he 'has had to learn how to do every bit of that', while other people, from his perspective, do it naturally.

My car developed a frustrating fault. Sometimes – but not always – the lights wouldn't come on. More dangerously, sometimes they would suddenly go out, not a nice thing to happen after midnight on country roads. A new switch left the problem unresolved. My mechanic deduced that there must be a broken wire somewhere in the system even though to outward appearances everything was intact. To strip out every wire would mean hours of work. He made the car serviceable by somehow "hot-wiring" the lighting circuit. Now the lights worked, but at the expense of losing the security of fuses and the warning beep that would let me know if I left the lights on after turning off the ignition. Our children are rather like that car, except that stripping out all the brain wiring is not even an option. After years of stabilisation with us, of making belated attachments to us, of learning about themselves, of developing compensatory mechanisms to overcome the harm of poor early attachment, they can and do conduct themselves appropriately in almost every social situation. But an unexpected stress can still occasionally catch them out for the lack of a fuse or a warning beep. And since I suspect that none of us enjoyed a totally perfect attachment relationship with our parents, that is probably true, at some level, for us all.

Impulse control and victim empathy

Once our children had begun to build trusting, attached relationships with us, we could begin to share frankly with them our tentative but growing understanding of their behaviour. Gradually we learned to avoid ploughing through the details of early difficulties, and concentrated on the simple premise that aspects of their early experience led them to develop patterns of behaviour which were no longer helpful. We began to try to take the line that it appeared to us that the child found some things difficult – getting up in the morning, leaving other people alone when they wanted to be, reacting calmly to implied criticism, playing games fairly when losing, eating moderately, whatever – how might we help? With this approach, behavioural change was presented as something that could be learned, like bicycle maintenance or quadratic equations. The change had to be a wanted change, wanted, that is, by the child. If the demand wasn't there, we had to use all our marketing strategies, including group pressure, to create it! We learned – painfully – that we could not change our children's behaviour against their wishes. We could only change our own, by working on how we tried to relate to the individual child, to the whole group or sub-groups, to each other. We could change our reactions, and how we expressed our feelings. And once the child was responding by indicating some motivation to change, the key to learning would often be in the areas of development of impulse control or victim empathy.

We tried to help children to identify how they felt immediately before things started to go wrong, and to have a range of options available. There might be a mantra to repeat, an incident to remember. One remarkable exchange involved Kate asking one of our boys what he felt when he was about to "lose it". He was unable to frame an answer. She asked him what he heard. This time he could answer, and described, in mounting distress, an insistent loud buzzing in his head from which he could only escape by being violent. Her next question might have seemed nonsensical, but not to our boy. 'What colour is the buzz?' It was brown. 'Try changing it to pink,' she advised. It was effective. Changing modality, or using a different sense, can often help us to take control of feelings.

Some psychologsts believe that personality disorders can be overcome simply by encouraging people to think in a different language which they have learned to speak after an original traumatic event. Certainly we encouraged children whose emotional reactions were at a pre-verbal level to use language, aloud or silently, to describe the stress to which they were reacting, which would immediately transfer activity to a less dangerous, more reasoned area of the brain. When children reacted to stress with physiological symptoms – shallower breathing, or increased muscle tension, perhaps – we would rehearse with them and practised a way of regulating the symptoms, and that too could help them to take control.

Sometimes the options would include some sort of displacement activity – banging the drums, smashing snooker balls around the table –

or a calming one – going for a cycle ride, stroking the guinea-pigs. Moderating damaging behaviour could be a step on the road. Swearing at people who are "doing your head in" is infinitely preferable to thumping them! Often the options would include walking away from the overwhelming situation, and we had to try to remember that walking away from us was often a coping strategy rather than rudeness. Teachers often find this difficult to accept, and need help with it.

Sometimes we could see the tension rising, and intervene, directly or indirectly, by reducing the stress. We would reduce surrounding noise levels, or create a calm distraction. Offering a neck massage or a hair brushing, or a favourite drink might help. Opening a window, ensuring that the child doesn't feel hemmed in, lighting a perfumed candle, playing soothing music, dimming the lights, might all help. Alternatively, for some children on some occasions, the security of a hug might be the antidote to mounting stress, but the attachment relationship needed to be well formed for that to be welcomed. If we said anything at the point of stress, it had to be positive rather than negative, and calm rather than agitated. Only once the stress level was reduced was it helpful to find an opportunity to talk about what had happened, what had been felt, what had been avoided, what had been learned.

Children who have not become attuned to their carer in infancy have difficulties in understanding, "reading", or even acknowledging other people. There must be links here with Asperger's Syndrome and mild autism. Many of our children showed little interest in knowing other people's names, and less in remembering them. One was well through primary school before understanding that most first names are gender-specific – he would eventually learn, for example, that friends of ours were called Jean and Ken, but could never remember which was which. Infants neither know nor care what their mother is feeling when they cry – they know only the effect (food, warmth, comfort) which they hope to prompt. Children with attachment problems can be blissfully unaware of how little Nicola feels when her toes have been trod on, and can seem to lack the capacity to understand when told. We learned that it was a mistake to ask our children, 'How do you think Nicola feels?' The likely response was 'I dunno,' – an honest answer – or blankness, as to an incomprehensible question. Where children lack the ability to identify emotions and talk about them objectively, such a question might as well be asked in Lithuanian. And if the question is asked accusingly, the child's response may say more about their confusion, fear, or need for self-defence at all costs, than about their awareness of Nicola.

We needed to tell our children what Nicola felt. Over and over again. And we needed to tell them stories that would give them insight into the world of the feelings of others, and to talk about our own feelings, good and bad, and to enable them to learn from one another's feelings, and to play games that generate "artificial" emotions, from Ludo to Monopoly, and talk about how we feel as we play, and to look at pictures of people (the classic "Happy Families" cards were good) and guess what they might be feeling, and so on. I have been privileged more than once to be present at what seemed to be a dawning of empathy – almost overwhelming – as a child suddenly has a sense of what it might mean to be starving on the plains of Africa, or to have lost parents in a train crash, and starts to see the world as lots of individual people like him, rather than a collection of more or less impersonal resources to be plundered. It is a vision which can start off as fleeting, even frightening, but which can grow with practice.

I have been involved in recent years in various discussions about the merits of on-line learning for adults. Amidst its many advantages, a disadvantage often mentioned is the difficulty of learning alone, without other people at hand who can share the experience and bounce ideas and insights to and fro. I believe that our children benefited greatly from learning social behaviour as a group. A singleton child in a foster family is isolated in learning, and often isolated in perceived failure, especially if there are birth children in the household to whom socially acceptable behaviour appears to come naturally, or if their foster carers do not or cannot acknowledge openly their own ongoing learning and efforts to manage their feelings. Our children learned from one another, and from one another's friends, as well as from us. They still do.

This approach required us increasingly to see inappropriate or "bad" behaviour as being inevitable while our children were still learning ways of seeing the world and reacting with it within which appropriate or "good" behaviour would become more and more possible. If they could do that, the problematic behaviour would reduce. We – and they – had to keep focussed on the future, rather than allowing ourselves to be distracted by the particular alarums and excursions of today. Mistakes are useful to learn from. A lot of the learning – because we all had to live together, and with our neighbours, and with our local community, at a sustainable level of co-operation – had to be derived from today's problem, since individuals and communities are not endlessly tolerant, and difficult behaviour has consequences which may have an immediate harmful effect.

However, where we could, we tried to take the positive, long-term approach of 'How do we make happen what we want to happen?', rather than the despairing, short-term, limited approach of 'How do we solve these problems?' If we made it possible for the right things to happen, the "problems" would gradually fade away. So where we could enable children to identify and express their own goals – 'I want to be in normal school'; 'I want to have nicer friends', 'I want to be able to manage my own money' – we could then say, 'How can we help with that?', and work out ways of building the future that *they* wanted, rather than imposing our own development plan. After all, as Alice remarked in Wonderland, 'If you don't know where you are going, how are you going to know when you've got there?' This, when we could produce it, was the language of empowerment, and our task as parents, foster or otherwise, is surely to empower or children to become what *they* want to be. However, if people are to want to be something more social, more convivial, than the control freaks that they need to be to ensure their survival as dependent infants, they need to incorporate their growing awareness of other people into some sort of moral code.

Developing a moral code

Morals rarely trump the survival instinct, we discovered. I have often wondered if my pacifist beliefs would hold up if I were being attacked by a hostile intruder with murder apparently in mind. For some of our children, on arrival with us, moral scruples were luxuries they could ill afford and scarcely imagine. How were they to survive in this alien environment? How foolish of us to imagine, as we did, that anything was obvious. Our first task was to stabilise. We had to make expectations clear and simple so that children might know quickly what would be regarded as "right" and what as "wrong" behaviour. Consistency was important: "right" behaviour would produce smiles and nods of approval, thanks and "well dones". "Wrong" behaviour would produce, first, an instruction about what would have been "right", trying not to appear punitive, followed by frowns, headshaking, firm reminders, if the "wrong" behaviour was repeated, increasing in intensity if it continued to be repeated. We realised the importance of shame as a mechanism for the self-regulation of behaviour, that it is positive and necessary, provided that it is short-lived and followed by a sign of normal relationship being resumed. So we became skilled at exaggerated expressions of displeasure which could be quickly recognised, and replaced by re-accepting smiles as soon as they had been registered and understood with the necessary effect. All of which had to go on in a context in which new, healthy attachment was steadily, consciously being built.

So far, so good. We are forming the first base of a moral code: if I do good or bad things, good or bad things happen to me. This was a huge step for some children whose experience of life had been so chaotic that the very notion of cause and effect, of predictable rather than random outcomes, was new and wonderful. Now we had to move on to play consequences – considering them, not just experiencing them. This was where the "guided discussions" come in, the ones that don't fit the punishment book. There was no point in playing consequences while children were struggling with the concept of cause and effect. We had to tailor our reactions to each child to the stage of development of their moral code that the child had reached. The child's chronological age or apparent level of intelligence would not be sufficient to tell us how far their moral code had developed. This was easy to forget, and we found that teachers and well-intentioned friends and relatives would need to be reminded of it frequently.

Talking about consequences leads development along two strands closely relating to the development of impulse control and victim empathy. It helps the child to begin to be able to consider *delayed* good or bad consequences to themselves of "right" or "wrong" actions. It also gets us moving on the process of considering good or bad consequences to others.

As imagination, verbal and emotional vocabulary, and awareness of (and interest in) the world outside the immediacies of home and school develop, there is scope for further development. We were able to help our children to think about complex decisions, where there could be a mixture of good and bad consequences, and a judgement has to be made, or where the consequences involve unknown people. This is the stage at which we could move on from:

'Please don't leave that bottle on the beach – we'll have to pick it up and take it with us.'

'Why?'

'Because it's against the law and we could be fined a thousand francs.'

to:

'Because if we leave it, it could get broken and cut somebody's bare foot.'

Incidentally, that exchange includes another ploy – changing the subject of the unacceptable behaviour from "you" to "we" – immediately less threatening, leaving the conversation less likely to be diverted by "survival" tactics of self-defence. Stories, real or embroidered, help, shared memories even more:

'Do you remember when Josie got that piece of glass stuck in her foot and we had to spend a whole day taking her to the hospital?' or:

'My sister (a sprinter in her youth) had to miss an important athletics match once because she stood on some glass and wasn't able to run.'

And, of course, the size of our family group helped, because the lesson, whatever it was, could be borne in upon several children at once – singleton children have to make all the mistakes themselves.

Some might say that in the above, relatively trivial, example, the request, 'Don't leave the bottle . . .' is unnecessarily negative; I could have started with the positive 'Let's take it with us.'

I would disagree. The "don't" bit is helpful to add significance to the incident, which might otherwise be scarcely noticed, and to produce the moment of shame which assists learning; the positive which follows comes as a helpful suggestion, signals the reintegration of the "offender" and avoids being a command – 'Pick that bottle up!' – which is again likely to arouse hostility and resentment.

Incidentally – and this may seem very British – we were very scrupulous about making polite requests of our children, rather than issuing orders. 'Please', 'Would you mind . . .' and 'Thank you' were, I hope, rarely forgotten. When they were – and I was more likely to be guilty – Kate would point it out. Politeness is an indicator of respect, and there are other everyday indicators – punctuality, apology, keeping promises, doing what you said you would do – which create a climate of respect in which children grow to feel valued, to experience security, and to know that they are no longer excluded from that majority in our society who enjoy the luxury of being able to make moral decisions. They no longer need to be outlaws.

And yet, in our own way, we were all outlaws. We had substituted our own definition of "family" for society's prevailing (though changing) norm. And it was increasingly apparent to our children that we felt that moral choices were important, that our own moral positions were relative and open to change, and that we felt that many questions of morality and choice were far from straightforward. They knew that we were not satisfied with the simplistic slogan approach to morality of the tabloid or the soundbite. Often our mealtime discussions and arguments about current affairs or conflicting philosophies or the underlying messages of television programmes will have passed over the heads of many of the family, but their importance was in the fact that they were happening, and that contributions from anyone around the table were welcomed. In such an environment it is easier for children to move on from envisaging particular and individual consequences of individual actions to looking at 'How would it be if everybody did . . . ?', and then to 'Should I be thinking more carefully about . . . ?' They learned, we hope, that a variety of moral views was tolerated, but that the development of some moral positions which could be argued and defended was an expected part of growing up – expected not only by Kate and myself but by other children in the family as well.

We don't learn our verbal vocabulary from being immersed in "the cat sat on the mat". We gradually make sense of being surrounded by a richness of spoken and written word, most of which we don't understand for a long time. Our grasp of moral concepts seems to grow out of a similar immersion in moral issues. In both areas of development, late arrival simply means that some structure has to be superimposed to guide the individual through, along with some patient deconstruction of previous survival mechanisms that might block out learning.

As adults, each of our children has, I think, a reasonably clear moral code. They like to think about issues and are not satisfied with superficial analyses. On many issues there would be a broad spectrum of views, but all are fundamentally kind people. None of them got into serious trouble with the law as children; two had court appearances and prison sentences as young adults, when impulse control and victim empathy gave way to more primitive responses to new stresses. This is more likely to happen, it seems, when other early childhood deprivations are compounded by the experience of trauma.

Trauma

Children joined us who had been looked after children for years, yet a clear picture of the trauma they had experienced in their parental homes, or in previous care settings, or both, seemed to be known only sketchily, if at all, to their placing social workers. The children could not or would not talk about it. Often it was pre-verbal, and they had effectively blotted out details from their accessible memories, although the feelings and psychological scars remained. Kwesi, for example, had and still has no recollection of the horrors he must have endured or witnessed in Uganda in the early 1980s, as the Baganda people, to whom he belonged, were systematically wiped out. Others began over the years to recall or trigger memories, often fragmentary, of appalling physical and sexual abuse, of neglect, of domestic violence.

In the early years we were naïve enough not to postulate these traumatic experiences while we tried to puzzle out the children's behaviour, their fears, their perceptions, their reactions to stress. As we learned more about trauma and about post-traumatic stress disorder, we began to find some explanations for the seemingly irrational terrors, the panic attacks, the nightmares, the phobias, the apparent inability to concentrate or remember simple instructions, the lack of self-esteem, the propensity for self-harm or reckless behaviour, the outbursts of aggression. We became more able to separate out the symptoms from the cause. This is a distinction I now make frequently when supporting foster carers who are finding their children's behaviour hard to live with and resistant to traditional sanctions. The behaviour, I point out, is symptomatic, something to be managed or contained as best we can while our main energies go into understanding the message and addressing the causes, which are likely to be found in the child's perception of their environment.

The first priority for traumatised children is, once again, stabilisation. We would try – sometimes successfully – to maintain calm and serenity, to be the "still centre" for the agitated child, and to pilot them into our sheltered harbour. We (more often Kate, for she is good at serenity, as well as needing less sleep than I do) spent hours holding a child who was kicking and screaming, lost in a private rage and fear inaccessible to anyone's reason, least of all their own. She would repeat calming words, minimise damage, provide hands to be squeezed or scratched rather than allowing more serious harm to be done. My job was often to ensure that the rest of the family remained reassured that the situation was under control and that nobody was coming to harm, whilst organising people to keep supplies of tissues, drinks and soft cushions coming, and generally maintaining the ongoing life of the household on an even keel. We spent more hours sitting up in the middle of the night with children waking in terror from a nightmare or struggling to send a sudden intolerable flashback memory back into oblivion, mopping brows, sharing soothing drinks, gently easing the child back into a more restful sleep. Day after day, night after night. Kate used to joke that she wore jeans to hide the bruises and glasses to hide the bags under her eyes. It helped that Plainlands was a big detached house with thick walls. Well-meaning neighbours calling out the police would not have been helpful.

Following on from stabilisation comes integration – not integration into the family in this context, but integration of past and present. Once Liam, for example, began to feel more secure with us, he was able to admit to his fear of the dark, rather than going to inordinate lengths to contrive or manipulate situations so that he didn't have to be in the dark in the first place. Helping him to talk about his fear of the dark and its origins – gently, so as not to unearth details of traumatic memory too hot to handle – began to integrate the past into the present and make a coherent story which lessened the psychologically disruptive power of the memories. As an interim measure we could then look together at how to address the fear of dark places, most often encountered on the unlit lane between town and home – the half-mile of horror! We could arrange that he would phone for a lift if he couldn't face it, or arrange to meet another member of the family.

The final goal, of course, was adaptation. Once the traumatic content of the memory is decommissioned by integration, the dark doesn't seem so scary, and behaviour can be modified. It is now under more rational control. This process may take a long time. In the meantime – and it has taken me virtually all my fostering career to learn this fully – there is little to be gained by assuming that children are able to exert control over behaviour which is not governed by reason simply because they are told that that behaviour is unacceptable. Smokers and nailbiters will have an inkling of what I'm talking about. They need to be motivated to change the behaviour – which can mean sometimes nothing less than turning their whole perception of reality upside-down – and they need to be offered committed, individualised help in doing it.

As with so many aspects of children's long-term care, the involvement of a trusted and sensitive social worker from the placing authority is a valuable asset. As children stabilise, they may want to talk about emerging memories of their past, to ask questions about their social services records, to revisit relationships with birth family members or previous carers, and all this is much easier if the relationship with the social worker has been maintained. Moreover, some of our children were aware of trauma's potential for contamination. They wanted to keep it away from their new home, and didn't want us or other children in the family to be somehow fouled by the events of their past.

Our experience of field social workers was variable. Most, especially in the 1970s and 1980s, wanted to work with us. They stayed in post for several years, had the will and the freedom to build up important and supportive relationships with the children and with ourselves, and were concerned to help us reflect on the children's needs and attempt to understand them in the light of their earlier experience. Others moved on quickly, or showed little interest, or appeared to see their role in terms of protecting "their" child against possible shortcomings in our care. The reaction to disclosures of poor or abusive care in previous placements was disturbing: one social worker was effectively silenced by her management, prevented from investigating disclosures made about abusive practice in a previous children's home, and was not replaced when she left the job suffering stress; another literally disappeared, taking the file with him, after the beginnings of serious disclosure relating to residential care settings. His local authority only acknowledged his disappearance four months later after repeated attempts on our part to talk to someone, by which time the child was so disturbed by events that he would not or could not disclose again. The damaging effects of these events, not only on the two children concerned, but on the stability of the whole family group and on our own emotional health and ability to hold everything together, cannot be underestimated. However stable children may seem to be in placement, the supportive presence of known social workers, backed up by their employing authority, as a guaranteed link with the past and potential safety-net in the present and future can add enormously to their personal integration and well-being.

Teenagers

Kate and I recently attended a foster carers' conference where Kate spoke at length about the damage done to the developing brain by poor infant attachment and early traumatic experience. A minority of the delegates took issue with her, because, in their view, their work was with teenagers, and they could see no relevance for them in what she had been saying. But this sort of damage doesn't simply disappear over time, like nappy rash. On the contrary, as distorted perceptions and maladaptive behaviours become more embedded, the problems get worse. Children become physically stronger, the stresses in their lives become greater, society becomes less tolerant of the challenges they pose, and their capacity to cause serious harm to themselves or others becomes far, far greater.

Only four of the children who stayed with us long term joined us after they had reached secondary-school age. All of them wanted to come; they could see something in our household, our way of living together, that they wanted to be part of. Without that, we would have had enormous, possibly insuperable, difficulty. As it was we did not have the luxury of time stretching far in front of us, the ability to take the pressure off and help the children to stabilise and grow almost at their own pace. With these older children, the pressure was on, because the demands of hormones, examinations, careers, social integration and imminent adult independence loomed close. We felt appalled, let down, by the record of previous, often expensive, placements, which had scarcely contained the problems, let alone work on them in any positive or therapeutic way.

We tried to accommodate to our older arrivals as we might to a foreign exchange student – welcoming with a light touch and respect for their individuality. Always listening, always learning, keeping frameworks to a necessary minimum. One wanted to learn about country pursuits and go out all night with ferrets after rabbits. We accommo-dated. One wanted to keep goats in the garden. We accommodated. One wanted to learn about computers (this was 1990, when home computers were still not common). We acquired one, and found a friend with residential care experience who came and gave lessons. We accommo-dated, with difficulty, to a level of "self-medicating" dependence on a variety of substances, to sexual risk-taking, choosing carefully what to challenge and how to challenge it.

Two of our teenagers showed themselves to be outwardly conformist, but challenged quietly and deviously; two were outwardly challenging, but much more open. We had to learn how to get alongside and establish a partnership on the basis of : 'If you can work out what you want to do (and we might be able to help with that), then we can see if we can help you do it'. I had worked like this with teenagers in the special school where I had taught – unable to make any headway with teaching a curriculum devised by me or by some external agency, I would sit down with 15-year-old boys individually, and point out that in a year's time they would be in one-sided competition with others leaving mainstream schools and brandishing exam certificates – maybe we should look together at subjects they felt they could have a go at, and find a curriculum that would suit? The aim – with these boys as later with young people joining our family – was for them to have the maximum possible control of the agenda. And much of the help we could give within the family was exactly the same as with the younger children – help with identifying and expressing emotions, with understanding how the way they perceived the world and reacted to it might differ from others, with controlling impulses and with empathy, with reflecting on choices that had proved to be unhelpful, all in a context of stability and commitment. There is some evidence (Johnson, 2002) that successful work with adults labelled "personality-disordered" can be carried out along similar lines.

Becoming a tribe

Perhaps more than in any other chapter of this book, what I have written here is coloured and informed by hindsight. I learned how to help our children by trial and error, and by very gradual assimilation of the theories and ideas of others. For many years Kate had a much clearer vision than I had of what we were doing and how we were doing it. It was her vision that enabled me time and again to put the incident of today in the context of a lifetime, to temper my immediate anger and frustration, to realise that the apparent resolution of today's problem was less important than helping our children to work towards long-term stability and connectedness with the world around them. In the early years, particularly, she would pull me back from over-reaction to a misdemeanour which was no more than a symptom of stress, and help me to project patience and understanding which was hard to feel. Now I try to do the same for parents and carers who feel at breaking-point with the children for whom they feel responsible.

Insights from the field of social anthropology helped. The writing of Jean Liedloff (1989) showed us how many tribal approaches to living allow those who stray too far outside the expectations and conventions of the tribe to be lovingly tolerated and re-incorporated. Sanctions can become symbolic. Our society has lost the art of tribal living – in tiny nuclear families, disagreement, disaffection and anti-social acts become personalised. Parents feel personally aggrieved by the actions of their children, and individually responsible within a disapproving and blaming society. Our household, our family, was numerous enough to have some of the attributes of a tribe. We could feel collectively responsible for one another – indeed, we all had a vested interest in one another's survival. The writings of Daniel Quinn have helped us to understand this (e.g. Quinn, 2000). I can honestly say that never in twenty years of shared living did Kate and I feel that battle-lines had been drawn and it was "us against the children". Within that "tribal" framework we could be gloriously inconsistent. We never had to feel that we must behave in such-and-such-a-way towards A because last month we decided to react in that way to B's behaviour. The numbers were large enough, the relationships varied enough, for comparisons to be largely irrelevant. What was important was for us to understand what each child needed from us, and from the rest of the family, each day, and to work out how best to provide it. That was a constant puzzle – it helped that we usually found it both a worthwhile challenge and fun.

Key factors

- Accepting that facilitating emotional and behavioural development cannot be left entirely to other professionals.
- Understanding that a punitive approach to inappropriate behaviour will be unlikely to succeed and be counter-productive.
- Minimising use of arcane systems of rewards and privileges, whilst stressing and identifying the social benefits of pro-social behaviour.
- Ensuring that consequences of inappropriate behaviour are logical, proportionate, and capable of being understood by children.
- Recognising that children with chaotic previous experience will need help with understanding cause and effect.
- Recognising that children with attachment disorders will have difficulty in acquiring an understanding of emotion, and a language in which to express it.
- Finding ways through shared stories to do this emotional education.
- Taking care to model for children the behaviour and values that we expect from them.
- Learning to recognise when children experience stress and how to help them to reduce it.
- Ensuring that our physical environment is designed to reduce stress.
- Accepting that our children may not understand their own behaviour, and trying to explain it to them in a non-blaming way.
- Helping children practically with impulse control.
- Keeping attention focussed on long-term outcomes rather than being distracted by temporary apparent setbacks.

- Facilitating through open discussion the development of individual moral codes.
- Maintaining respect for each child as an individual, whilst missing no opportunity to be inclusive in words and actions.
- Being alert to triggers of earlier trauma and reacting appropriately.
- Never underestimating the long-term effects of early damaging experiences.
- Allowing children to take risks.
- Using the strengths and influence of the whole group.
- Valuing appropriateness above consistency in response.
- Relishing the puzzle of learning how other people tick.

9 Self-care skills
Developing practical skills for 21st century living

Domestic tasks

If a looked-after child is developing healthily and age-appropriately on all the previous counts, it would be strange indeed for him or her not to be developing alongside many appropriate self-care skills. Many aspects of self-care are intimately linked to health and social presentation, considered in Chapters 3 and 7. The skills required in keeping one's person, clothing and surroundings clean are not difficult to acquire. Whether or not they are exercised in adult life is more a question of motivation and personality than of ability. This is linked in turn to social inclusion – people who see themselves as part of a societal group are motivated to conform to the conventions of that group and to learn whatever skills they need to learn to do so.

As adults, all the children in our family have reached a point – at the moment – where they are no longer socially excluded or at immediate risk of social exclusion as a consequence of their childhood experiences or consequent effect on their personality.

In a large household as ours was there had to be some element of sharing out of domestic tasks. There were those who enjoyed cooking, or lawnmowing, or buzzing about with a vacuum cleaner, ironing, even – and those who didn't. But we had no rigid system of allocating tasks (I dislike the negative word "chores" – there is no reason why any of us can't adopt a positive attitude to housework and find it in some degree satisfying). We simply expected everyone to contribute a bit from time to time. Group pressure helped, as ever. Most learning was from observation – as is the case, I think, for most young people.

I wish I could say that we totally avoided sexism in our household management. However, Kate and I both grew up in households which were fairly traditional in gender-allocation of roles, and change for us has been only gradual. Kate is a confident cook and I am not – the family's recollection, amid gales of laughter, of culinary disasters served up by me on days when Kate was away, is perhaps a little exaggerated, but recognises my favoured role as kitchen porter, not chef. If we are together, I prefer to drive, Kate to be driven. My skills with needle and thread are rudimentary and involve much sighing and swearing. But I wield a mop or vacuum-cleaner with vigour and zest, enjoy ironing, and would be a valiant competitor in "Supermarket Sweep", whilst Kate mows the lawn quite often, and is more likely to be able to repair the washing machine than I am. The message to the children was, I hope, that we would each have a go at most things, whilst recognising individual preferences, strengths and weaknesses, and acknowledging that we still had much to learn. Handing a tea-towel to Kate's father and watching his apparent bewilderment as to its purpose became a family joke.

It helped greatly that none of our family faced the spectre of knowing that they would have to "leave home" at the local authority's insistence before they felt ready to. Most began, naturally enough, to show more interest in the skills required for independence at the point when they were beginning to consider leaving for reasons to do with work or further education. Some – as many young people do – had a rude awakening to reality, but knew that they could come back and ask for advice on those aspects of household management which had somehow passed them by. They could also – and do – ask their older brothers and sisters in the family. It wasn't totally "sink or swim". And the motivation to learn was high, because the peers with whom they now compared themselves were young adults who were getting their lives together rather than those who weren't.

There were – of course – exceptions. Karen needed all her intelligence and drive towards self-preservation to learn how to be a wife and mother when she eloped shortly after her sixteenth birthday and set up home with her young husband and baby in a town near ours some months later, cutting herself off from us for a couple of years. Liam battled through years of post-traumatic stress disorder, confusion and drug addiction, often in considerable disorder, emerging in his mid-twenties to begin piecing together a more "normal" life. Without the support of all the rest of the family, practical and emotional, always available but never imposed, these two, at least, might have foundered in their late teens or early twenties.

Personal management

If we extend the definition of self-care skills beyond the practical skills of cooking and personal care, we must look at skills of what I shall call "personal management". Some of these skills are related to securing and retaining employment, other than study skills and social relationship skills which we have considered elsewhere. They include time management, personal organisation, the ability to access and use transport, and an understanding of the frameworks of society – how the world works. These and other skills – the ability to budget and manage money, to understand contractual and social obligations, and to select, acquire and maintain appropriate possessions, also relate to securing and retaining accommodation. And beyond that we get into the skills needed to form and maintain relationships and to be a parent oneself, which are the real test of whether a child's experience "in care" has been instrumental in breaking the "cycle of deprivation" which can so often carry on through successive generations.

I have always had a "thing" about punctuality. When our children were battling through issues of attachment deprivation or unresolved childhood trauma, I learned to understand how and why time and its passage had little importance for them, but I never found it easy to live with. As they became more able to be aware of the needs of others, I would talk often about the importance – as I saw it – of keeping to agreed deadlines, not holding others up, predicting how long a planned task would take and reviewing this at intervals, and so on. I would annoy them by repeating pedantically 'If you say four o'clock you mean four o'clock, not ten past . . .' Or 'If you tell me you'll be down in a minute, that means 60 seconds, not half an hour!' I still wince when I hear parents being imprecise with their children about time – 'I'll read you a story in a minute or two . . .', meaning something very different.

It has rubbed off – on some of the family at least. At least they are all aware of the expectations of others. So far as I know, none of them have lost jobs as a result of poor timekeeping. Their employment records have been full and good – and success breeds success.

As they have reached adulthood, our children have come to realise that our household when they were young was a considerable daily exercise in logistics. It has enabled them to see that the busy, complex lives that most of us have to live nowadays are possible, with some thought, ingenuity and mutual co-operation. Those who are parents have become skilled at organising their full days cheerfully, tending to see new complications as challenges rather than problems, recalling our family round-the-table discussions about how we were going to fit everything in today AND get Kwesi to his football match in Southampton, which he, as the youngest, took for granted then, but reflects on now as he combines his office job as a mortgage adviser with evening and weekend work as a disc jockey and a busy social life.

Our filing systems, like everything else in the house, were unlocked, and we encouraged the children to find things for us there occasionally, and were happy to discuss anything which aroused their curiosity. This exposed them unobtrusively to the value of this kind of organisation, and to the fact that time needs to be devoted to it. Unfortunately, children in residential homes rarely get to see this side of the lives of the staff who care for them, and I suspect that many parents, and certainly many foster parents, regard these aspects of life as "personal", and of no relevance to the children.

Financial management was an important part of this. Our children received pocket money once they could demonstrate an adequate grasp of simple arithmetic to deal with the sums, and a reasonable level of impulse control and discrimination. As soon as they could demonstrate some ability to manage that, and if their understanding of time reached the level at which they could understand and imagine a month, they had their pocket money on a monthly basis.

Pocket money never had to be used for essentials, and was never linked to work or behaviour, except on rare occasions when some level of reparation, on a manageable instalment basis, seemed appropriate for deliberate or reckless damage. But as the children reached teenage years, we would introduce them to allowances for non-school clothing or for school dinners, say, which we would pay to them monthly or even quarterly in advance – by cheque. That meant some learning about bank or building society accounts and helping them to choose and open one – or even two, because some preferred to have a separate savings account. Then pocket money would become payable by cheque as well.

Of course there were repeated crises as they ran out of money in the first week, but lessons were painfully learned. I was not averse to acting sometimes as a bank if requested, but the children were in control. Sometimes we needed in individual cases to revert to more frequent payments. But there were advantages, as ever, in peer competition – nobody wanted to appear too inept at money management if others in the family could do it – and in expectation – younger children would look forward to being "promoted" to the world of cheques and bank accounts like the older ones. Some developed quite an interest in comparing the relative advantages of various accounts, and at one stage Kwesi had little pots of money in several building societies as he waited hopefully for demutualisation to throw windfalls his way! His knowledge of fluctuations in interest rates rivalled his knowledge of football league tables.

Not all of the family have been consistent in their money management as adults. We live in a world where debt is commonplace and financial security over time uncertain. But most have ventured into the world of financial management with their eyes open, undaunted by the apparent complications of mortgages, housing benefit, council tax, loans, pensions and investments. They have all learned the basic lesson, that considerable restraint, organisation and planning are required to balance the flow of money in and the flow of money out.

As our family home was, officially, a registered voluntary children's home, we had to keep detailed accounts. Fortunately, I am one of nature's Treasurers – I actually *enjoy* the book-keeping, the tabulation, the projections, even the hunt for the elusive 99p which would take me round in circles at the end of the year when preparing to present my accounts. And although poring over my cashbooks in my study was often a good excuse for a necessary hour's peace away from family demands, I liked to ensure that each of the family looked at the accounts with me from time to time and could see just how much we spent on clothing, or fuel, or food. And if expenditure seemed to be running out of control, we chose to consult the family on where and how to economise. Lessons were learned about the economies of buying second-hand, avoiding over-hyped brands, carrying out maintenance, or reading the small print, which I see being frequently put into practice in our children's own family lives today.

Dan has written about his horror at the debt problems experienced by many of his friends, adding, 'I think that in part I have avoided this because we were not raised to place much value on material things. Sure, I like nice things, but I like peace of mind more! The sensible part of my brain seems to set reasonable limits that work. For this I am undoubtedly indebted to the approach adopted by my parents.'

Living in a rural area, personal transport was vital to us. For much of the time while the children were growing up, we were a three-car household: a car for Kate, usually a seven-seater estate-car; a car for me, usually something smaller and older which the children could learn to drive in and borrow without the insurance premiums being totally prohibitive; and a twelve-seat minibus, used for whole-family outings. This was not extravagance, but a way of ensuring that we could manage the logistics of ensuring that we could all get to wherever we needed to go. It also meant that the children were able to learn to drive on reaching 17, and were able to start transporting themselves and even transporting the younger ones from time to time. Interdependence again! I became quite a skilled, if unqualified, driving instructor, complementing the skill and patience of the local driving school, and gaining a close acquaintance with various hedges and ditches near our house. It was good for my relationship with each of the children at a sometimes delicate stage. It proved to be so helpful to many of our family in their early adult lives to be able to write "full driving licence" on a CV. And quite apart from the practical skill involved, the process is a helpful rite of passage towards the development and recognition of responsible maturity. I believe that local authorities should provide driving tuition for young people "leaving care" as a matter of course, recognising that it takes some people much longer to learn – and therefore more money – than others.

The same would now be true of computer skills. If we still had ten children at home, I would feel it right to have several computers in the house, and to be embracing enthusiastically the potential of networking, not so that the building could echo to the endless beeping of computer games, but so that computer skills could easily be practised and utilised by everyone without too restrictive a need for time rationing. I can visualise the possibilities for developing email as another way of communicating at times within the household – personal yet not physically oppressive, instant yet allowing time for reflection before response, enabling the sharing of ideas and responses among the group.

Aspects of all our work with children translate into self-care skills. People who have learned how to stand back from themselves and see themselves as others see them, are able to present themselves effectively at interviews and conduct themselves appropriately at work. People who have lived in an atmosphere of learning continue to learn and acquire the knowledge and know-how they need to keep abreast of an ever-changing world. People who have been helped to see links between diet, health and behaviour are likely to eat more nutritiously. And people who have experienced parenting which is competent and sensitive enough are more likely to be effective parents themselves, if they have been able to overcome and tame the legacies of any early damage or trauma. Two of our children, still teenagers themselves, had children adopted at birth in the 1980s. Lynn has recently written movingly about how her own experiences of abandonment as a young child and her later understanding of the responsibilities of parenthood combined to make adoption the only course of action she could consider when she was pregnant at 18. None of the children born to any of the family since then has ever been in care or on a child protection register – all are thriving.

Key factors

- Recognising the importance of motivation and role models.
- Sharing household tasks – but not rigidly or oppressively.
- Striking a balance between domestic chaos and fastidious order, and prioritising accordingly.
- Avoiding gender-specific sharing out of household responsibilities.
- Accepting that most independence skills will be acquired only when the need arises, so being available then to advise and teach.
- Remaining available to young people after they have left home to live independently.
- Being clear and consistent in allocating and defining time, and keeping to deadlines.

- Giving particular thought to how children learn to manage money, and allowing for learning from mistakes.
- Involving children in household decision-making and budgeting.
- Ensuring that young people have the opportunity to learn to drive.

10 The carers' experience

Liberation and liberalisation

It is difficult for me to have any clear idea of the person I would be today if my life had developed differently. If I had stayed in Northern Ireland, if I had studied different subjects, made different friends, met and married a different person – any or all of these "ifs" would have resulted in me being a very different person now. We are changed constantly by our environment and our interaction with it, just as our children were and continue to be.

I cannot say with any conviction what sort of people our children might have become if they had grown up in some other setting. Similarly I cannot look at myself now and see precisely how I as an individual or we as a couple would be if we had not shared our life with our family. Kate and I have had years of self-examination and reflection, necessary to ensure that we were working as best we could with our individual strengths and weaknesses to become more like the people our children needed us to be, so we are probably quite self-aware. We can track changes and developments in our outlook, our attitudes, our values, our beliefs. But we cannot isolate with accuracy the particular factors which have made us what we are today. Nevertheless, this chapter is an attempt to identify some of the ways in which we feel we have been changed by the experience of sharing half of our life so far with this particular group of people. Much of it will be very subjective, and therefore may seem to be of little relevance to anyone else. The exception is the section where I refer to secondary traumatisation – the sometimes devastating consequence of living with children who have been traumatised.

Our family life may not be the sole reason why, for example, there are now many words which I find much harder to define than I did thirty years ago. One of these is "work". For people employed in "residential care", time spent with the children they care for is deemed to be "work", and regulated accordingly. For adopters this is apparently not the case. Foster carers are increasingly paid a salary, yet few would be described as "working a 168-hour week". Our "work" with our children was inseparable from the rest of our life.

My diary contains a series of commitments. Many of them have to be exercised with a sense of responsibility. For some of them I will be paid, but not for others. Some of them I will enjoy, others less so. Some can be altered more easily than others. Some will tire me more than others. The result is that I can no longer be clear which of them constitute "work", and for that I am grateful. The insistence of my local authority employer that I require permission to undertake "work" in any other capacity during the remaining 130-odd hours of the week leaves me uncomprehending, as does the insistence of the European Parliament that we should regulate our "working hours".

The effect of losing my grasp of the meaning of "work" has been liberating. I hope that it has been liberating for the children too, for it seems to me that children do not thrive if they see themselves as the object of "work", as the raw material being "worked" on. They need to know that the adults who care for them take an unexploitative pleasure in sharing their space, that the living group to which they belong is joyfully interdependent, a tribe in which younger and older members support each other thoughtfully and prosper together. I would now find it impossible to take on employment in a "residential care" setting with children, leaving behind at home all the accoutrements of living that make me a rounded person who, in my entirety and my connectedness to the rest of society, may have something to offer to children who are dislocated from that society.

I have also lost my understanding of much of the vocabulary associated with crime and punishment (see Chapter 8), right and wrong, good and evil. I have come to understand that many of the actions of all of us are based on our reactions to pressures and stresses, themselves a consequence of our earliest experiences and their impact on the shape and structure of our developing brains. I have become aware of the combinations of stresses and emotions, the accumulation of experiences, that shape my own behaviour from moment to moment. There are few actions, however antisocial or "out of character", about which I could say categorically, 'I would *never* do that.' My experience in trying to find clues for the puzzles set for me by the perceptions and behaviour of the young people with whom I have lived has greatly reduced a tendency to be judgemental or dogmatic. I have come to find questions more interesting than answers, and answers rarely complete. I am ever more suspicious of ideologies, of panaceas, of final solutions. When the tabloid press reacts to the latest murder or rape trial with shrieks of "Monster!" or "Evil!", I see only damaged, frightened individuals whose perceptions have been distorted by events, circumstances and relationships.

But my faith in people has grown. I have come to marvel at the resilience of our children and others as they have overcome many of the obstacles which early experiences placed in their way. They have taught me about courage, and perseverance, and humility. They have demonstrated to me a remarkable human capacity for healing, for rising above pain and suffering, given space and time, stability, and an infinitely adaptable environment conducive to recovery.

Providing this environment has been exciting, but tiring. I have no doubt that athletes are absorbed in what they do, and committed to it, but the constant mental, emotional and physical effort required cannot be carried on indefinitely. Similarly, the level of constant activity and concentration on detail demanded by looking after several children with very particular needs, seven days a week, cannot be maintained for ever, at least not by me. When Kwesi reached the age of 18 in 1997, we knew that we should not continue actively looking after children, even though we were still under 50, an age when many people first take up caring for separated children. We could feel our energy levels reducing, and knew that our time had come to move on from actively caring for children to finding ways of helping others to do it. We had planned for this from at least seven years earlier, when we consciously agreed that Liam would be the final child to join us. The children knew then that this was our intention, and that the plan would mean that we would have to move on from Plainlands. But that would not be an ending, only a transition for all of us. What would link us all would no longer be a house, but our feeling of belonging together because of our shared history and love for one another. We all have other things to do. Kate and I find that, by comparison with many of our peers, our energy levels are still high, our capacity for "work" still considerable. Perhaps this demonstrates that the physical demands upon us a decade or two ago were great indeed; perhaps we enjoy a natural resilience that enabled us to "bounce back", even stronger, after a few particularly challenging years in the 1990s.

Another part of the decision to stop adding to the family was a sense that it had reached a size beyond which it could no longer *feel* like a family, particularly as partners and the next generation of children attached themselves to it. Three years after the last of our children has moved out of our home, we still have a sense of being actively part of a large family, even if relationships are inevitably at any given time closer with some members than with others. Our bid to redefine the concept of "family" has been more than window-dressing, more than affectation. The links with and within our family are something that we feel – they are not a pretence. At the same time, we have been able to let our children go and find their own level of relationship with us and with one another, taking pleasure in their autonomy, in a way that often seems difficult for smaller families. We have no need to place on them a burden of expectation, so no need ever to feel disappointed. That can only be beneficial for them, and liberates us all from an ongoing sense of unending responsibility or dependency.

Insofar as the outcomes for our children constitute "success", I applaud their determination. We have not made them the people they are. I have learned the important lesson that the only person whose behaviour I can attempt to control is myself. As we learned this, we became increasingly less interventionist in the detail of the lives of the children, knowing that we could advise, suggest, or guide, but never realistically nor respectfully insist, demand, or control. What we could control, choose, modify and fine tune was the environment we built, physically and emotionally, for the children to live in, and our own reactions to the various ways in which they communicated with us and told us about themselves through their words or actions. The most important question for us to ask on a day-to-day basis, we learned, was: 'What is this child's experience of living here, with us, today?' The answers led to follow-up questions: 'Can we work out what we might do to make the experience better?' and 'How can we make the necessary changes?' This needs a lot of active listening, and a lot of what I call "reflective talking", trying to put the child's experience into words. I wish I had learned this more quickly.

But the learning has been deep and, I hope, permanent. I now have more understanding of what it feels like to be a frightened child, an abandoned child, a neglected child, an abused child, than I would ever have developed as a classroom teacher or even as a local authority social worker. And as a white person who has shared his life intimately for many years with children of colour, I believe that I have come to understand the insidious effects of racism more fully than would normally be possible from a position of liberal white privilege.

The world becomes an ever more interesting place to us as the question, 'How does it feel to be that person, here and now?' becomes the one we most readily ask. When Kate and I travel to other countries, or to other parts of our own country, we find ourselves slipping off the tourist track, finding the areas where "ordinary people" live, and asking ourselves that question. We have become more inquisitive, and, I hope, more perceptive. And we are aware, too, that our perceptions are shaped by our own interaction with what we are seeing and hearing. On days when we feel positive, we see a wealth of determination, dignity, resourcefulness, strength and love. On days when we feel low ourselves, we see more fear, rage, aloneness, desperation and hopelessness. Just as it was with our children.

Our experience of caring for children has, it seems, strengthened our marital relationship enormously. Our many disagreements have taken place in a situation where we each knew that it was imperative to heal the rift quickly and completely, for not to do so would rapidly destabilise the children's environment. Given their previous experiences, that could be very damaging indeed, undoing long periods of careful work. We could not afford the luxury of long, smouldering conflicts, of affronted silence, of petty acts of tit-for-tat. A disagreement was like a crack in a load-bearing wall – it needed immediate attention, and the repair could not be botched.

We have become very aware of the fragility of each human life. One of the vulnerabilities which we had to accept as we took on responsibility for our family was that there are only two of us – if one of us should die while the children were still dependent, there would be a huge commitment for the other to continue to carry out alone. The practical issues were too great to leave to chance. We made careful financial provision – and careful emotional provision, too, by talking often about how it might be if one of us was left alone. We were about as prepared as one can ever be. Now, with the children all grown and gone, the practical consequences of that inevitable first death will be less demanding, and the emotional preparation is done.

We have had to learn to work as a team, juggling and re-assigning roles almost minute by minute to meet developing needs, assessing new situations and reaching decisions quickly. The applicability to the work I have done for the past decade, managing out-of-hours emergencies in a social services department, is obvious – the ability to re-prioritise constantly, to assess the significance of new developments, to decide immediately what requires immediate attention and what can safely, or even usefully, be left to simmer or resolve itself, is something acquired and honed over the course of our years with the children.

Because we often had to divide forces, and because our days were very full, we came to appreciate all the more our precious uninterrupted hours together. Our friends often talk of needing a few days to "wind down" into a holiday – for us, winding down became of necessity a much speedier process. After the children had all reached adulthood, Kate took on employment which required her for a couple of years to be London-based from Monday to Friday most weeks. We bought a flat in London which became her main home during that time. Many of our acquaintances assumed that our relationship must be foundering. In fact, we relished the excitement of looking forward to meeting up again after a few days' separation, either in London or in Gloucestershire. Kate could feel "on holiday" in either place. The total unpredictability of our life as carers has meant that we have had to develop our ability to defer gratification, to find gratification in small things, and to be flexible enough usually to accept unexpected change as an interesting challenge. It has made our life more exciting.

Secondary traumatisation

When we live with children whose predominant emotions are the fear, the rage, the aloneness, the desperation and the hopelessness that arise from previous traumatic experience, these emotions affect us too. They are incredibly powerful, and transferable. Secondary traumatisation is this phenomenon of transfer. As carers, we could see the terror, the panic, the desperate attempts to avoid the triggers which would plunge our children once more into the unspeakable horror of past traumatic experience. They could only feel it, uncomprehending, lacking the emotional vocabulary to understand or the narrative to remember what was prompting the behaviour that could be so hard to live with. And at times the power of those wordless feelings swept us up into themselves. It was as if the emotions and memories became ours, and the agitation, the panic, the fear, the urge to violence, became our reactions too, followed by the hopelessness, the erosion of self-worth, the sense of increasing isolation from all the other people whose world neither comprehends our world nor overlaps with it.

This is the price we often paid for daring to enter the emotional world of suffering children. Just as they found everyday life unbearably stressful, so our own stress levels rose. At times we became unnaturally hypervigilant, not able to properly take in what was happening around us because we too were scanning the horizon for danger signs. We would read a page of a book over and over, several times, before we could take in what was written. We became unresponsive to ordinary stimuli, emotionally numb as if our emotional box was full. This threatened our ability to relate consistently and responsively to those of our children who were untraumatised, to our friends and colleagues, and to each other. We suffered sleep disturbance and grappled with nightmares that left us exhausted. We lost our capacity for joy, for wonder, for contentment. We could easily have sought temporary relief in abusing alcohol or other drugs. (For a much fuller treatment of the causes and effects of this secondary trauma, see Cairns, K (1999), Chapter 5.)

It is so much easier for carers to allow their own defence mechanisms against this "trauma infection" to come into play, and to maintain an emotional distance between themselves and the child. But this way the child's scary behaviour will become increasingly uncomfortable to live with, and very soon intolerable, and the placement will break down, reinforcing the child's sense of failure and worthlessness and jeopardising future placements before they ever start. This pattern sends many looked after children down a path of more and more changes of placement and increasingly out-of-control behaviour until they emerge from the care system totally unable to face themselves or the world or to cope with independent living. It may keep the adults sane and functioning, but it does nothing for the child. Severely traumatised children need carers who are willing to travel through hell with them.

Fortunately we did not always have to travel through hell unsupported. Sometimes, as we made these journeys (most often, I must admit, Kate made the journey with the child and I tried to hold the rope to secure her from a relatively safe distance), we had frequent access to a skilled supervisor who knew and understood what we were doing and why, and who could act as a safe deposit for a muddle of fears and emotions and as a link to what we would dimly remember as reality. When we had no such rock to lean on, we could easily have been swept away.

At these times especially we found it difficult to maintain social links with friends and relatives, who through no fault of their own were unable to comprehend what we were going through. To meet the social expectations of others we would have to talk about our family life and our day-to-day experiences. That would either be too painful for us, or impossible because we would recognise our friends' inability to respond appropriately to what we would have to be saying. A frequent and perfectly understandable reaction would be for them to distance themselves from us or to reject the child. We would often be conscious of the image used by one of our children to describe his own sense of being dangerous to anyone who got too close – 'It's like there's a bomb in me that could go off at any moment.' Kate developed that image in a vivid paragraph that demonstrates the far-reaching effects of the gradual explosion of that bomb (Cairns, K, 1999, p.6): *Like blast from a bomb, circles of harm spread outward . . . making victims of any who stand in its way. At the centre are the children, the primary victims who will bear the scars for ever. Then there are those closest to them – whoever loves them enough to feel the wounds and suffer harm because of them – secondary victims through loving those who suffer most . . . And beyond is the whole social order, for where there is corruption, no part of the social fabric can escape the taint.* We felt at times like carriers of toxic fallout that would poison anyone whom we allowed to come close to us.

Moreover, there was the question of confidentiality. For people outside the immediate family to understand the child's pain and its effect on us they would have to know more of the child's history than it would have been right, then, to tell. No doubt the friends of "residential" carers accept without difficulty that carers may not talk in any detail about the children they care for when they go home after a shift. The friends of foster carers may be able to live with knowing little about the child who is a transient visitor in their friends' home. But we were building a potentially permanent identity as a family. It was vital, we felt, for our children to build real relationships with the people who were important to us, and yet it was impossible for those people to be told the horrors that those children were re-experiencing with us on a daily basis. We owed it to everyone in the system to adopt a "professional" attitude to this sort of sharing of information.

The worst of these periods of secondary traumatisation was towards the end of our time of direct caring for children. We were carried through it by a combination of skilled supervision and other factors. We had a clear sense that what we were doing was necessary and right, and that we would and could find the strength to cope at a spiritual level. We had a growing understanding from our own reading and learning of the effects of traumatic experience on the brain, and could see that our own symptoms of secondary post-traumatic stress disorder were to be expected. And we had developed the ability to take the long-term view, to recognise that change is constant and always possible, that gain lay through pain. That ability to think long term, to focus on what you want to be possible for the children in your care, not today, but in ten or twenty years time if you can only get through today and the next few tomorrows, is essential for successful child care.

I often recall a conversation I had with a young Palestinian whom I met in the occupied West Bank in the early 1970s. I had been staying in his family's house, and was amazed by his measured and matter-of-fact response to the bulldozing of the house next door during the night by army tanks – the owner was being punished for his involvement in publishing political pamphlets. 'How long,' I asked my friend, 'do you think it will be before there is any sort of peaceful coexistence in this country?' 'Not long,' he replied. 'I believe that we shall all be living as friends within two hundred years.'

I am increasingly conscious of the shortness of human life, and the shortness of childhood within it. Our aim as carers for our children was to initiate and facilitate a process which might, we hoped, effect some sort of social rehabilitation, not just for the children themselves, but for their children over the course of several generations, where only the prospect of continuing social exclusion existed before.

If some of this book has unintentionally made the choice to live for over twenty years with such a large group of children and young people from such varied backgrounds seem easy and problem-free, read the last few pages again. There were many moments of despair, of uncertainty, of frustration, of anger, when we lost perspective or felt inadequate, and rightly so. Those moments were very difficult, but without vulnerability the job could not be done. But the difficult and painful times have been, and continue to be more and more outnumbered by the good times. It is the predominant good times that we remember. We have enjoyed our family life. Its variety has enriched and educated us beyond measure. In that we feel that our children may be happier and more fulfilled today and in the future than they might have been if they had not come to us, we feel satisfaction, and joy in sharing in their achievement.

That is as true in relation to our "home-grown" children as it is to those who joined us later in their childhoods. We feel that the uncon-ventional childhood experiences of Sal, Tom and Rich did them no overall damage, and considerably enhanced their understanding of the world and their ability to relate to a wide variety of people. We live in an increasingly risk-averse society, and there will be some who will feel that by requiring them to grow up with so many other children, all with their own emotional baggage from elsewhere, we were placing their development at risk. They are old enough now to assess that for themselves, and their thoughts comprise the next chapter. Whatever their view, Kate and I owe them a great debt – they have been "children who foster", as have the other children in their turn, since they all contributed to the environment where they and others could find safety and healing. They have shared their parents and their siblings, apparently without resentment. They have willingly cared for others, for us, and for each other at vulnerable moments. They have been bridges and conduits to help us all understand one another a little more and to bring us together when we have threatened to drift dangerously far apart, on tides of misunderstanding or intolerance. They and their partners continue to be a vital part of the glue that continues to hold the family together and enables it to continue being a live and active system of mutual support.

11 The "birth children"

The particular experience of foster carers' birth children, long ignored, is gaining belated recognition, but is not yet widely documented, despite the raising of the issues by Gillian Pugh (1995). In this chapter, Sal and Tom consider aspects of their experience. Rich adds a reflection which was first published within an article written by Kate in 1999 titled 'The frozen terror' in *The New Therapist*.

Sal:

In the course of my studies and professional and personal life I have come across case studies and anecdotes of where, even in the best intentioned households, the relationships between "birth children" and foster siblings, just as between "birth children" and their parents have been negative, damaging or at best distant. This was not our experience.

When the subject was first raised, it was clear to me that the experience and role within our family of Tom, Rich and myself was different from those of the other two distinct groups – parents and foster siblings. However, it has been difficult to identify usefully just what the differences were. I read the first nine chapters of this book and then tried to think of my/our experience in the context of guidance for would-be social workers and foster carers. What can our experience teach about the needs of any "birth children" within a foster family? It seemed impossible to make any universally valid statements. Maybe I was trying to be too academic. Through the course of our discussions the three of us have found that we had three very distinct experiences, which may be true of any three siblings. As such we have concluded that the easiest way to approach this is for two of us to tell our own story and then to try and draw some general conclusions. Dad will then be given freedom to edit as he sees fit (one of our shared beliefs being that we trust our dad not to misrepresent us!).

Dad discusses the seven facets of child development. I have used some of those headings to try and make sense of my own experiences.

Identity

Given an opportunity to introduce myself I might say the following.

My name is Sarah (or Sal depending whether this is a professional meeting or a private encounter). I am a Probation Officer. I live with my partner of ten years, Simon, and two cats. I am one of 15 children, ten boys, five girls. I'm white, middle class and British (or possibly European). My politics sit left of centre although I am able to accept that market economics is here to stay. I was brought up as a Quaker and Quaker teachings continue to offer guidance in my daily life. I could go on.

The bit of the above I am most often asked to expand on is the 'I'm one of 15 children'. The questions I face include:

Half brothers and sisters?
Are your parents Catholic?
Are your parents mad?

I often find the question difficult to answer. When I say that some of my brothers and sisters are fostered I am left feeling that judgements have been made. It's almost as if people think, 'Oh well! That doesn't count.' Assumptions are made that my relationship with my genetic brothers is bound to be different from my relationship with the others and that our relationship with our parents is bound to be different. The message I would wish to convey is that all 15 of us have a different experience of our relationship with Kate and Brian and that is about us being individuals. For myself, being born to them is just part of my history, just as having had a choice of five last names when he joined the family was part of Dan's history. In other words it is important to my identity that my family is viewed as valid and as "real" as the next.

I have often wondered, particularly since embarking on this project, what it is like to be one of my foster siblings explaining to a third party that they are a member of the Cairns family. On occasions when the number of siblings has been queried, I have tried to be vague about whether or not I was one of the homegrowns. For example, I will say, 'Some of us are fostered'. However, this inevitably leads to the question,

'Were you?' Clearly the question of genetic origin is important within our society. Having said this, I only started having to offer explanation once I left home. In our home town the family was just accepted.

Dad discusses ethnicity in his chapter on identity. I was always aware as a child that we were from a number of different ethnic backgrounds. Looking back I'm surprised that the obvious differences such as skin colour did not raise questions from our peers at school. My experience as a child and something that has been taken into adulthood was accepting ethnic background as just one factor that creates diversity and that diversity is something to be embraced and cherished.

As Dad describes, my identity is ever evolving but there will always be some fundamental aspects of that I share with my siblings whether fostered or not.

Family and social relationships

I have already attempted to describe how I do not differentiate between my foster and natural siblings. However, it is important to note that coming from a large family means inevitably that some relationships are closer than others. Of my siblings there are four or five with whom I am in regular contact and whom I am likely to see outside of visits home to see mum and dad or big family gatherings. It is the case that my two natural brothers fall into this group. We do have a lot of shared interests and as such it is easy to speculate that there may be some additional genetic bond between us that is not present in my other relationships. I don't know if this is the case and on one level I don't really care. It seems to me that these relationships can be as ever changing as other relationships within my life and, providing my current closeness to Tom and Rich does not exist at the expense of other relationships, then that is fine.

I think the important thing here is that at no time have Tom, Rich and myself ever thought of ourselves as a subset within the family. At no time have we ever pursued the three of us having a shared relationship to the exclusion of our other siblings. My relationship with Richard is separate from my relationship with Tom, just as it is separate from my relationship with Liam and so on.

Looking back, for several years (from 1978–1983) the three of us (Sal, Tom, Rich) held the position as the youngest three in the family and there was a four year age gap between me and Dan. Kwesi was added to the younger end followed by Karen and then Pete at the older end. Finally Liam was added in the middle! I think now if Mum and Dad had left it that all of their foster children were going to be four years older or more, our sense of identity may well have developed along more 'them and us' lines. As it was, the impact of having siblings close in age to the three of us was experienced on an individual basis. There was no sense of having a private clique intruded upon.

As an adult I can see that having foster brother and sisters close in age to us was important to achieve balance within the family. However, it was these relationships that were experienced on the most intense level and which, in my, view set our experiences of childhood apart from our peers who did not grow up in a foster family. I know that Tom and Richard would be able to give numerous examples of the difficult and not so difficult times the experienced following the arrivals of Kwesi, Karen, Pete and Liam. For me, Karen's arrival in the family had greatest impact. Karen is ten months older than me and I am almost exactly the same age as her "natural" sister, to whom she was very close. I can remember being very excited prior to Karen's arrival about having a new sister and one so close in age to me. However, things did not work out quite as I had envisaged. Over the next three years, mine and Karen's relationship was characterised by short periods of being very close to longer periods of hating each other. We can both look back now and analyse the processes that were being played out. But this was a difficult time for both of us. We now laugh about the time that Karen punched me full in the face and then ran off into the hills surrounding Stroud, disappearing for a worrying six hours (about the same amount of time as it took for my nose to stop bleeding!).

By the time Pete joined us I had, I think, begun to develop awareness of Mum and Dad working professionally as foster parents. I had some insight into the functions and processes of the family and I had learnt and grown through my experiences with Karen. Pete and I, although in the same school year, were never particularly close. I think now that I may have unconsciously opted to keep a distance between us due to the inevitable proximity of being so close in age. It must have been difficult for Pete coming into a school year where I was already established and had my friends. The main quandary I faced was when Pete fancied my friends, or more difficult still was if one of my friends fancied him (we were, after all, 14 years old). There was a brief period when Pete and one of my friends were going out with each other. Somehow, I'm not sure how, the three of us managed to get through this period without Pete intruding into my life and social network or mine into his.

Throughout my childhood I always enjoyed having a number of close friendships and rarely suffered bullying. However, there were, I now realise, ways in which being part of a foster family impacted upon my social relationships. I was recently chatting to my closest friend (we have maintained a friendship since we were aged two) about this book and my contribution. Liz was commenting on how life in the Cairns household was always busy with never a dull moment. But she reminded me of how she was the only one of my school friends who spent significant periods of time in our household. She was my only friend who regularly visited for tea. This was in part due to the geographic closeness between our two families but it was also, I think now, to do with her having grown-up with us, her parents being both friends and colleagues of my parents and grandparents and her sense of ease in our home. I remember when I was about six or seven inviting another school friend to tea. As we all sat down at the table to eat, my friend burst into tears, completely over-whelmed by the whole experience. It was the only time I was allowed to take my tea (and my friend) to eat in front of the television. That friend never came to tea again. Along a similar theme I, unlike my friends, tended to shy away from having birthday parties choosing instead to have a birthday treat with maybe just one or two of my closest friends.

My social relationships in adulthood remain varied and, I'm grateful to say, plentiful. I am a reasonably confident and outgoing person and am able to hold my own within most social settings. I think one of the things I can be most grateful to the family and my upbringing for is a sense of assertiveness that enables me not to get drawn into complex, duty-bound, tangled, dysfunctional relationships.

Emotional and behavioural development

I have already touched upon these issues above. I would expect that my emotional and behavioural development as a child would have been viewed by my teachers, and any social worker who might have wanted to observe, as "normal". I laughed, played and cried as a young child, I developed an interest in how I looked and boys as a teenager. I became stroppy and uncommunicative with my mum for a few months when I was about 13. I rebelled a little bit when I was 15, 16, 17 by smoking and participating in infrequent bouts of underage drinking and when I left home and went to university I smoked cannabis. These are experiences I was likely to have gone through regardless of whether or not I had foster brothers and sisters. However, there were aspects, I think, of my emotional and behavioural development that set me apart from my peers in non-foster families and that were directly linked to my experience of being a birth child.

Members of the family often describe me as the "peacemaker". I don't think this is a truly accurate description, as trying to come in between or sort out disputes was not something I particularly did. However, I did from a young age concern myself with family affairs. An early memory (I must have been eight or nine) was listening at the pantry hatch to mum and dad having a "discussion" with John. In other words John was in trouble! For some reason I felt like I needed to know what was going on so that I could do everything possible to either help make things right or stop things getting worse. By "things" I think I mean the smooth and harmonious functioning of the household. I can remember on later occasions realising, often together with Dan, that things were not necessarily calm on the western front, and deciding it would be a good idea to lay the table or hang the washing out or do something that would relieve some pressure off mum and dad.

As I got older I found myself almost appointing myself as a "deputy parent" to my younger brothers (Tom, Liam, Rich and Kwesi). I was in some ways the archetypal bossy older sister, but I actually think this ran deeper. Discussing this with Tom recently, he told me that he and Rich often curbed or thought twice about their behaviour because *I* might have been displeased. Between the years of 1991 and 1994, Mum and Dad found their inner resources increasingly stretched, due, I felt, to a number of reasons, but predominantly the result of cutbacks in the availability of external resources (e.g. adequate professional supervision). I think during this time I took on increasing levels of responsibility towards my younger siblings ranging from the practical – cooking, shopping, cleaning – to the more emotional – trying to advise and offer guidance.

I think that these roles within my life were not comparable to the experiences of my peers. However, I do not think that this was in any way harmful to me. I believe that my late teenage experiences actually enhanced my emotional and behavioural development and I consider that if there had been any hint of the growing responsibilities I took on within the family having been too much, Mum and Dad were aware and would have intervened.

There is another element to emotional and behavioural development that links with the above. That is the expectation that birth children will cope. We will not go off the rails and we will succeed in most aspects of our lives. I'm not saying that Mum and Dad themselves placed this expectation upon us. But we were aware from quite a young age about the links between early childhood trauma and subsequent behavioural or emotional problems. Such awareness enabled us to understand the sometimes difficult and stressful behaviour of some of our siblings and in understanding we were able to support them through recovery. Such understanding, however, meant for me that (for want of a better phrase) being "good" was a conscious process. It also meant that, in my self-appointed role as deputy parent, my chastising of Tom and Rich was more severe than any condemnation I may have had for Kwesi and Liam.

Health

There are, I have found, some links to be made between health and emotional and behavioural development. I have always enjoyed reasonably good health both physically and mentally. I believe my general good physical health is down to my having always been taught to eat healthily and enjoy a balanced diet (something I maintain in adulthood – never having had need to diet!). Mental health is, in my view, something that can be vastly more vulnerable than the physical body. Above I mentioned a difficult period for the family between 1991 and 1994. Towards the end of this period, events had started to take a toll on the mental health of both Mum and Dad. This worried me greatly, particularly once I had left home to go to university. I needn't have; Mum and Dad surrounded themselves with the right people (and the right GP, etc) to ensure that they recovered quickly. However, I do think that my mental health could have taken a battering during this time had it not been for the external supports that Mum and Dad had always ensured we had around us. Gran and Grandad, Fred and Dan were rocks to me during this time (and I assume to each other). Friends were also important. I really do believe that fostering is not something a couple can do alone; external support, both in terms of the extended family and perhaps more structured professional support, is vital.

It is difficult to be objective about being a birth child in a foster family because it's about being me. I'm the subject. I guess the message is that any child has only one shot at childhood and the decisions their parents / carers make determine what that is going to be like. For me my mum and dad, overall, did an allright job! I can't change that, I'm one of 15 and frankly I wouldn't want to because that would be to change me!

* * *

Tom:

There are some questions people always ask when I mention my family – or at least, when they find out about its unusual make-up. Since I'm inordinately proud of my family, very fond of the sound of my own voice and enjoy meeting new people, this happens a lot.

The questions posed certainly say something about the "outside" view of a foster family. I hope that this brief survey of my answers reveals something of my experience of childhood. I have focused on what feels important to me. If I don't touch on all of the seven dimensions of development it is either because I see my childhood as having been fairly "normal" in certain regards, or because I feel I have little to add to Dad's analysis.

So how many real brothers and sisters do you have?

Of course, the quick answer is that they're all real – imaginary siblings were not a recourse I felt I needed while growing up! On the other hand, I know that people have a need to relate my experience to theirs and I usually concede to their criteria rather than get bogged down at first base. I happily declare that I do have a natural brother and a natural sister along with 12 foster siblings. And yes, I am my parents' natural child (which seems to matter a lot to people).

I worry, though, that people tick the box that says "foster family" and don't appreciate the deep, permanent nature of my relationship with my acquired family. On the day I was born, I had seven siblings, and the family continued to grow, as families do. The difference was only that people didn't enter the family at age zero and didn't have as much shared genetic material. (OK – there were other differences. My foster siblings had reviews and social workers, they could leave if they really wanted to, and they had their own birth family. But these things are pretty nebulous to a young child.)

I really cannot put my finger on a way that I relate to Sal and Rich that is different from the way I relate to everyone else. There are people in the family I see more of than others; there are varying levels of shared interests, and indeed of shared history. Sharon is eleven years older than me and moved out of home when I was six – of course my relationship with her was less important to me as a child than that with, say, Rich, Kwesi, Sal and Karen, with whom I played ball games and hide-and-seek, and with whom I walked to school year-in year-out.

If there was a difference, it was an inequality of experience. Sal, Rich and I never knew any other family environment. Not that I envied the others their experiences with their birth families or in children's homes but, certainly, those different backgrounds were apparent. They led to differences in modes of behaviour, especially when people were very new to the family. They also meant that some of my siblings had birthday and Christmas presents from more than one family – most unfair, I thought at the time.

As birth children, I think Sal, Rich and I all felt we ought to be "normal". We didn't have the same difficult backgrounds that mitigated difficult behaviour, and besides, among the chaos there had to be a certain stability. I don't know whether this sense of being the "solid rock" of the family was communicated to us, or whether we simply reasoned it out by looking at the family's make-up and assuming our natural role in the dynamic. I think we all handled it differently. Sal took it on board to the *n*th degree, assuming an active role in organising the family and making peace when problems arose. Rich, I think, rebelled more against this typing, especially in his teenage years. Perhaps because he was deeply affected by the problem behaviour of foster siblings and recognised that that *did* give him the "right" to have his own problems. Or maybe because of the old 'I didn't choose to be in this family' line (of which more later). For me, I always felt I *co-existed* with the family as an organism. Not that I lived a detached life but, when things got difficult, my tendency was to leave them all to it.

Didn't you miss out on attention from your parents?

It's true that Mum and Dad often had more pressing concerns than what their birth children were up to. Whenever there was a crisis point with one of my siblings (and there often was), attention was keenly focused on that person, that problem and how they and we could all get through it and grow past it. Since I didn't create much in the way of problems, I suppose I would have to lose out to other siblings in an analysis of "attention given".

I never felt a lack of attention or love, though, and I can see several reasons for this. For a start, Mum and Dad were all too aware of the risk of the needs of some children leading to a paucity of interaction with others. There were always times of keenly focused attention, whether it was having stories read as a young child, the goodnight kiss, or the banter while getting a lift to some social event. And of course, given that my parents were employed as care-givers, there wasn't the necessity for them both to work; for most of my childhood either Mum or Dad was at home full-time, or they were job-sharing and – *quid pro quo* – sharing the role of house-spouse. This meant there was that much more parent time to go round.

Another aspect of the caring dynamic in such a large family was that my elder siblings were also there as care-givers, taking on some of the tasks of looking after me while I was young. Later and in a more general sense, a whole network of siblings and extended family acted as a complex socio-emotional environment. In such a model, I think, there is less intense dependence on one or two people for approval, support and affection than in the now more common nuclear family. This inter-reliance continues to this day, and it makes me happy to be able to offer support and help to my siblings whenever possible, be it because I can drive (and therefore pick Josie up from the bus station for family events), because my design skills come in handy, or merely (as in the last few days) because I'm tall enough to reach the best-looking apples in Gran and Grandad's garden.

It must have been difficult growing up with kids from such mixed-up backgrounds . . .

There's no doubt that fostering isn't usually a recipe for a quiet life, and in a big group of big characters my childhood was never dull. Several of my siblings had problems with anger management and I sometimes found myself on the wrong end of aggressive behaviour. Looking back it isn't difficult to see why. When I was four and a precocious reader, I was often the target of Josie throwing her weight around. She was 11, twice my size and – the nub of the issue, I think – not finding reading so straightforward. To have a four-year-old correcting her grammar must have been wearing. Later, Karen held a great deal of resentment towards me for a year or so after she joined the family. I was in the sorry position of being the same age and having the same name as her natural brother, which must have stirred up the ambivalence she always struggled with about her birth family. Perhaps even worse, I was "posh" (apparently) and therefore a natural candidate for bullying by a fiery, street-wise 11-year-old.

Dealing with these experiences was made easier by the fact that the family was always realistic about where such behaviour came from. Even if a seven-year-old's bruising isn't made easier to bear by knowing that little Johnny has attachment difficulties, it does help in piecing together an explanation after the physical wound is healed. From what I remember, my strategy for dealing with aggressive behaviour was a combination of self-reliance and readiness to seek backup from the big guns. Where the assault was verbal, lightweight or fleeting, I followed the usual childhood dictum against telling tales and weathered it as best I could, often by just taking myself out of the situation. On the other hand, if an attack left me feeling seriously threatened or anxious, then I remember having little compunction in approaching Mum and Dad with the story. Partly this was to do with the awareness that we were in a therapeutic environment and that keeping secrets or letting problem behaviour go unchecked was not going to be good for anyone involved, particularly the "perpetrator". Partly, of course, it was due to being a rattled and aggrieved child in need of parental tenderness. Oddly, I recall that if I ever modified the facts in reporting a skirmish, it was as often as not to play down someone else's bad behaviour or cast their motivation in the best light: an early awareness that people don't always choose to act the way they do, I suppose.

A compromise between total self-reliance and telling tales was to seek the support of other siblings. This didn't count as snitching and could be very effective, whether because having someone else aware of the incident stimulated embarrassment or shame on the part of an aggressor, or just because a friendly presence makes any problem lighter. In my large family, there were always those outside a dispute who could be called on to referee or provide succour, and one week's enemy could easily become next week's ally.

This shared support among the siblings was crucial in an environment that had more than the usual incidence of heated arguments, police visits and tantrums. I have vivid memories of the way the process worked. As tensions rose or a problem presented itself, someone would sensibly suggest that it might be more easily dealt with without a crowd of spectators – sometimes this would be Mum or Dad; often it was one of my generation taking on a guiding role. Those of us not involved with whatever was going on would then repair to other parts of the house, either to our own devices (I often ended up in my bedroom with a book) or to take comfort in each other's company. Away from the chaos, we made jokes, discussed the issues, peeked through the banisters or just distracted each other. This gave us a valuable feeling of continuity by emphasising the relationships that were unchanged by the crisis, while at the same time giving Mum and Dad the space to deal with the situation. As I grew older and talked to my friends about their problems at home, I valued this more and more. The easy companionship we shared even through difficult events was very different to the feeling of isolation and impotence experienced by, say, an only child hearing her parents battle their weary way towards divorce or the younger child of a single mum watching his older brother beat her up on a daily basis.

We all had other relief valves when things got difficult, too. Having Gran and Grandad along the road was no accident, and meant there was another source of compassionate adult support when times were hard. Sport – whether on the rugby field or mountain-biking in the local hills – played an important part in giving Rich something to do with the tensions of family life. For me there was always the escapist world of books, while as I entered adolescence, my friends became more and more important. On a tangential point, I think it's worth mentioning that as far back as I can remember, I invited friends home and I don't remember any sense of awkwardness at having to explain the family set-up. Indeed, in my secondary-school years, my home became the regular centre for get-togethers among a group of friends who appreciated my parents' laissez-faire attitude and the acres of space to run around in.

Do you wish it had just been you and your parents?

This is the big 'what if' and, like any such question, can only be answered speculatively. Is it possible to imagine what it might have been to grow up with just two siblings? I rarely considered the matter as a child, though I suppose I probably did make comparisons with friends from medium-sized middle-class families in the understanding that that's what we would have been. What I didn't realise then was that, as Dad pointed out earlier in this book, the choice they were making in the early 1970s was between a large therapeutic group family or none at all, making the Mum, Dad and three kids scenario still less conceivable.

What I can do is hazard some guesses at how my relationships with Sal and Rich might have been different. I am sure that Rich and I, both high achievers, and proud of it, would have had a more directly competitive relationship. The complex dynamic of the foster family cast us more often as allies than rivals and, I think, counteracted a lot of the testosterone-fuelled in-fighting that is normal between adolescent males.

I can also draw comparisons with "normal" families, and in most of these I conclude that my childhood has been richer and equipped me better for life than many. The large-family system provides both a rich support network and a great deal of individual freedom, whereas most families I know sit uneasily between the extremes of neglect and over-protectiveness. Perhaps because my parents had already raised ten teenagers I found, when I reached the point, that there was none of the struggle for independence that some of my friends faced – I was never the rebellious teenager. I also feel there was an emotional literacy among my siblings, essential to deal with the deep and complex problems thrown up by painful backgrounds, which meant that we always addressed problems and kept lines of communication open. I used to feel sorry for friends who really didn't speak to parents or siblings, because they hadn't the shared language to do so.

I never wished that I had the standard nuclear-family upbringing of my peers (though even that is a shorthand – by the age of 15 I suddenly noticed that I was unusual among my friends as one of the few who still lived with both parents!). I was perhaps more affected not by the fact that my family was different in its detail but by the realisation that it was planned – that so may of its aspects were the way they were because of concrete decisions on the part of my parents. I always knew I was part of a therapeutic grouping and consciously wanted to play my role within it, but I didn't realise until I read *Groups and Groupings* (Cairns and Cairns, 1989) just how constructed it was, right down to family traditions and myth-making. My first response was to feel a kind of betrayal – this family which was supposed to be as close as possible to a "normal" family, that seemed so organic and natural, was planned in detail.

On reflection, however, this is where the great benefits came in. In all areas – whether the need for education which led to such a great quantity of books around the house, or the need to deal with the health require-ments of looked after children that meant I was that much better informed about drugs, mental health, etc. – my parents' role as foster parents informed their provision of parenting generally. I am convinced that the exercises and processes of good foster care are just as applicable to parenting across the board. If more people were conscious of the decisions they make, the environment they inhabit and the ramifications of the dynamic within their family, the world would be a happier place.

* * *

Rich:

Fear is transferable

You stop, arm raised, fist clenched, your knee pressing down on my solar plexus, crushing my breath. In that instant our eyes meet. Somewhere deep inside, your finger drops from the trigger. A single tear rolls down your cheek. Dear God! Who put such fear in your eyes? An explosion, nervous energy, and you are gone. Running, fleeing. I should follow, reassure you. Prostrate and hurting, the image of your eyes like a branding iron on my soul, I slip instead into darkness.

I grew up with injured children. Not physically injured – well, not necessarily. More fundamental scars these, sabre-like slashes across the fabric of growing minds. My brothers and sisters, for such will they always be, weren't as fortunate as I was. They were experienced in violence, rage and harm long before anyone thought to show them love.

The destruction

As a young child I was shielded through ignorance from the reality of fear and pain that plagued the lives of the other children with whom I lived. As awareness developed, however, so too did the realisation that something here was wrong. Very wrong. It is no easy matter to try to understand the root of another being's pain. To do so requires an engagement, an attachment. Empathy. And if that pain is a terror struck to the foundation of that other being's existence, what then for the developing mind? Fear is primordial. It is also transferable.

To grow healthily as a child, certain assumptions must be proven correct. If I cry, someone will come. I will be fed, clothed, cleansed and supported. People more capable than me will provide for me, play with me, teach and cherish me. As I grow, my assumptions change. I become stronger, more learned, better able to fend for myself. But what if these assumptions fail? Not directly for me, but in another for whom I care. How can I accept life in a world where someone so similar to me can suffer such pain? As my assumptions are shattered, I experience danger, panic and rage; the transferring of fear and, with it, rage volcanic in its intensity.

Thus I too became dangerous. Vulnerable and afraid, I see myself impacting with venom on the lives of others, hitherto fortunate others, unaware that the world stinks and that people are not trustworthy, are to be feared, shunned and harmed. I too run, blindly, drunkenly, lashing out. Standing alone in the dark screaming into the wind. What need have I for schooling, for play, for love? What need for anything? Life hurts, and we are all bastards, alone in our misery.

The regeneration

There is a difference between those damaged, terrified children with whom I lived and me myself. At the beginning of my story, when I was little more than a blank page, the assumptions on which I must rely were not disproved. I was far older than they were when first I had to deal with disillusion. For me the terror was no less real, but my foundations were more solid. The influence of people bearing me no harm could reach me more easily, and I had known love. The knowledge that children are abused, that people deliberately psychologically maim the utterly defence-less can never sit well with me, but gradually my shattered assumptions began to reform with an acceptance of this altered reality. I was afforded sufficient safety.

Time is a great healer: time and perspective. As time passes, so too does the immediacy of a given event. It can be possible to relearn that there are other states than pain, other modes than violence. Strength is often developed through damage. As a rod of steel may be tempered by applying the right amount of heat, or physical, muscular strength be gained through controlled tearing of the muscle fibres allowing new, stronger tissue to grow, so too may psychological strength develop out of traumatic injury. It is possible to harness the power of rage, to remember its intensity, and then to attempt to use such energy constructively, to impact positively on the lives of those around you. The experience of growing up with people who have suffered the intense bio-psycho-social injuries of childhood is hard. It is a difficult choice to care for someone whose only mode of interaction is an attempt to cause pain, for that is all they themselves have experienced. It can be overwhelming, and some are overwhelmed. Not everyone survives. But if a safe place can be found, it can be a source of strength and positive personal development.

Some years have passed, but now you are here. I hug you, hold you close, trying to give you my strength, my support. Trying to be your brother. Our eyes meet. For once you do not flinch. It's still there, the pain. Buried, perhaps, for now, but still real. There's something else too. Something bright. Could it be hope?

12 What's transferable?

An inspector from the former Social Services Inspectorate visited us one day around 1980. After his visit he wrote to us stating that our registration (as a voluntary children's home) should be discontinued unless we employed more "care staff", working on a rota basis. A correspondence ensued, in which the inspector was asked for his reasons. It appeared that he had found little of substance to criticise in our shared life at Plainlands. However, he had made frequent references to his own experience of caring, and the difficulty of looking after just one fostered child. His argument was that if it was difficult for a couple to look after one child long term, it must be impossible for us to look after six or more.

The argument was won, partly because we compromised by "recruiting" for a time various relatives and friends who visited us regularly in any case. But it serves as an example of a common professional view which holds that what we did in caring for our family "cannot be done". There may be a parallel in the scientific theory which solemnly propounds that it is theoretically impossible for a bumblebee to fly.

There have been others who have conceded that what we did *can* be done, because we can now demonstrate that we and others have done it successfully but they often add the rider that we must therefore be "very special people", and that therefore it would be impossible for others to replicate our model with any hope of success. This chapter challenges that view. Firstly, I argue that for some children in some circumstances, our model of care may offer the best hope of "success", if that is defined as enabling children looked after long term to become stable, coping, socially connected adults. Secondly, I suggest that various aspects of our approach might usefully be incorporated within other structural models of caring for separated children.

*   *   *

Finding the right foster carers

The world is full of special people. We need them. We need special people to nurse people who are suffering from acute mental illness, or who are profoundly disabled. We need special people to be firefighters, lifeboat crews, overseas aid workers in war zones. Special people manage prisons humanely, perform major surgical operations day in, day out, become vicars of inner-city parishes, defuse landmines, serve their communities as councillors or their countries as politicians and ministers of state. Special people raise families successfully in inner city wastelands, set up effective residents' associations on run-down estates, devote themselves to campaign unstintingly for human rights, environmental awareness, or world peace. Special people spend decades painstakingly developing research that may or may not one day benefit people they have never met. Special people push their strength to the limit in training for and running marathons, in sailing across oceans, in climbing perilous peaks.

I find it difficult or impossible to see myself doing any of these things, yet they are done by thousands of people every day. I have no reason to assume that the supply of people to fill these roles is going to dry up. I cannot think that people who would be able and willing to live a family life similar to ours should be any harder to find. The attitudes, aptitudes and skills required may not be universal, but are not in such short supply, and the examples of other "specialisms" given above suggest that human beings are capable of developing and learning many abilities with the right motivation, opportunities and support.

Any of the jobs or roles listed above could be given a job specification and a person specification. Many of the job specifications would be challenging for most people, and similarly the job of permanent carer and "familybuilder" for a growing group of separated children would not present itself as a sinecure. But what would the person specification comprise? I contend that it would be demanding, but far from impossible to meet. It would include self-awareness, a deep interest in people, a capacity for committed long-term relationships within a large family group, and determination to see a task through despite setbacks. It would attract people who are looking for a comprehensive way of living rather than for work that can be compartmentalised into one corner of a life –

our main tool was ourselves, and it had to be all of ourselves, and not just a part of ourselves that we were prepared to hire out. I would look for a good educational standard and commitment to continuing education, and a knowledge of child development and emotional development or ability to learn about them quickly and comprehensively. Emotional maturity and groundedness would be essential, as would capacity to empathise with other people and tolerance of differences. Honesty and integrity are important, and the ability to inspire trust within a well-developed but not rigid moral code and a principled adherence to the values enshrined in social work training. I would look for patience, a capacity for joy and wonder, a flexible and creative approach to unforeseen problems. I would want articulate people who can negotiate sensitively with a wide range of others, who can listen carefully and express themselves clearly, people who can notice detail without losing sight of the big picture, people who can keep several balls in the air at once. Special people, certainly, but not so special as to be an endangered species.

So what would be the motivation for the rather-special people who could find their life's work and purpose in building families like ours? The desire to live in a group of people is not so uncommon. Despite the tendency of the contemporary media to demonise children and young people, most of us like the involvement of children in our lives. The wish to do something useful with one's life is present in many. Long-term projects with visible end results appeal to many of us. There are enough people who are not totally risk-averse, not afraid of commitment, prepared to gamble a little with their own emotional well-being if the potential gain is personally satisfying. Enabling people to fulfil their potential can bring great satisfaction. It can also help us to fulfil our own potential – to become the people our children need us to be.

The concept of motivation includes reward – indeed, most of us in making choices about our careers and lifestyle do a constant cost-benefit analysis, and the costs and benefits are both tangible and intangible. Many of the intangible costs and benefits for me and for Kate will have become apparent elsewhere in this book. The long-term nature of the commitment may be seen as either a cost or a benefit – there is something reassuring about knowing what you are going to be doing for the next twenty years. The intangible benefits have included a considerable degree of autonomy in running our day-to-day life, flexibility in allocation of time, opportunity to work closely together and to blend work and leisure. As for tangible benefits, we have been able to live in a beautiful environment in an attractive part of the country; we have never lacked for company; we have been reasonably financially secure and comfortable and have been able to plan to ensure, as far as anyone can, that that security will continue in retirement.

Our society is at last moving beyond sentimentality to recognising that caring for looked after children is indeed a job, an often difficult and demanding job, that merits adequate and appropriate payment. The payment must take into account the unusual level of commitment required. Looking after children on a permanent basis, as we did, is by definition not a job from which one can or should readily resign after a few months or years. It is neither a career, with its connotations of advancement up a career ladder, nor a vocation with its other-worldly sense of noble altruism that rises above the mundane need to pay for the necessities of life, and a few luxuries as well. We have become used to the concept of balancing out income over a lifetime: carers taking on a job like ours will need to know that they will be able to afford to live at a standard of living equivalent to that of others doing important professional jobs in public service, that they will be able to make a smooth transition into other work when they are no longer caring for children at home, and that they can provide or be provided for in their old age at a level that takes into account the unusually large number of people to whom they will wish to continue to relate as "family". They will, for example, want to live at that stage of their lives in spacious enough accommodation to enable their children and grandchildren to visit (perhaps not all at once!), to be able to mark birthdays, Christmas and anniversaries appropriately, to attend a succession of weddings, christenings, reunions, funerals, to visit their grown-up children and their families, to help out at times of illness or family crisis, to stay in touch by telephone or email, and this will cost them more than it would cost most older people with just one or two children.

These carers will also need to know that the day-to-day costs of managing this sort of family will be properly covered. There is considerable capital expenditure, but in this era of steady appreciation in house prices this can be seen as an investment. Plainlands increased in value more than tenfold in the 20 years after it was purchased for our use in 1976. Our children needed space – space to grow into their own individualities, space to escape from one another and from us to do their own thing or just be alone, space for noise and stress to dissipate. They needed space indoors, and space outdoors – and so did we. Plainlands had a floor area of around four hundred square metres, and an acre and a half of garden, and when I am asked what made it possible for us to do what we did, my usual first answer is the single word, "space". And the space needs to be appropriately (not necessarily expensively) furnished and equipped, and well maintained, whatever demands the children and their lack of impulse control may place upon it. We could not allow our space to become shabby and apparently neglected. It had to be attractive, well heated and comfortable, a both relaxing and stimulating environment for all who lived in it. Both children and carers have to feel valued and respected, and that respect has to be evident in the surroundings that are provided.

Permanence and commitment

Opportunity should never be lacking. The need for long-term, "permanent" care for separated children does not go away, either in the UK or elsewhere. As a society, we continue to seek adoptive parents, recognising increasingly that for many, possibly most of the children we seek to place, the circumstances of their separation will have set in train difficulties that may socially disable them for ever. Yet we shy away from describing the task of enabling these children to recover and thrive as "work", and we remain muddled about whether adoption services are services for parentless children or for childless parents. We expect the financial cost to the state of such arrangements to be low, yet do not factor in the costs of adoption or placement breakdown, of drug abuse or crime if things go wrong, or the costs of an odyssey through ever more expensive placements "in care" for children who do not "find parents".

The children who were placed with us had the good fortune to be placed by local authorities who were prepared to bite the bullet, to make a long-term commitment to secure a child's future. Such children are still there on the caseloads of social workers in the UK. In the present "mixed economy" of child care it should not be impossible for private or voluntary agencies to recruit and support some of the people who would establish families like ours, given the chance. A revised regulatory system would recognise this as a category of care subtly different from the present classifications of residential care, fostering or adoption, and present a regulatory framework that would enable such families to live as outwardly "normal" a life as possible whilst being protected against potential institutional abuse.

The salient factor is commitment and permanence without ownership. There is a long history of children being seen as the property of their parents. State involvement in raising children has often been seen as unwarranted and unacceptable interference, whether in the establishment of compulsory schooling, the regulation of children's working hours, or the banning of "smacking" children. Our society is still a long way from assenting to the words of Kahlil Gibran in *The Prophet*:

Your children are not your children.
They are the sons and daughters of Life's longing for itself.
They come through you but not from you,
And although they are with you, yet they belong not to you.
You may give them your love but not their thoughts,
For they have their own thoughts.
You may house their bodies but not their souls,
For their souls dwell in the house of tomorrow, which you cannot visit,
    not even in your dreams.
You may strive to be like them, but seek not to make them like you.
For life goes not backward nor tarries with yesterday.

Our way involves a permanent commitment based on trust, not on legislation or ownership. Carers take on responsibility, but not possession. Its vulnerability is its strength, for the carers, the children and their birth families can recognise that there is always the possibility for change. Children may be able to return, temporarily or permanently, to their birth families, as children or as adults, but the relationship can continue. The change does not have to be seen as breakdown. Children may reject the carers and the substitute family, but the door remains open. Illness or dangerous behaviour may mean that children have to be cared for in a different environment for a time, but the option of returning remains, and contact is maintained. As they move into adulthood, children may move away, and come back again if things don't work out.

Slightly further afield, many European nations find themselves left with huge "orphanages" and abandoned "street children" as a legacy of previous regimes and social instability. There is an awareness that the needs of the children living in these settings would be better met by the experience of family living. Many of these governments are working hard to move children out of institutions into foster homes, but the sheer weight of numbers involved often means that pre-placement checks are of necessity perfunctory, and aftercare minimal. Sadly, abuse in such generally unregulated systems is likely to be rife, and understanding insufficient of the needs of children who have unmet attachment needs or whose development has been distorted by experience of trauma.

Our model provides an opportunity for larger groups of children to be placed together with permanent carers who approach the caring task in an informed and professional manner, seeking to respond to disturbed and disturbing behaviour constructively rather than trivialising it as "naughtiness" or demonising it as "wickedness". In such settings, supervisory and therapeutic support can be provided more cost-effectively. Where there is a commitment to permanence, so that there is no artificial cut-off point at the end of childhood, supportive lifelong relationships can be built.

Moreover, Europe has a fine and long tradition of the profession of social pedagogy. The quality of care provided for separated children in the UK might well rise if this were to become a recognised and accepted discipline here. Indeed, the development of children's trusts, bringing together much more closely the provision of education and social services to children, may catalyse the development of social pedagogy in this country. It is a profession in its own right, combining in the training it offers many of the values and skills of social work, child psychology, and education. Social pedagogy graduates are to be found in many of the European continent's special schools, residential homes, pupil withdrawal units, young offenders' institutions, and so on. I can see no reason why young and enthusiastic social pedagogues with a little experience could not be recruited and supported to live their family lives in settings not dissimilar to ours. In the British context, suitably motivated carers may well be found among carers previously employed in residential homes who have become disenchanted by the ethos of negativity and neglect in which they frequently find themselves working, and yet retain a professional vision which they realise they could turn into reality on their own premises.

We know of one project, Nadomak Sunca, in Croatia, where such a vision is being worked out. Here, four couples, with a range of backgrounds in social pedagogy and related subjects, have established four families, each with six to eight children. Children are placed by the local Centre for Social Welfare, with whom the carers sign foster care contracts. The project owns four family houses in the small town of Oprtalj, which had become depopulated. The families are each involved in some farming activity that provides a cohesive element of interdependence and self-sufficiency, and the presence of the children has enabled the primary school in the town to reopen after a period of closure. The project is supported both by the Croatian government and by voluntary organisations in Germany and the Netherlands. (There is a mainly Dutch language website: www.kinderdorpkuberton.nl) Young volunteers from Germany and Austria can fulfil their national service obligations by coming to spend a period helping with the children or on the farm and being available in the community to broaden the horizons of the children (but living separately from the families). No further expansion is planned in Oprtalj, so that integration into the wider community is not jeopardised, but the model appears to have been successful over nearly a decade, and the possibilities for duplication elsewhere in the region seem real. Similar potential exists in other parts of the world where rebuilding is taking place after conflict, or where social care systems for children are being established.

Professional support

Carers will also be attracted if they can rely on support. In the UK, carers are increasingly attracted to the better private foster care agencies because they know that, as well as reasonable remuneration and status, they can expect dedicated support in their work around the clock from equally committed social workers who are knowledgeable and well acquainted with them and with the children they are looking after. There is no obvious reason why the necessary level and quality of support cannot be provided consistently within statutory organisations. It is a question of priorities, of understanding, and of political will. It requires a professional recognition of carers as specialist colleagues, not as junior assistants whose homes and families can be utilised insensitively as an impersonal "resource". It demands a willingness to share responsibility rather than delegating it and forgetting it, or shuffling it off.

Support workers need to develop an understanding of what it is like to *live* with children whose reactions to stress are harrowing or frightening, and an ability to share some of the emotional burden without themselves becoming overwhelmed by it. They need to be skilled observers, assessors, reflective supervisors. They must have the ability to help carers to form and hold onto a vision of their long-term aim for each child and for the whole group, and to bolster the carers' own resilience, self-confidence and self-esteem. They, too, must be rather special people, backed up by a responsive system that has rapid access to practical assistance, creative solutions, and funds. But a stream of rather special people come into social work and related professions, and this sort of work is what many of them trained to do and like to do if they find an opportunity.

It is only worth setting up services if they are going to be effective and efficient. The outcomes for our children have been good. Children have reached their potential. The early outcomes for Nadomak Sunca also appear to be good. Considered over the lifetime of each child, the cost to the public purse will not have been high, and those who have been successful against the odds will be a net boost to the country's resources rather than a drain upon them. The lifetime cost to the state of long-term unemployment, poor physical and mental health, repeated crime, housing dependency, abusive or neglectful child care, and all the other features of the measured outcomes of much "standard" child care provision is enormous.

Group size

I contend that the size of our family group has been a very beneficial factor in its success. It has given our children emotional space for recovery and a sibling group for lifetime support. They have been able to feel secure without feeling compromised, isolated or pressurised. Belonging is easier in a broad church. The size of the group has offered them opportunities to assume responsibilities and lay them down again, and to learn from the mistakes and successes of others as well as their own. It has allowed them to lead when they have felt confident, and to be protected when they have felt vulnerable. They have learned about sharing and the joys and advantages it can bring, and have been motivated to become sharing members of the society in which they live, included in it and able to offer inclusion to others.

To summarise, it is possible to imagine structures within which families like ours could be seen as a viable and potentially successful way of caring for separated children who need long-term placements or permanence. There exists a pool of potential carers, and a larger pool of children who need them. The size of the group does not at all have to be seen as a negative factor, either deterring potential carers or compromising the likelihood of success. The capital costs required to provide and equip premises are not a problem. In many parts of the world property is cheap; in more affluent places the servicing costs of loans add only a small percentage to the running costs of the care provision, and the asset should not depreciate. If the work is valued in terms of status and reward and properly supported, this model of care can make a very effective contribution to child care in many places.

* * *

Whether or not our family group model of care is duplicated in its entirety, many of our approaches could perhaps be adopted helpfully within other care environments, particularly where children are learning to overcome the legacy of earlier damaging experiences. The "Key Factors" at the end of each of Chapters 3–9 may provide many points for carers to consider in the context of their own caring environments, and could form the basis of a regular audit, either of individuals or of a whole home. The word "home" is deliberately ambiguous here: each of us will have a collection of images, generally positive, I hope, of what constitutes "home" for us, and possibly a very different collection of images of "children's homes". I want to blur and conflate those collections. A colleague was once proudly shown round a new, purpose-built children's home by its manager. As he locked the final door, he asked, 'Well now, don't you think your children would like it here?' My colleague tried to imagine her two daughters living there, and answered apologetically, 'Actually, no, I don't think Emma and Jane would like it at all.' After a few moments' incomprehension, the manager laughed and said, 'But of course I didn't mean your *own* children!'

I have tried to pick out several themes of our approach to caring for the children who grew up with us which, I think, pervade the detail in the previous chapters, and have relevance in any environment and may help carers to make their environment a better place for children to be. They are about Sharing lives, Enhancing the physical environment, Responding to the messages of children's behaviour, Inspiring a love of learning, Encouraging relationships, and using the Strengths of the group. Conveniently, they can be remembered as an acronym – SERIES – and could form the basis of a series of reflections which carers might undertake with supervisors at regular intervals. Although in some form they were part of our philosophy from the outset, sometimes more implicitly than explicitly, their importance to us, and our ability to see *how* to put them into practice, increased as the years went on and we reflected on what was happening. I wish that I had realised their significance more from the very start.

Sharing lives

This means at the very least living in the same place as the children. Children need to know that people want to be with them, not just for the hours on a rota. Carers certainly do not need to be spending every moment in direct contact with the children – all of us would find that oppressive – but it adds enormously to children's sense of self-worth to know that adults don't have to put geographical distance between the children and themselves before they can relax. In a traditional residential care setting, it makes such a difference if at least one carer, the head of home, perhaps, actually lives on the premises, and is content to do so.

However cosily domestic a care setting feels, it is unsettling for children to feel that they are the only full-time residents. The boundaries become unclear between who "belongs" and who is a visitor. The feelings experienced by the children can be either an intoxicating and inappropriate sense of control which they lack the maturity to exercise, or a disconcerting sense of instability, or a sense of being rather like livestock, tended by visits from the farmer and his labourers, or possibly a sense of being prisoners, guarded by a succession of wardens.

Even if the home is not run totally on a family model, the presence of carers who are living out their personal life among them opens up for children great potential for observing, learning and sharing – social workers know that we gain a fuller picture of people if we see them in their own homes surrounded by what is important to them. There is scope to observe carers' adult relationships, and their relationships with their own children. There is opportunity to observe the carers' emotions from a safe distance, to see how they put their various life skills into practice, to have some contact with the carers' social network. There are casual encounters, chance conversations which might not happen in the context of busy "shifts", constant opportunities for carers to demonstrate courtesy and respect. There may be shared activities – the resident carers may enlist help in putting up shelves, preparing for a birthday party, servicing a car. The living environment becomes more "real", less artificial. Children will feel less socially excluded.

Even when looked after children are accommodated by carers in their own homes, there is often untapped opportunity for sharing. I have met foster children who know little about the carers with whom they may have lived for several years. For example, they may not know what the carers do when they go out to work, or when they bring in a babysitter and have a night out. They may never have heard about their carers' personal histories, where they were born, what their childhood was like, what twists and turns their lives have taken. They may have no idea about why their carers chose to become carers, what they see as the costs and benefits of the role they have undertaken, what their future plans are, what their views are on politics, religion, etc. They may have the dimmest notions of their carers' family structure. The carers might say that the children had never shown any interest, that these matters were of no relevance to them. But part of caring is to help children to find and make links between themselves and the world around them, to add texture and colour to their possibly monochrome view of life, to develop awareness of difference and variety, of options and choices, of feelings and emotions. It is also, as carers, to permit the children we care for to effect change in us as well as changing themselves. All true relationships are reciprocal, and to care for children in ways that do not allow this to happen can border on emotional deprivation. What easier or more affirmative way to do build trusting relationships than to say, 'I trust you (but do not burden you) with my life. You are a part of it – share it with me.'

Enhancing the physical environment

The surroundings in which children are cared for must be designed with the needs of the children in mind. We were indebted to some of the thinking of early champions of the "planned environment", such as David Wills and Bruno Bettelheim. Designers of children's homes need to produce buildings in which both children and carers feel at home, and where informed thought has been given to the children's needs for stability, privacy, relaxation and stimulation. Foster carers and adopters may need to set aside some of their own tastes in use of space, furnishings and gardens, and look at the space they are providing in the light of its potential to enhance the healing and growth of the children placed with them. The environment must be able to soak up hard physical treatment yet still look and feel welcoming, unthreatening, embracing. Sometimes it is right to choose fabrics and furniture which may be short-lived and require replacing sooner rather than later, simply because they are beautiful and enhance their surroundings. Colours should be uplifting but never harsh, lighting warm, textures soft and comforting. There should ideally be a choice of places to be where children can find community, intimacy or solitude. A balance should be struck between obsessive order and disorienting muddle, with different approaches to different shared spaces in the house. There must be interesting things – glassware, pottery, wood, stone, textile – for children to look at, to touch, to ask about, but nothing must be overwhelming or excluding. Let there be paintings on the walls to suit all tastes. We often brought back a new piece of artwork from a family holiday, usually chosen by several of us together.

Carers need to think about noise. Materials which absorb sound rather than bouncing it around will do wonders for the sanity of everyone. Doors which always bang are no good for reducing stress – considerations of safety may suggest self-closing doors, but in practice the constant noise and the physical barriers they automatically set up are not conducive to children's well-being. It is better to go and find someone than to shout. Telephone tones can be chosen with care. Music is fine, but if one person's music is another's white noise, there is need for continuing discussion and compromise. The German shepherd dog that we acquired in 1995 barked very loudly when anyone came near our front door – she was excellent as a guard dog, but if we had had a house full of younger children at that time she may have had to learn quickly or find a new home, for her habit was not conducive to restfulness and calm.

Open access, like open lives, symbolises and encourages trust. Carers need to think carefully about what areas, if any, really have to be off-limits to children, and why. Secrecy is an enemy of trust, and a catalyst of fear. Locked doors are easily experienced as an affront, a threat, or a challenge. We were asked from time to time by inspectors why our children were not able to lock their bedroom doors to protect their property and maintain their privacy against unwanted intrusion. We outlined our philosophy of promoting mutual respect of property and privacy, and our feeling that, by preventing that respect from being freely chosen, we would be hindering its development. It was a discussion we regularly had with the family. For most of them it was the absence of locks that made the house seem a safe place to be, because it gave a message of mutual trust.

Nomenclature is important – the nuances of words say so much, which is one reason why carers must be able to choose their words to children with precision and care. In terms of our living environment, we preferred "study" (a domestic term) to "office", and avoided institutional concepts such as "dayroom", "bootroom", or "laundry" to denote a space. Similarly, a "corridor" sounds more impersonal, less cosy, than a "hall", "landing", or "passage".

I visited the home of experienced foster carers recently, after a placement breakdown. One of the reasons for breakdown had been the child's "lack of respect" for their home. The high-ceilinged rooms echoed to every footfall on the highly-polished wooden floors. Every inch of shelf space in the sitting-room (furnished with a white suite) was devoted to family photographs – weddings, christenings, graduations – but never a foster child in sight. The dining-room featured a wonderful display of dolls, carefully arranged – the child had apparently earned disfavour by moving the dolls around. In my view this was not an environment in which a child could easily relax or feel, 'This is *my* space too'.

Responding to children's behaviour

Carers must be the champions of their children. Looked after children need champions in a society where they are stigmatised, and where any difficulties they have in relating to the expectations of the confusing and stress-laden world around them are likely to be magnified and derided both by peers and by adults in positions of authority or influence. They need to be clear that carers are trying to understand and trying to smooth their passage rather than joining the ranks of the disapproving and dismissive.

I suggest some simple guidelines for carers. Criticise the behaviour, not the person – 'That was a cruel thing that you did', rather than 'You are cruel'. Don't attribute your own feelings to the child: 'When you . . ., I feel . . .', rather than 'You make me feel . . .' Attribute responsibility, not blame, 'You caused that to happen', rather than 'That was your fault'. Look for natural consequences rather than punishments – we are educators, not judges. Accept that children have deep emotions, and less skill and experience in living with them than you do – so in conversation with friends, 'B is finding life very difficult at the moment', rather than, 'We are having dreadful problems with B . . .. Remember that you have taken on the responsibility to make it possible for children to grow and change, but you cannot *make* the change happen, and you cannot be expected to. Many inappropriate responses from carers are the result of panic, of feeling too great a burden of responsibility for effecting what seems today, at this moment, to be impossible. If we keep tending the ground, the seedlings are likely to flourish – we should always think long-term.

All this may sound very trite, and far removed from the reality of young Wayne who has just smashed the telephone against the wall, young Gemma who is locked in the bathroom hacking at her wrist with the nail scissors, or young James who has been turned off the school bus for using foul language and bullying younger children for the third day in succession. Yet it gets to the root of therapeutic and effective caring. It assumes that the child's behaviour is not itself the problem, but is a message, an indicator of a problem. The task of the carer is to read the message, understand it, and find ways to address its content together.

Children are likely to be more accustomed to adults who choose in such circumstances to express their own emotions and exercise whatever power they may have arbitrarily, forcefully, and self-righteously. As time went on and I understood, more and more, the inappropriateness and unhelpfulness of this sort of reaction, it was good for me to repeat to myself frequently the contents of the previous paragraph to programme myself to react more rationally, less violently. The mantra becomes the reality. With it comes an awareness of the importance of listening to children before jumping to conclusions, whilst recognising that they too may be repeating a different sort of mantra, a learned formula that has served before to divert blame, deny responsibility, control pain, avoid overwhelming emotion. So the listening includes helping the child to get beyond the stock response. That requires patient building of trust, trust that lowering defences will not result in disaster.

I believe that it is important to avoid formulaic responses to children's anti-social behaviour. Children learn little from a tariff system of fines and deprivations, groundings and humiliations, except that the system and those who operate it – and become its slaves – have little interest in them as individual people. Consistency in dealing with children in a group is not about treating every child in the same way as every other child – it is about maintaining a consistent and insightful response to the particular needs of each child and allowing that response to change with the child.

Other members of the group can be helped to recognise the appropriateness of this and to reinforce it.

Hasty reactions are also to be avoided, if possible. There is plenty of time. It is better to under-react while both child and carer are processing what has happened, and while emotions are running high, and to return to the matter having ensured that the situation is calm and safe, and some trust has been established or re-established. None of us can think clearly and rationally at the point when whatever constitutes our personal sabre-toothed tiger is about to pounce. Difficult discussions are easier after some time for reflection, and accompanied by a drink and a slice of cake. The greatest fear of many looked after children is rejection, the ultimate disempowerment, to the extent that they may provoke rejection in order to feel that they were in control of the situation. Any sign that a discussion of what has gone wrong, however challenging and discomfiting, will take place in the context of ongoing commitment, will be conducive to openness and honesty.

Just as nomenclature was important with respect to the physical environment, so carefully-chosen language – both words and body language – is a vital element of responding to children's behaviour. How is the child understanding what we are saying? How far does our choice of words demonstrate that we are able to put ourselves alongside the child, to understand what the child thinks and feels is happening? Are we giving a message of hope or of despair, of commitment or alienation? Do we seem to be reaching out or pushing away?

Carers can help themselves and their children by being demonstrably prepared to learn about the effects of past damaging experiences on the child's feelings and perceptions. This brings us conveniently to the next element of the SERIES.

Inspiring a love of learning

Children who have lived through uncertain or frightening circumstances in their early months and years will have missed out on a great deal of learning. They will have learned what was necessary for survival in a hostile or unpredictable world, and this may have so preoccupied them that there will have been neither time nor space to learn much more. They may not have had the benefit of an attuned relationship with a trusted carer who can direct their gaze outward, imbue the new with excitement rather than threat, talk to them calmly and consistently so that out of the meaningless babble of noise meaning begins to take shape. Since much learning is hierarchical, the more specialised learning that children are expected to take on as they grow older may have no foundation on which to build, and the child may well give up trying to do what feels impossible.

But once children have experienced stability and have begun to experience trust, learning may recommence. It will come more easily if the newly-trusted carers are excited by learning themselves, and can express their own wonder at the world clearly for all to see rather than bury it under a fashionable urbanity or world-weary cynicism. A world in which children will learn, almost in spite of themselves, is a world which is full of stimulation and conversation, a world of books and newspapers and machines and computers, of people with interesting points of view and tales to tell, television and radio programmes which are selected, listened to and talked about rather than serving as background noise. It is a world where questions are asked – 'I wonder why . . .' – and answers sought out and debated, where interests are nurtured and passions encouraged. In this world there is always something more to see and do just round the next corner – our family holidays would each notch up a formidable list of castles and museums and nature reserves and impressive old town centres visited and explored without complaints from the children that they were "boring". A Baltic beach covered in huge jellyfish became a reason for learning a lot about the strange world of the jellyfish, rather than simply a reason to pile back into the minibus and find another beach. A teatowel featuring a list of the kings of Denmark, brought back from the same trip, provoked endless speculation about the attributes and activities of Gorm the Old, Harald Bluetooth and Sven Forkbeard. Opportunities for the stimulation of imagination and painless learning are everywhere.

In such an environment it is easy to encourage formal education. Where carers are learning themselves – and presenting it as something enjoyable and satisfying rather than a chore – it is easier to motivate children to do the same thing. This applies just as much to learning practical skills as it does to academic learning. Perhaps it's the Tom Sawyer principle –

painting the fence becomes an attractive proposition if someone else appears to be deriving pleasure from doing it.

One of the easiest ways of persuading someone to read a book is to say, 'There's a bit about you in it'. A couple of weeks before writing this chapter, I sent copies of most of the earlier chapters around the family, inviting comment. Several phoned me back within a day or two to say that they 'couldn't put it down'. I am not to be fooled that this has anything to do with the quality of the writing – it is to do with the fact that we like to hear about us (especially if we like compliments and expect to get them). We don't often walk past a mirror without looking in. We should always share with children what we write about them, both as a learning tool and as a courtesy.

So it should not be difficult to encourage children to learn about themselves. I keep returning to the concept of working *with* the children we care for, not *on* them. As we try to fathom the puzzles our children set us, as we read and gain understandings about the basis of difficulties they present, it is incumbent upon us to share those insights, those tentative explanations, with our children. Without wishing to direct them towards a lifetime neurotic consumption of psycho-analysis, we can teach them that we can go beyond 'That's just the way I am'. We can model our own growing self-understanding – 'I used to be . . . then I asked myself why and realised that . . . so now I can aim to become more . . . and this is how I'm working out the steps to take along the way'. We can enlist the help of our children, just as we do of our partners if our relationship is good, to support us in our own personal growth, provided that becomes in no way burdensome for them and remains within a framework of healthy interdependence. It will make it much more natural for them to recruit us to help them learn to achieve their own personal goals. It will also give them the tools with which to support one another.

Encouraging relationships

Looked after children have become disconnected from society. Unless the missing links are made or remade, the resulting social exclusion may be lifelong. Being part of a functioning family is often a passport to social inclusion, which is why adoption is often an effective arrangement.

Children who live in closed communities struggle to be included. The growing child's links to the rest of the world are not only mediated through their carers, however committed, but also come through being woven into networks of peers and communities.

It is the carers' task to facilitate the formation of these networks. Children cared for together need to have a framework within which their understanding of one another as real people can be developed and their relationships with one another valued and encouraged. Just as important are the relationships with the communities in which they live. Children need role models in people they can relate to directly, not just people they see in the media. They need opportunities to make real, dynamic relationships with other adults – teachers, club leaders, carers' friends and relatives, neighbours, friends' parents, shopkeepers as well as social workers and independent visitors. To facilitate this, carers should ideally be involved members of the local community themselves. Meeting new people and learning about their lives can be part of the agenda for any holiday, any day trip. The carers need to ensure the safety of the children within these relationships, but with that proviso it is good actively to encourage the formation of such relationships, and to know when to withdraw into the background.

A wide variety of friendships with other children should also be encouraged, and friends need to be welcomed in the care setting and helped to feel comfortable when they are there. Any decision that a child should attend school other than within the immediate community has to be questioned and rigorously justified. Enabling children to become fully involved in clubs, societies, sports teams, etc., has to be given a high priority, whatever the logistical or financial difficulties.

Children are likely to need help and guidance to learn and practise the social skills required to manage all these relationships. Carers have to be aware of the need and sensitive as to when and how it can be met. Much can be done by modelling, both by the carers and by the more socially able children in the group. So many little things can help – unforced smiles, brief but sincere expressions of appreciation, matter-of-fact introductions, random acts of kindness, in an ethos where there is a fundamental assumption that other people are interesting, benign, and worthy of respect.

Using the strengths of the group

Human beings are sociable beings. We like to be part of a group, and are socially most effective if we can claim membership of a variety of groups in and out of which we can move comfortably. Some of these groups will have memberships that overlap. The groups to which we belong help us to shape our identity, and provide us with systems of mutual support and group norms for our behaviour. To be accepted in a group raises our self-esteem.

It will have been clear in a variety of ways that Kate and I devoted a great deal of energy and thought into encouraging a group identity to evolve in our family, whilst also nurturing the individuals within it. When our children look back on their childhood, they are as likely to talk about growing up 'in the family' as about growing up 'with Mum and Dad'. When we still had several children at home, and friends would ask, 'How's the family?', we were very likely to think about the overall state of the group, and answer on that basis, than to think immediately about its individual members. And at the end of a day, when we would reflect on how things were going, we would often exchange views about the current state of the family group as an organism in its own right.

We would feed these reflections back to the rest of the family group in the course of the mealtime discussions that were so central to our shared life, and discuss possible reasons, and ways to change things if the developments seemed to be undesirable. In the event of an incident which seemed to have the potential to affect us all as a group, we would bring everybody together to talk about it. The event might be an argument between two family members which had got out of hand, or the discovery of damage to someone's property, the death of a pet animal, some family news, good or bad, the imminent arrival of a visitor. Individuals could measure their reactions against the reactions of others, and a general group view would usually emerge. Where one person's reaction was different, we could often help the rest of the group to understand, support and modify, and healing work could go on without our direct involvement. We were using similar skills to those used by the leaders of therapeutic groups, but much less formally and often less consciously.

Decisions to welcome a new child into the family were always made after discussion. I was often touched by how ready most of the family were to give somebody else the chance of sharing their life. Because of the level of trust generated in the group, we felt able as time went on to explain to the family some of the potential difficulties the newcomer would experience, given what we knew of his or her previous history, and we could rely on the established children to take this into account as they helped the newcomer to integrate. Potentially difficult situations about to happen could also be shared with everybody – contact with a birth relative, an examination, a social services review, a change of school. Mark has written to me movingly about his feeling of belonging as he marched off to secondary school on the first morning, under the wing of his older 'brothers and sisters', wearing the same uniform as they did.

Our group was generally a forgiving group. Whilst it was never discussed in these terms, the concept of reintegrative shame seemed to be internalised. When one member of the group had somehow fallen from grace, the disapproval of the rest would be clear, but there would usually be a clear desire to find a way to re-incorporate that person in the group by including them in some group activity. On the occasions when Karen, and later Liam, were taken away from the group for several weeks because their difficulties had become too great, the level of concern from the rest of the group, wanting news of their progress, was high and sustained, and their welcome back on their eventual return was genuine.

Our family group was not a democracy. Kate and I remained its non-elected leaders, and are only now relinquishing that position, with some relief. But it was a group often consulted by its leaders, and its leaders were, I think, open to suggestion. It was also a group whose members expected responsibilities to be delegated within it, and where those responsibilities would be exercised on behalf of the group, and not just on behalf of the leaders. It was a group with a clear sense of its bound-aries, and a pride in its own being. Primarily, I like to think, it was a group in which individuals felt valued. Within this group, each of us could grow. Mark has described the process he went through as 'un-ravelling' himself and 'being set free'. His metaphors paint a telling picture of the child in care, tied up in knots of fear and anxiety, and cut off from the rest of the world. For others, it seemed that they felt in danger of unravelling or disintegrating before they came to us, and needed a safe and supportive framework within which they could put themselves back together.

I am completing this chapter immediately after a weekend during which 11 of our 15 children have joined together with other family and friends to celebrate Kate's father's 80th birthday. I could observe little that indicated rivalries or grudges, competitiveness or jealousy – far less than I would expect to observe within a more conventionally formed family. It seemed that the group, as it learned to do as children, has remained self-regulating, tolerating easily the wide range of outlook, values, and income that have developed within it, and refusing to allow its easy flexibility to be threatened. I observed shared joy in recent births and forthcoming marriages, welcoming of new partners, pooling of knowledge, skills and experience on business and child care matters, concern for those who were not present, and a lot of hugs and laughter. The demons of the past may not all have gone away, but they have lost much of their power to destroy.

13 The afterword

Here are some further extracts from letters, emails or recorded conversations with our foster children after they had the first nine chapters of this book in draft form.

Dan:

My earliest memories of Plainlands are fairly sketchy, but I can recall it being much more homely than our previous house. It is not a fair comparison as I spent most of my formative years there and this sense of warmth is in part due to the number of years spent living there. It was an instantly more inviting building and more adaptable to family life. Once carpeted, it gained a cosiness that our previous house never had. It had large spacious gruonds too, but was less isolated in its location – we had neighbours! It was important to have a sense that other families thought this a good place to live.

Plainlands had a greater sense of being "normal", less on the fringes of everyday life. It had a lot of space and was set in idyllic surroundings. Without being nostalgic it is fair to say that it would be hard to find many such properties on this scale that could still offer that sense of warmth that makes a building a home. Over the years it was adapted and tailored to our changing needs and this only increased its sense of homeliness. Like many others of the family I felt genuine disappointment when the day came and it stopped being our family home. It was in many ways a wonderful place to grow up and I felt at home there.

I live in the countryside now, and while the bright lights of the big city had a lure for me during my university days, I have since returned to my roots by moving to the wide open spaces of the Derbyshire Peak District.

* * *

I am fairly sure that I have done more than I would have with my education as a result of growing up in our family. Why? By being encouraged to see the value of learning, having educated parents who showed an interest, and having access to books from an early age. The fact that I had stability in my schooling was invaluable. I had one primary school and one secondary school. By the time I finished A-levels, going to university felt like the natural thing to do.

* * *

I feel that our numbers brought more advantages than disadvantages. I'm glad I did not grow up in a family where a board game for four would gather dust in a cupboard. Had our number been two or three it would have been different but not necessarily better. I think that my ability to relate to people and ease with large groups is a direct result of having to acquire the skills to cope with just such situations. Going away to university was something I took to easily, but some were returning every weekend because they found it difficult to adapt and integrate into their new surroundings.

* * *

I only had one fear regarding the family – that perhaps the next addition would be "a bridge too far". Over the years I came to see myself more and more as an integral part of the family and our expanding number as my brothers and sisters. But I can remember family get-togethers that were called when a new addition to our family was being proposed or lined up. My feelings were mixed at this time, not because of any real objection to any new addition to our number, but from a fear that perhaps the next person to arrive could be the trigger for everything to go horribly wrong. This was a fear that lessened as time went on as a result of my own greater sense of security and the fact that my fears had not come to anything yet. I came to realise that our family was both resilient and adaptable. We all were. I also realised from a fairly young age that the potential for family breakdowns existed to the same extent in more "normal" family circumstances. Divorces were common among the families of friends of family members as we were growing up.

* * *

I don't think that there was a moment where I said, 'I trust Mum and Dad'. It was more of a gradual process than that. A case of: 'Until I am given any real reason to *dis*trust Kate and Brian then I have no need to.' This acceptance is almost certainly linked to the fact that I joined the family quite young, and because as far as I could see they were as good as their word.

The trust came from a sense of stability and the fact that I never really felt any personal sense of being let down. It was cemented on the occasions when I did something wrong or let myself down but was still shown love and understanding. Trust is in no small way linked to love that is unconditional, not just reserved for when you are good or doing well at something.

* * *

I don't think it took me long to decide I was staying in the Cairns household. I had been there almost from the outset and was comfortable with my position within the family. The family did grow and evolve around me (amongst others) but that was certainly an easier role to adjust to than that of one of the later arrivals. It must have been for them more like an outsider coming in than an insider looking out. I certainly felt like an insider, part of the established group. As the years went by and the number of additions grew, I became increasingly confident of the family unit's ability to survive and grow still further.

The resilience of our family unit was good for my confidence and I was happy with Mum and Dad's leadership. I can honestly say I never really entertained the notion of staying anywhere else. Indeed, I had other friends who were quite envious of where I lived and how I was allowed to grow up.

I was always comfortable about bringing my friends home. Some friends found our family numbers more daunting than others, but they (certainly the ones that I regarded as my closer friends) coped well with this on the whole. More than anything some found our organised mealtime rituals daunting, but all this meant was that those who found this aspect particularly difficult would decline offers to stay for tea more often than not.

On the whole I feel I made friends with accepting types who rather liked our unusual family set-up; one is well remembered for having an uncanny knack of "just passing" as we were about to sit down for tea. I think in part that my own sense of confidence with myself and the position I occupied in the family made it easy for me to let "outsiders" into my world. I think it follows that those who were perhaps less secure in themselves and in their place in the family might well have found this a far more difficult exercise.

*　*　*

With a family the size of ours it was easy to choose to spend time either with people if you wanted to, or to take yourself off separately to be on your own. Friends offered a further outlet as visiting them was a further way of removing oneself from our sometimes hectic environment.

Over the years I would say that my understanding of and for my siblings has grown, perhaps most noticeably with those whom I found more testing at times in my childhood. I feel that we all continue to move forward and progress, and are as strong a unit as ever.

Lynn:

Growing up in a big family had its advantages. There was always something to keep you occupied, or someone to play with, be it just two of us or all of us. I can still remember people saying, 'But isn't that a children's home?' The answer was always, 'No! It's my home, my mum and dad, and my brothers and sisters'. It felt so good to be able to say that. Although I did let them know that I was fostered, and proud of it, because that meant I was wanted. It also meant I didn't have just have one or two brothers and sisters, I had loads.

*　*　*

There were a lot of changes to Plainlands. But one thing stayed the same. We were a family, and nothing could change that. If there was any leaving to be done, then it was by our choice, not Mum and Dad's.

*　*　*

A closure was meeting my birth mother, when I was 16, and realising that Mark and I had the best thing going for us. I have not seen my birth mother since and have no intention of doing so. The family I have now are what I consider to be my real family.

Fred:

No words can express the meanings and benefits of what was achieved. I was potentially a very selfish person. That is what I would have become without experiencing the 'family brotherhood of mutual understanding, tolerance and caring'.

*　　*　　*

I didn't like conforming. But in our family I could enjoy big open spaces that gave me a feeling of freedom. Somehow there was an absence of direct pressure and competitive aggression which are highly destructive.

*　　*　　*

In my business life I have learned the importance of synergy created by using the strengths of the group. I learned that from how we worked to everybody's strengths in the family.

Karen:

I don't believe for one minute that people I meet would guess I had grown up in care! Being a part of the family taught me how society would expect me to behave as an adult. Prior to living in the family I believed that I could do what I wanted – there was no way people were going to tell me what to do.

*　　*　　*

There have been times when I think, 'Who the hell am I? Where's my mum? Do I look like her?' But I consider myself to be a competent caring person who copes very well with my roles as mother to five boys and wife. Although I find it very hard to trust, I have managed to form trusting relationships with people who are well-adjusted individuals. Most of the time I feel as able to cope with daily life as most people do. I feel very strongly that this is down to having lived in our family group where I was provided with the safety and structure of a loving family in which I could work through my past traumatic experiences and begin the healing process. It was here that I encountered what it was like to be cared for, to trust and to be trusted.

Mark:

Dad and Mum, Brian and Kate, over several years helped all of us to "find ourselves". We were shown love, trust, caring and understanding. We were carefully guided and picked up with kind gentle hands and a warm smile, as we slowly unravelled ourselves to find a new person longing to be set free and loved. We also learned the art of caring, loving and having respect for our brothers and sisters, no matter what their colour or their background was. Over time we learned to feel safe, loved and wanted, not something to be discarded in the corner of the room or out of sight. Here was someone willing to listen – no, not a joke, this was real – someone who listened and responded with soft gentle words to understand and make you feel better.

*   *   *

This family unit is very special to me. It has given me security and safety, something all of us might never have known if we had been left where we were. To some people, it's not a "real" family. But what is a "real" family? A family is a group of people living and growing up together through thick and thin, loving, supporting, being there when needed.

References

Broad, B (1998) *Young People Leaving Care*, London: Jessica Kingsley

Cairns, B and Cairns, K (1989) 'The family as a living group', in Brown, A and Clough, R (eds) *Groups and Groupings*, London: Routledge

Cairns, K (1999) *Surviving Paedophilia: Traumatic stress after organised and network child abuse*, Trentham Books

Cairns, K (2002a) *Attachment, Trauma and Resilience: Therapeutic caring for children*, London: BAAF

Cairns, K (2002b) 'Making sense: The use of theory and research to support foster care', *Adoption & Fostering*, 26:2

Department of Health (1991) *Patterns and Outcomes in Child Placement*, London: HMSO

Fratter, J, Rowe, J, Sapsford, J and Thoburn, J (eds) (1991) *Permanent Family Placement: A decade of experience*, London: BAAF

George, V (1970) *Foster Care*, London: Routledge and Kegan Paul

Gibran, K (1972) *The Prophet*, London: Heinemann

Gilligan, R (2001) *Promoting Resilience: A resource guide on working with children in the care system*, London: BAAF

Jackson, S (ed) (2001) *Nobody Ever Told Us School Mattered: Raising the educational attainments of children in care*, London: BAAF

Johnson, B (2002) *Emotional Health*, York: James Nayler Foundation

Liedloff, J (1989) *The Continuum Concept*, Arkana

Mather, M, Humphrey, J and Robson, J (1997) 'The statutory medical and health needs of looked after children: time for a radical review', *Adoption & Fostering*, 21:2

Napier, H (1972) 'Success and failure in foster care', *British Journal of Social Work*, Vol 2

Office of National Statistics (ONS) (2003) *The Mental Health of Young People Looked After by Local Authorities in England*, London: HMSO

Parker, R (1980) *Caring for Separated Children: Plans, procedures, priorities*, London: Macmillan

Parker, R, Ward, H, Jackson, S, Aldgate, J and Wedge, P (1991) *Looking After Children: Assessing outcomes in foster care*, London: HMSO

Pugh, G (1995) 'Seen but not heard? Addressing the needs of children who foster', *Adoption & Fostering*, 19:1

Quinn, D (2000) *Beyond Civilisation: Humanity's next great adventure*, NY: Three Rivers Press

Rowe, J, Hundleby, M, Cain, H and Keane, A (1984) *Long-term Foster Care*, London: Batsford

Schofield, G, Beek, M and Sargent, K, with Thoburn, J (2000) *Growing Up in Foster Care*, London: BAAF

Stein, M and Carey, K (1986) *Leaving Care*, Oxford: Blackwell

Ward, H (ed) (1995) *Looking after Children: Research into Practice*, London: HMSO